"Alan Reifman's book is comprehensive, easy to read, and covers almost all the domains one would need to know about to understand emerging adulthood. The breadth of this work is outstanding. This book is a must-read for parents, educators, policy makers, and emerging adults themselves."

Seth J. Schwartz PhD, *University of Texas at Austin*

"In this book, Dr. Reifman takes us on a journey through emerging adulthood – the developmental processes, cultural variations, and multiple domains of the lives of emerging adults. The book captures the key aspects of the fast-growing research in emerging adulthood in recent decades. As a long-time researcher in emerging adulthood, Dr. Reifman masterfully translates research into this easy-and-fun-to-read book to a broader audience."

Ming Cui PhD, *Florida State University*

Journeys through Emerging Adulthood

Journeys through Emerging Adulthood takes the reader on a tour of contemporary transitions to adulthood, reporting on the latest cross-national and cross-cultural research into young adulthood and separating fact from fiction about this important life phase. Alan Reifman shows how today's youth are taking more time to enter traditional adult roles and explores the benefits and disadvantages of this gradual emergence into adulthood.

This essential textbook navigates the research that reveals the substantial variety in young people's paths to adulthood. It covers the spectrum of the young-adult experience, examining the influence that parents have on their grown children's progress and identity as adults and considering the impact of traditional milestones such as higher education, establishing a career, forming romantic relationships, and becoming a parent. It examines key topics including mental health in emerging adults and the likelihood of substance abuse, and how young adults might reach out into the community through volunteerism, religious involvement, and political activism. Each section includes examples and studies conducted in a range of countries, exploring how the journey to adulthood can vary according to cultural context as well as individual circumstances. The book affirms that while there is great variety in how one transitions to adulthood, there is no correct path, and most people fare well – or even thrive – in adulthood.

Featuring end-of-chapter summaries, quizzes, and activities, *Journeys through Emerging Adulthood* provides an accessible yet comprehensive overview of this significant life stage, connecting fundamental psychological theories with modern social phenomena. Reifman's text is essential reading for both undergraduate and graduate students of psychology, human development, and sociology, as well as students and researchers of any discipline interested in the path to adulthood.

Alan Reifman is a Professor of Human Development and Family Sciences at Texas Tech University, USA. He received his PhD from the University of Michigan and was inducted into Texas Tech's Teaching Academy in 2008, reflecting his skill and commitment in the classroom.

Journeys through Emerging Adulthood

An Introduction to Development from Ages 18-30 Around the World

Alan Reifman

Routledge
Taylor & Francis Group

NEW YORK AND LONDON

Cover image: Getty

First published 2023
by Routledge
605 Third Avenue, New York, NY 10158

and by Routledge
4 Park Square, Milton Park, Abingdon, Oxon, OX14 4RN

Routledge is an imprint of the Taylor & Francis Group, an informa business

© 2023 Alan Reifman

Library of Congress Cataloging-in-Publication Data
Names: Reifman, Alan, author.
Title: Journeys through emerging adulthood : an introduction to development from ages 18-30 around the world/Alan Reifman.
Description: New York, NY: Routledge, 2022. | Includes bibliographical references and index. |
Summary: "Journeys through Emerging Adulthood
takes the reader on a tour of contemporary transitions to adulthood,
reporting on the latest cross-national and cross-cultural research into
young adulthood and separating fact from fiction about this important
life phase"–Provided by publisher.
Identifiers: LCCN 2022004825 (print) | LCCN 2022004826 (ebook) | ISBN 9780367742034 (hardback) | ISBN 9780367742041 (paperback) | ISBN 9781003156567 (ebook)
Subjects: LCSH: Young adults.
Classification: LCC HQ799.5.R45 2022 (print) | LCC HQ799.5 (ebook) | DDC 305.242–dc23/eng/20220202
LC record available at https://lccn.loc.gov/2022004825
LC ebook record available at https://lccn.loc.gov/2022004826

ISBN: 978-0-367-74203-4 (hbk)
ISBN: 978-0-367-74204-1 (pbk)
ISBN: 978-1-003-15656-7 (ebk)

DOI: 10.4324/9781003156567

Typeset in Bembo
by Deanta Global Publishing Services, Chennai, India

Please visit the Companion Website: www.routledge.com/9780367742041

To Sylvia,
Your quick wit and loving heart make me feel so fortunate that our respective winding roads through emerging adulthood and beyond brought the two of us together and ended my status as an "educated single."

Contents

Acknowledgments

This book represents the culmination of 20 years of conducting research on emerging adulthood and 13 years of teaching the course "Development in Young Adulthood" at Texas Tech University. I have so many people to thank.

My Texas Tech faculty colleagues and students are too numerous to mention (that's what happens when you're at a place for 25 years). Still, I would like to recognize a few. Judy Fischer, Nancy Bell (late), and Jean Pearson Scott all served on the faculty for roughly 35–40 years before retiring. Their spunk, heart, and wisdom made them highly valued colleagues and role models for Sylvia and me. Michael O'Boyle (also a retired colleague) kindly took time from his guitar playing and enjoyment of the New Mexico vista to read a draft of my chapter on the brain and cognition. Thanks also to the Texas Tech Library, whose extensive catalog of online books and articles saved me a lot of time and effort in locating the materials I needed.

Within the broader academic community, I would like to thank Jeff Arnett, a force of nature in building the field of emerging adulthood, both intellectually and organizationally. Jeff has always supported my academic efforts and collaborated with me (and another valued Texas Tech colleague, Malinda Colwell) on the original Inventory of the Dimensions of Emerging Adulthood (IDEA) scale. I hope Jeff won't mind some friendly competition in the textbook arena! I would also like to thank Jon Grahe for keeping large, multi-investigator research projects on emerging adulthood going for nearly 20 years. My friends and mentors from my research position in Buffalo, graduate training at the University of Michigan, and undergraduate school at the University of California, Los Angeles (UCLA) – with many of whom I'm still in touch after 30–40 years – also mean a great deal to me.

Lastly, I would like to thank members of my family. My mother Estherly and father Leonard (late) provided love and support during my emerging-adulthood years and beyond and set positive examples with their community engagement. My sister Lynn, her husband Jeff, and my nieces Ari and Jordy – my two favorite emerging adults – and my brother Steve are always a pleasure to visit with (virtually, in the COVID era). My uncles David and Irving (and Irving's late wife Myra) nurtured my interest in law and politics during my emerging-adult years. While I was still a UCLA undergraduate, Irv took me to meet future US Vice-President and environmental champion Al Gore at an event and lined up a summer internship for me in the local Los Angeles office of US Representative Henry Waxman. I have also enjoyed sharing and watching the transitions to adulthood of my cousins from the "Irving side" of the family.

Finally, as seen on the dedication page, I express my love and gratitude to my dear wife Sylvia. I also appreciate her parents Ursula and Manfred and brother Oliver in Germany for the support they have shown over the years.

Foundations

1

Introduction

> *It is clear that young adults face a less scripted and more individualistic transition from teenager to full adult.*
>
> *— Waters and colleagues (2011, p. 3)*

This book is about a journey. It is a journey that takes longer now, on average, than it did 50 years ago. The duration of your personal journal will likely be affected by what country you live in, which region within your country you live in, your career aspirations, your economic conditions, and probably many other factors. There is no universally agreed-upon endpoint, like a finish line in the 100-meter dash, to tell you when you have reached your destination. Nor is there, as writer Elizabeth Segran (2020) terms it, an exit sign on your metaphorical highway through life. Still, you and the significant others in your life will probably have a good idea when you have gotten there. It is the journey to adulthood.

Becoming an adult is a gradual transition, and, as we will discuss, it is not unusual for people in their twenties to feel like they are an adult in some ways but not in others. Some of you may feel confident in your progress toward adulthood or even that you have attained it, whereas others of you may feel lost and confused. In the United States (US), the culture has a number of somewhat humorous references to the sometimes uncertain, incremental pathway to adulthood, such as the quote "I'm an adult, but not like a real adult" that appears on T-shirts, coffee mugs, and other items. Also the word "adult" has become a verb, as in "I'm in the process of adulting." Different people have their own idiosyncratic views of when they became an adult. Maria Walker, a youth-development specialist at the University of Nebraska-Lincoln, who co-hosts a podcast on the topic (Benes & Walker, 2021), said the following:

> I knew I was an adult not when I moved 1,000 miles away from my family of origin, not when I married my partner, not when I entered certain graduate studies, etc. It's when [her husband] Joel and I bought our first washing machine [laughter] for our rental home … Like, I'm getting serious now, this is not a

DOI: 10.4324/9781003156567-2

rented machine or going to the laundromat ... I think I was 26 – maybe – at the time ... just felt super-confident in my ability to adult ...

Popular singers such as Britney Spears ("I'm Not a Girl, Not Yet a Woman"), Fergie ("Big Girls Don't Cry"), and Martina McBride ("This One's for the Girls") have also addressed themes related to becoming an adult.[1] Numerous television shows (e.g., the longtime viewer favorite *Friends* and the recent Netflix shows *Atypical* and *Sex Education*), movies (e.g., *Failure to Launch*; *Juno*), and even classic (e.g., *Pride and Prejudice*) and modern literature (e.g., *On the Road*) have done likewise.[2] I absorb ideas wherever I can find them, including the media. However, first and foremost this book is a work of social science. Hence, most of the material will come from scientific theories and research.

The scientific method as applied to human behavior has many components. These include definitions of the concepts we wish to study, theories of why people act the way they do, ways to measure these concepts (such as questionnaires or behavioral observation), statistical analysis to test if things go together (e.g., does marrying later reduce the risk of divorce?), and inferences and conclusions based on our findings. As we'll soon discuss, many aspects of development during young adulthood (e.g., the typical age at first marriage) have changed dramatically in just a few decades, so theories in this area will need to address how societal changes have affected individual behavior. If a particular set of methods for investigating a problem becomes well established, it is known as a *paradigm*. Let's begin our scientific inquiry by reviewing three ways or paradigms to study the onset of adulthood.

Three Ways Scholars Have Studied the Onset of Adulthood

As noted, defining our concepts is one of the earliest steps in scientific inquiry. Defining different stages or phases of the lifespan is not an easy business, even for academics and health professionals, and there is not always complete agreement. Take adolescence, for example. Sources such as the World Health Organization (2001) and the Society for Research on Adolescence (Kirkpatrick Johnson et al., 2011) define adolescence as the second decade of life (ages 10–19), whereas others use puberty to mark the onset of adolescence (Steinberg, 2014). How about middle age? Many of us would probably think of the forties and fifties as representing middle age, yet roughly half of people 65–69 and one-third of those in their seventies consider themselves middle aged (Lachman, 2004)! Defining when people first reach adulthood is no exception to this ambiguity. Rather than there being a single, universally accepted starting point for adulthood, therefore, experts have addressed the issue from multiple paradigms. We review three major ones, which I refer to as the *tripod* of the transition to adulthood (Figure 1.1).

Milestones/Roles

Henig and Henig (2012) observed that "Traditionally, five milestones have been used to define adulthood – completing school, leaving home, becoming financially independent, marrying, and having a first child" (p. 3). These authors also note that some people never achieve all five of these statuses and, among people

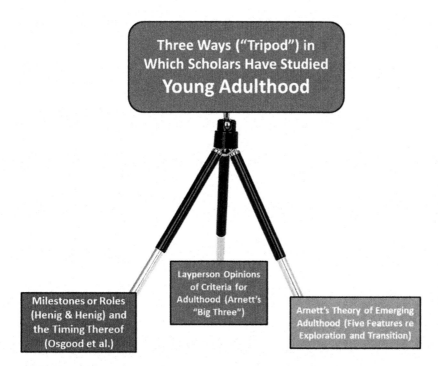

FIGURE 1.1 Tripod depiction of three ways (paradigms) of studying the transition to adulthood ("re" = regarding).

who reach most or all of them, the order in which they do so can vary from person to person.

If we define the onset of adulthood based on attainment of the above milestones, it is clear that, in the US and other Western industrialized nations, young people today are reaching adulthood several years later, on average, than did their counterparts half a century ago. Whereas in 1970 the median age of first marriage in the US was 23 for men and 21 for women, as of 2020, men's median age at first marriage was approaching 31 and women's had reached 28 (US Census Bureau, 2020). Internationally (as of 2016), the median marriage age for men in several countries (Italy, the Netherlands, Germany, Ireland, Hong Kong, Australia, and Japan) ranged from 31 to 35, whereas in women the range was from 29 to 32 (Buchholz, 2019). Similarly, in 1970, US women tended to have their first child at around age 22 (Mathews & Hamilton, 2002), but by 2019, this age had risen to 27 (National Center for Health Statistics, 2021). (For readers who haven't taken a statistics course, a median is a central dividing point, so that a median age of 23 would indicate that half of the people married before 23 and half married after 23.)

Using these milestones to define adulthood only gets us so far, however. We all probably know people in their thirties, forties, fifties, or older who have never married or had children, but whom we would still consider adults. A more nuanced use of milestones has been to divide young people into groups based on how quickly or slowly they are moving toward traditional adult roles (Osgood et al. 2005; Sandefur et al., 2005). Illustrating this approach, Osgood and colleagues surveyed 24-year-old respondents from Detroit, Michigan (US), in the 1990s on whether they had attained various milestones. Had these young adults gotten married, had children, graduated from high school and college, lived independently, worked full time, and so forth? Then, using a statistical technique that groups similar people with each other (for you Harry Potter fans, like the "sorting hat" that places like-minded students into the same house), Osgood and colleagues revealed six subgroups of these 24-year-olds:

- *Fast starters* (12% of participants; distinguished by their high rates of marriage and having children, living away from parents, and working full time, but rarely having received a college degree). Hence, even though the *average* young adult is delaying marriage and other traditional adult milestones well past the early twenties, the fast starters are a relatively small subgroup defying the larger trend.
- *Parents without careers* (10%; this group, like the previous one, has a high rate of being married with children and living apart from parents; however, parents without careers have not advanced very far in their work or education beyond high school).
- *Educated partners* (19%; high rate of being married or cohabiting, large majority with a bachelor's degree and possibly in graduate school, generally without children).
- *Educated singles* (37%; similar to the previous group, except – as the name implies – they were not romantically partnered and largely lived with their parents or in apartments). I was the poster child for educated singles! Neither during my undergraduate years at the University of California, Los Angeles (UCLA, 1980–1984) nor my graduate training at the University of Michigan (1984–1989) did I have a serious romantic relationship. In fact, I did not marry until age 47.
- *Working singles* (7%; again, as the name implies, these individuals are in the labor force, with a high rate of living with their parents).
- *Slow starters* (14%; this group had shown little progress toward living independently from their parents and finding work with long-term prospects).

Researchers have identified similar subgroups in the United Kingdom (UK; Schoon et al., 2012) and Finland (Räikkönen et al., 2012; Salmela-Aro et al., 2012). These American, British, and Finnish studies have consistently yielded subgroups embodying the following configurations. There is typically a group exhibiting early attainment of multiple roles, as well as ones that amassed extensive education while single or around the time of getting married and perhaps starting a family. In addition, there are groups that put certain pursuits at the center of their lives, such as work (with a lower likelihood of marriage or childbearing than in other groups) or parenthood (with lower work and educational involvement than in other groups). Finally, there is typically a slow-starter group. The different pathways uncovered by Osgood and colleagues (2005) and the other researchers support the idea quoted at the beginning of this chapter that becoming an adult is an "individualistic transition." Within whatever constraints people face (such as the need to earn money for one's family), each person can take on whatever adult roles they like, in whatever order (Henig & Henig, 2012), and on whatever timeframe.

Of course, role statuses are not permanent. Married persons may divorce, non-marital romantic partners may break up, people living in their own apartment may have to move back in with their parents (known as "boomerang kids"), college students may drop out, and so forth. Cohen and colleagues (2003) investigated life changes from ages 17 to 27, both the ups and the downs, in participants from upstate New York via in-depth interviews. The researchers created an elaborate scoring system (known as Transition Levels or TL) for each domain studied – residential, financial, romantic relationship, and parental life – where 0 represented most childlike and 99 represented most adult-like. In the residential domain, for example, living with one's parents and having no responsibilities at home was scored as 0, living with parents but taking on some household responsibilities might be scored at 25 or thereabouts (depending on the person's exact situation), moving to a college dorm 30, living in an apartment with friends 40, living alone 70, etc. When the researchers plotted TLs vs. age, with each participant receiving their own line, the graphs for residential, financial, and romantic life looked like plates of spaghetti. Cohen and colleagues' residential transition graph appears in Figure 1.2. (Note that, to illustrate general patterns without unduly cluttering the graph, Cohen and colleagues show curves for only a subset of participants.)

A few participants exhibited completely horizontal lines, indicating that their residential status never changed from ages 17 to 27. One person's trend (or trajectory) showed a rise in residential TL from around 30 at age 17 to 65 at age 20, signifying increased independence in their living situation, then stagnated. Another person's trajectory rose from around 30 at age 17 to 55 at age 22, only to plummet down to a TL of 0 by age 27. Finally, other people's trajectories rose from ages 23 to 27, perhaps as a result of graduating college, with one person's residential TL score

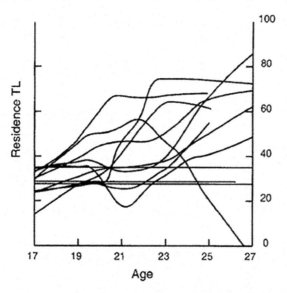

FIGURE 1.2 Many male participants' attainments of adult-like residential statuses (e.g., sharing an apartment with friends, living alone) had their ups and downs from ages 17 to 27. Cohen and colleagues' scoring system for residential transitions yields the above graph, which looks like a plate of spaghetti (each curve is a different person, representing 10% of the men in the study; residence transition level [TL] scored from 0 = most childlike to 99 = most adult-like).

Source: From Cohen et al. (2003, Figure 3 in original work). Reprinted with permission. Copyright © 2003 by American Psychological Association. Reproduced with permission. Cohen, P., Kasen, S., Chen, H., Hartmark, C., & Gordon, K. (2003). Variations in patterns of developmental transitions in the emerging adulthood period. *Developmental Psychology*, 39, 657–669. https://doi.org /10.1037/0012-1649.39.4.657

reaching all the way up to 85 (equivalent to getting an apartment with one's fiancé or fiancée). The maximum score of 99 would be warranted only if "the participant carried all the responsibilities of establishing and maintaining an independent residence," presumably full home ownership (Cohen et al., 2003, p. 660). As noted, the graphs for financial and romantic life (not reproduced in this book) were similarly spaghetti-like. One exception was parental life (0 representing "no children and no interest in conceiving a child in the foreseeable future" and 99 representing "a highly committed involvement in child rearing," p. 660). For parental life, nearly all the trajectories were steadily upward (except for people who did not have children). Downturns were rare, possibly resulting in a loss of custody rights.

Here's the bottom line on these spaghetti graphs. If your personal strand of spaghetti is not going straight upward in one or more life domains, you are probably not alone.

Laypersons' Criteria for What Qualifies One as an Adult

Jeffrey Arnett (a name you will come across frequently in this book for his research and his sharing of song lyrics with me) conducted a variety of studies based on a simple survey exercise. In one study conducted in the Midwestern US (Arnett, 2001), respondents were shown a list of 38 behaviors and accomplishments. Some of these were milestone-based, such as getting married, having at least one child, and being employed full time. Other behaviors reflected a sense of independence, such as "Accept responsibility for the consequences of your actions" and "Decide on personal beliefs and values independently of parents or other influence." Still other behaviors reflected a sense of responsibility for health and safety, such as refraining from illegal drug use, driving safely, and, if sexually active, having only one partner at any given time. For each behavior, respondents were asked to check off "yes" or "no" to "Indicate whether you think the following must be achieved before a person can be considered to be an adult" (Arnett, 2001). Take a moment to reflect for yourself on what kinds of behaviors and accomplishments you think are *required* before you would consider someone an adult. Then come back for the next paragraph.

Would you require that someone be a parent before you considered them an adult? I'm probably not going out on a limb to guess that you would not. In Arnett's (2001) study, hardly anyone did so (9% of teen respondents, 7% of people in their twenties, and 11% of people aged 30–55). People didn't consider other role transitions – marriage, finishing one's education, establishing oneself in one's work or career – as being necessary for adulthood, either. Nothing in these categories, in any respondent age group, received higher than 39% endorsement as a criterion for adulthood. One of the other role transitions noted by Henig and Henig (2012), moving out of your parents' home, received higher endorsement (53–61% in the three age groups).

What behaviors and accomplishments were most commonly considered necessary for adulthood? It was the independence-related behaviors: accept responsibility for one's actions (87–93% in the three age groups) and deciding on your own beliefs (73–83%). These two criteria, along with becoming financially independent of one's parents (69–72%), are now called the Big Three, as popularized in *The Atlantic*, a general-interest magazine (Beck, 2016). The magazine also noted that these findings hold up internationally:

These three criteria have been ranked highly not just in the U.S. but in many other countries as well, including China, Greece, Israel, India, and Argentina. But some cultures add their own values to the list. In China, for example, people highly valued being able to financially support their parents, and in India people valued the ability to keep their family physically safe.

In summary, reaching traditional adult milestones will not guarantee that people see you as an adult. You will also need to demonstrate independence and responsibility for yourself.

Arnett's Theory of Emerging Adulthood

Jeff Arnett, in addition to his research on laypersons' criteria for considering someone an adult, has also proposed a stage of the lifespan that he calls "emerging adulthood" in which, starting around age 18, individuals progress toward adulthood (Arnett, 2000). The theorized ending point for emerging adulthood has shifted over the years. Arnett (2000) originally specified it as age 25, but more recently he and his colleagues have put it closer to age 30 (Mehta et al., 2020). We'll be using the term *emerging adulthood* so much throughout this book that, if you don't mind, I'll refer to it as EA. The key to EA is the notion that this stage provides a "window" of opportunity for young people to explore freely various areas of their lives, in between two periods of restriction and responsibility. As Arnett (2000) wrote: "Having left the dependency of childhood and adolescence, and having not yet entered the enduring responsibilities that are normative in adulthood, emerging adults often explore a variety of possible life directions in love, work, and worldviews" (p. 469). This exploration may include travel, internships, volunteer work, or different majors in college (if one attends). These attempts by young people to learn about themselves and their place in the world can last for several years, "until their late 20s or early 30s cuts off the backpacking trips to Europe and brings [retirement plans], mortgages and children" (Barmak, 2010). People taking extra time to discover more about themselves and the world may also be one reason for the delays in marriage and childrearing noted above. I have created the accompanying graphic in Figure 1.3 to put those words into pictures.

It is important to note, however, *that not everyone age 18–30 experiences emerging adulthood*. For example, economic need may force some in their late teens or early twenties to work full time to support their families. It's hard to engage in the kinds of exploration described above when one is working 40 hours or more per week. A theme we will develop is that – based on their socioeconomic status (SES), country of residence, and other factors – some people are more likely than others to be able to take an extended EA.

Let's pause to take in what we have learned so far. EA is a stage roughly between ages 18 and 30, but only some people in this age group experience it. Here are some questions you might have at this point:

Why do we have a stage like EA? It seems clear that today's twenty-somethings are doing things differently from their same-age counterparts in prior generations. Whereas, in the past, people in their early-to-mid-twenties used to get married, start families, and work full time, today they obtain advanced education, try out different jobs, volunteer, or travel. Arnett (2000) looked at these trends and concluded that

FIGURE 1.3 Emerging adulthood as a window of time to explore different life options, in between periods of restriction and responsibility.

these changes were so profound – that they "have altered the nature of development in the late teens and early twenties for young people in industrialized societies" (p. 469) – that a new stage of the lifespan called "emerging adulthood" should be designated. Thus, EA is meant to describe the stage these milestone-delayers are going through and investigate their motivations, attitudes, and lifestyles.

Why are people in their twenties delaying marriage, parenting, and careers? Arnett (2015a) theorized that four "revolutions" have stretched out the number of years most young people take to reach traditional adult milestones.

First is the technological revolution, in which the economies of advanced nations have increasingly used industrial robots rather than human employees for manufacturing (Bharadwaj, & Dvorkin, 2019), thus putting greater emphasis on "information and technology skills" (Arnett, 2015a, p. 4). Bharadwaj and Dvorkin examined US job growth in four occupational categories. These include: *routine cognitive* (repetitive, mental rather than physical operations, such as sales and office work), *non-routine cognitive* (more varied and complex cognitive operations, such as management and professional work), *routine manual* (repetitive physical operations such as construction and repair), and non-routine manual (e.g., providing care or technical assistance for medical patients, working in the foodservice industry, and cleaning). One of these four types of work has seen major growth (30 million new jobs) in the US since the 1980s, another type has seen modest growth in that time (roughly 10 million new jobs), and the other two have declined in recent years. Before looking at the following graph (Figure 1.4), try to guess which of these types of work is the one with major job growth.

The rising need for information and technological skills also increases participation in higher education to achieve these skills. As *New York Times* columnist Thomas Friedman (2016) writes in a book about technological acceleration, "middle-class jobs … require more knowledge and education to perform successfully. To compete for such jobs you need more of the three Rs – reading, writing, and arithmetic – and more of the four Cs – creativity, collaboration, communication, and coding" (p. 211). A heavy commitment to advanced education in one's mid-twenties, of course, is likely to delay marriage, parenthood, and full-time employment.

Second is the sexual revolution, with the arrival of the birth control pill (providing greater effectiveness against pregnancy and greater convenience than some of the earlier methods; Goldin & Katz, 2002; Greenwood et al., 2019; University Health Service, 2021) and the liberalizing of societal attitudes about premarital sex in the US (Elias et al., 2013). Though the US Food and Drug Administration

Employment Level by Occupational Group

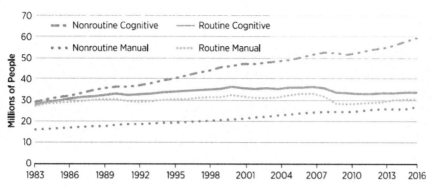

SOURCES: U.S. Bureau of Labor Statistics and authors' calculations.

■ FEDERAL RESERVE BANK OF ST. LOUIS

FIGURE 1.4 Employment trends in the US for four different types of work.
Source: From: Bharadwaj, A., & Dvorkin, M.A. (2019, July 10). The rise of automation: How robots may impact the US labor market. *Regional Economist*. (Figure 1 in original work). Graph provided courtesy of the Federal Reserve Bank of St. Louis. © 2019 Federal Reserve Bank of St. Louis. All rights reserved.

(FDA) approved the birth control pill in 1960, it took several more years for many single women to access it, due to state legal restrictions (Goldin & Katz, 2002). The sexual revolution is said to have made premarital sex more acceptable within large segments of society, hence delaying matrimony for many people. That is not to say that everyone abstained from sex until marriage before 1960. Some older surveys suggest that, among women born in the 1920s, around 20% engaged in premarital sex by age 20 and nearly 40% had done so by age 30. Among women born in the 1940s (1939–1948, technically), the percent engaging in premarital sex by age 20 had risen to 40% and the percent doing so by age 30 slightly exceeded 50% (Greenwood et al., 2019; see also Wu et al., 2017).[3] Continuing the trend, women born in the 1980s (1979–1988) are much more likely than their counterparts from earlier generations to have had premarital sex by age 20 (around 75%).[4] One might conclude therefore that the birth control pill, while not the impetus for the first-ever wave of premarital sex, was associated with an increase in this behavior. Goldin and Katz (2002), moreover, have provided statistical evidence linking the availability of the birth control pill to delayed marriage and attainment of a professional degree. These researchers demonstrated a link in young women between growing up in a state that made birth control accessible at age 16 without parental consent (compared to states with greater restriction) and a 2% reduction in getting married by age 23 (these data were available only for US women born from 1935 to 1957 and who completed college). Goldin and Katz also discovered that increased usage of the birth control pill in women born in the mid-1950s (compared to earlier decades) also was associated with about a 2% rise in women's attainment of professional occupations (e.g., law, medicine, business) from 1970 to 1990.

The third revolution (linked partly to the sexual revolution increasing women's control over their bodies) is the 1960s women's movement (also known as "Second Wave Feminism," as distinct from the "First Wave Feminism" of roughly 1840–1925, which concentrated on gaining women the right to vote). The 1960s women's movement – marked by such historical developments as the book *The Feminine Mystique* (Friedan, 1963) and the 1966 founding of the National Organization for Women (NOW) – gave voice to women's growing sense of independence and educational/career orientation and led to various legal changes. The landmark 1964 Civil Rights Act in the US, though best known for prohibiting various forms of racial discrimination, also barred job discrimination against women.[5] Many major US Supreme Court cases followed in the late 1960s and early 1970s (with a young lawyer named Ruth Bader Ginsburg, who later became a Supreme Court Justice herself, spearheading the arguments for gender equality), further increasing women's rights (National Women's History Alliance, 2021). The results of these changes were clear. In 1970–1971, for example, women earned slightly fewer than 10% of US law and medical degrees, whereas by 2009–2010, they earned nearly half of the degrees awarded in these fields (Cohen, 2012). Women's shares of law and medical degrees have not risen much since 2010, however (Rowe, 2018; Searing, 2019). Beyond the US, women's movements took place around the same time in many other countries, leading to equal-pay laws in Australia (state of New South Wales, 1958), United Kingdom (1970), and France (1972), to name a few (Cloudpay, 2019). Interestingly, a look at the most recent international statistics on pay equality shows that the countries that have most successfully minimized the pay gap between men and women come from many different parts of the world. Women in Luxembourg earn a few percent higher wages than do men; women and men in Colombia and in Costa Rica earn roughly the same; and women are within 5% of men's earnings in Bulgaria, Belgium, Romania, New Zealand, Norway, and Denmark (Organisation for Economic Co-operation and Development, OECD, 2021a).

Fourth is what Arnett (2015a) calls the "youth movement," referring to what he sees as today's young adults wanting to explore and enjoy their freedom, independence, and spontaneity. In contrast, the turmoil of the Great Depression (1930s) and World War II (1940s) made young people of that era eager to settle down. Part of Arnett's youth movement conception involves the idea of a "generation gap," when younger and older adults, on average, hold different views of the world and mistrust each other to some degree. Different age groups have differed in their political views in the US in recent years with, for example, 18–29-year-olds voting 60–36% for Democrat Joe Biden and those 65 and older voting 52–47% for Republican Donald Trump in the 2020 presidential election, according to exit polls (CNN.com, 2021). In addition, certain issues of particular relevance to younger voters, such as debt from college loans and being able to stay on their parents' health insurance plan until age 26, do come up in the US from time to time. To the extent younger adults see themselves as politically different from their older counterparts, therefore, they may approach issues such as marriage, family formation, and childrearing differently from how they perceived their parents' generation to have done things. Moving forward, demographer William Frey (2018) projects that future instances of a generation gap in the US will really be a generation–race/ethnicity gap. Whereas more than 70% of the Baby Boom (currently age 57–75) and older generations are White, a majority of young children in the US will soon belong to a minority group such as Black, Hispanic/Latinx, and Asian (Frey, 2018).

I would add a fifth revolution that may be contributing to young adults' delaying of marriage, childbearing, and other milestones, namely the aging revolution. With life expectancy continuing its longtime rise in the US (from 75 years in men and 80 in women presently to projections of 84 and 87 by 2060; Arias et al., 2021; Medina et al., 2020) and in other nations, people in their twenties will likely feel that they have more time to take on traditional adult roles. One young man quoted in Kimmel (2008) asserted that "I'm only 25, and I'm gonna live to what, 90? So, like, why hurry on the marriage and kids thing?" (p. 26). Beyond anecdotes, there is also some partial scientific evidence to support this claim. Anderson (2010) looked at data from 62 developing countries (e.g., Egypt, Ethiopia, Kenya, and the Philippines) and found that the longer a country's life expectancy, the longer its residents tended to delay marriage. (This finding was more robust in women than in men, and outside, rather than inside, of sub-Saharan Africa; Anderson suggests that the latter finding may stem from sub-Saharan Africa's AIDS epidemic, which can quickly alter countries' average life expectancy.)

Have the last 20 years or so been the only time in US history that people have delayed marriage until their mid-late twenties and early thirties? Actually, no. About 130 years ago (1890), men typically married at age 26, although women at the much younger age of 22 (Amato, 2011). It was really after soldiers returned from World War II that the typical marriage age really dipped, falling to 20 in women and 23 in men in 1950. These couples also had a lot of children, resulting in what is well known as the Baby Boom (births between 1946 and 1964). People continued to marry at these young ages until 1970, when a steady rise began toward older ages at marriage (Amato, 2011). Because ages at marriage have swung up and down in the past, therefore, they could turn again toward younger ages in the future. If so, we would have to come up with a new theory to replace or modify our notion of emerging adulthood (Arnett, 2007).

If not everyone between 18 and 30 is an emerging adult, how do I know if I am one? Let me start by clarifying that many researchers don't see EA as a binary status (i.e., yes, you are one; no, you're not). Rather, Arnett's (2015a) theory describes many of the characteristics people in EA are going through, so if you match most of these characteristics you are *for the most part* an emerging adult, if you match very few of these characteristics you are generally not going through EA, etc. Also, between 2001 and 2007, your trusty author, along with Jeff Arnett himself and my Texas Tech colleague Malinda Colwell,[6] developed, tested, and published a questionnaire to score people on the degree to which they fit the characteristics of EA (Reifman et al., 2007a). You can all take this questionnaire, known as the Inventory of the Dimensions of Emerging Adulthood (IDEA), at the end of the chapter. Arnett (2015a) proposed that these EA characteristics fall into five categories.

First, EA is a time of identity exploration and finding out the kind of person you are. EA identity exploration is a continuation of the identity exploration the famous lifespan theorist Erik Erikson (1968) postulated was the central task of adolescence. As we will examine more thoroughly in a later chapter on the topic, identity formation is not achieved by many adolescents, nor even by some emerging adults, and so is a continuing process. Linking back to an earlier section, Osgood and colleagues (2005) argued that their educated-partner and educated-single subgroups most closely resembled the notion of emerging adulthood, as their education could be considered a form of exploration. Second, individuals see the EA years as a time of open possibilities and open doors. Some people may be natural optimists, but also they may not have experienced the kind of setbacks – rejection from college, grad school, or a training program; washing out at a job –

that can signal their dream career is not for them (Arnett, 2015a). Third, EA is a time of self-focus, not in a selfish way, but in terms of taking on the kinds of self-sufficiency and responsibility that laypersons consider essential for adulthood (i.e., taking responsibility for one's actions, making one's own decisions, becoming financially responsible). The fourth aspect of Arnett's theory is that EA is a time of stress and instability. Individuals face stress and anxiety all through the lifespan, but EA presents its own challenges (e.g., doing well in school, getting a good job, dating and relationships). Also, the instability of EA appears in such mundane things as residential moves. Whether people go to college or not, there's a good chance they will move out of their parents' house and perhaps into and out of different apartments (perhaps living alone, with friends, or with a romantic partner). During my five years of graduate school, I lived in four different apartments and I always found packing up and moving to be very stressful! Fifth and finally, EA is a time of feeling "in between" adolescence and full-fledged adulthood. When Arnett (2001) asked people in their twenties, "Do you think that you have reached adulthood?" and gave them the options "yes," "no," or "in some respects yes, in some respects no," the most common response was the blended yes-and-no choice (50%), edging out the purely "yes" response (roughly 45%). In contrast, people aged 30–55 were near unanimous in saying "yes" (roughly 85%).

People in their twenties seem to grasp intuitively that, at their age, they can try to explore and find out about themselves in ways that they no longer will be able to once they reach full adulthood and become responsible for other people, not just themselves. A study by Russell Ravert (2009) captures this phenomenon nicely. Ravert surveyed nearly 250 university students,[7] asking them, "How often do you do or try something because you think you won't be able to do it later on when you settle down as an adult?" (from 0 [never] to 4 [all of the time]) and if they did, in what kinds of behaviors had they engaged (p. 381). The average frequency was around 2 (sometimes). Students' listed behaviors fell into eight categories:

- Travel (e.g., "random road trips").
- Social (e.g., "all-night parties").
- Substance use (e.g., "playing drinking games," "experimenting with drugs").
- Relationships (e.g., "lots of boyfriends," "mostly experiences with different women").
- Carefree (e.g., "being lazy," "do something a bit risky").
- Sports action (e.g., "rock climbing," "sky diving").
- Academic career (e.g., "study abroad").
- Independence (e.g., "getting tattoos," "dyeing my hair with funny colors").

Ravert's (2009) study supports the "window of exploration" aspect of EA (Figure 1.3). Other findings have supported Arnett's EA theory, as well. On the aforementioned IDEA questionnaire, Reifman et al. (2007a, 2007b) compared the age groups 18–23, 24–29, 30–39, 40–49, and 50-plus on sets of items assessing the emerging adult characteristics of identity-seeking, open possibilities, self-focus, stress-instability, and feeling in-between. For example, items measuring identity-seeking had respondents rate the extent to which this part of their life was a time of "finding out who you are," "separating from parents," "defining yourself," and "deciding on your own beliefs and values" (among other items). Results showed that the purported emerging adulthood features were highest in 18–23-year-olds and progressively lower as age increased.

Critiques of Emerging Adulthood

Arnett's (2000) theory of emerging adulthood is almost certainly the most widely used lens through which to study human development between the ages of 18 and 30. Thanks to the organizational work of Arnett and others, there is now a professional society for researchers, known as the Society for the Study of Emerging Adulthood, and a journal called *Emerging Adulthood*, in which to publish our studies. Still, there are some detractors of Arnett's theory of emerging adulthood, meaning that they do not believe it accurately describes how people act or structure their lives from 18 to 30 or that it offers useful ideas for further research. These critics do not necessarily have a problem with the way many people in this age group live their lives (e.g., delaying the onset of traditional adult roles) the way some other critics do. It's just the theory they do not like. Some critiques of EA theory appear below in Table 1.1, along with Arnett's responses.

The critiques, offered by journalists Robin Henig and Samantha Henig, psychologists Richard Lerner and Leo Hendry, education and psychology scholar Marion Kloep, and sociologists Michael Kimmel and James Côté, center on several key themes. Do we need the concept of emerging adulthood at all? After all, previous authors have proposed seemingly similar ideas, such as Erik Erikson's (1968) notion of a *moratorium* (a "time-out" from full adult responsibilities that those in their late teens and early twenties can use for exploration) and even Arnett acknowledges that EA may be relevant only in some societies during certain historical eras. How can EA be a stage theory if not everyone goes through it? Don't some people go through EA-like behaviors (e.g., considering a new career) at later ages than 30? Are people really as systematic in preparing for adulthood as Arnett says? Why doesn't EA have more to say about gender? And finally, is the "career exploration" Arnett talks about really just a matter of the youngest workers having little job security and switching jobs because they have to, not that they choose to?

Another set of EA critics, on the other hand, denigrate the lifestyle choices of many 18–30-year-olds themselves or other societal actors (e.g., parents, the media) that the critics believe facilitate unproductive behavior during people's twenty-something years. One critic in the latter camp is US Senator Ben Sasse, Republican of Nebraska, who wrote a book entitled *The Vanishing American Adult* (Sasse, 2017). In it, he refers to young people being in a state of "perpetual adolescence" and claims, perhaps with some exaggeration, that "Our kids simply don't know what an adult is anymore – or how to become one. Many don't see a reason even to try" (p. 2). We'll hear from other critics of today's youth – regarding their approach to education and politics, for example – later in the book. I'll present as much evidence as I can about how young people transition to adulthood so that you can decide for yourself whether you think most are successful at it or not.

TABLE 1.1 Critiques of the Concept of Emerging Adulthood (EA)

Critique	Arnett's Response
Concept of EA is not new; previous authors have written about similar ideas, just with different names (e.g., Henig & Henig, 2012).	Argues that EA captures the phenomenon of interest better than alternative labels such as "late adolescence," "young adulthood," "transition to adulthood," or "youth" (2015a, pp. 20-24). EA is a life stage, in and of itself, not merely a passageway to some other stage.
Lerner (quoted in Henig, 2010): For EA to be a life stage, all people must pass through a "universal sequence in stages that can't be skipped or reordered."	Individuals who do not go through EA between 18 and 30 may experience the same processes (e.g., exploration, self-focus) at a later time (quoted in Henig, 2010).
Hendry and Kloep (2007): (Regardless of age) "most of us are almost always in the state of being in between or emerging" (p. 75).	"more than any other period of life, emerging adulthood presents the possibility of change" (Arnett, 2004, p. 17).
Hendry and Kloep: EA is "limited to a certain age cohort in certain societies at a certain historical time with particular socioeconomic conditions" (p. 76).	"Eventually, the theory of emerging adulthood may be displaced by other theories as cultures and economies change in ways we cannot imagine today, but for the foreseeable future it will be an increasingly useful framework and model for the lives of young people" (Arnett, 2007, p. 81).
Kimmel (2008): "In an ideal world, [Arnett's notion of EA development] might be a dream trajectory. Yet Arnett's view of this stage of life is so sanguine, so sanitized, it's hardly recognizable. It's hard to square such serious self-reflection with the bacchanalian [heavy-drinking] atmosphere of a college weekend" (p. 39).	Individuals are not as irresponsible during EA as some people think. They "generally make very good use of [their time]. They do a lot of interesting things with their 20s. Things like join Teach for America, join the Peace Corps, try some interesting place to live or travel" (quoted on Today Show, 2010).
Kimmel: "One reason Jeffrey Arnett and his colleagues can be so sanguine about emerging adulthood is because there is nary a word about gender in their work. But how can one possibly discuss the age group 16 to 26 and not talk about gender? It's the most gendered stage of a person's development" (p. 41).	Arnett has not written heavily about gender during EA. This issue is discussed more extensively in Chapter 2.
Côté (2014): "Economists refer to unstable youth work histories as 'churning,' but Arnett reduces the churning experienced by many young people to freely chosen 'identity explorations' with various types of jobs rather than seeing their actions as coping with precarious, ambiguous, and exploitive job situations" (p. 184).	Arnett (2016): "social class differences … need to be taken seriously in public policy, especially in providing more opportunities for lower [socioeconomic status] emerging adults to obtain tertiary [college] education" (p. 232).

Review

You now have an introduction to the study of emerging adulthood. Many terms and ideas have been put forth, so to help you remember the major points, here's a summary in the format of the "12 Days of Christmas" (mine only goes through six). You should remember:

SIX pathways to adulthood: fast starters, parents without careers, educated partners, educated singles, working singles, and slow starters (Osgood et al., 2005).

FIVE features of Arnett's (2004) theory of emerging adulthood: identity-seeking, sense of open possibilities, self-focusing (personal responsibility), stress and instability, and feeling in between adolescence and full-fledged adulthood.

FOUR revolutions, Arnett (2015a) argues, led to the delay of marriage and other EA-related trends in the US and other economically advanced nations: the technological-information revolution, sexual revolution, women's movement, and youth movement (and a fifth one I proposed, namely the aging revolution).

THREE ways of studying the transition to adulthood: attainment of milestones, layperson criteria, and Arnett's EA theory. Also, THREE behaviors that most layperson observers say make someone an adult: accept responsibility for your own actions, decide on your own beliefs and values, and become financially independent of one's parents (Arnett, 2001).

TWO periods of restriction (relatively speaking) between EA's "window of opportunity to explore": childhood and adolescence (living under parents' rules) and full-fledged adulthood (responsibility for one's own family [potentially], house payments, etc.).

ONE plate of spaghetti (Figure 1.2) to emphasize the many ups and downs individuals experience in becoming an adult and how nearly everyone has their own unique pathway to get there.

Now, to help you and your classmates get some first-hand experience studying the transition to adulthood and emerging adulthood, I have some activities your instructor may choose to have you complete.

Possible Class Activities

1. How well do you fit the characteristics of emerging adulthood? Take the test!

Inventory of the Dimensions of Emerging Adulthood

■ First, please think about this time in your life. By "time in your life," we are referring to the present time, plus the last few years that have gone by, and the next few years to come, as you see them. In short, you should think about a roughly five-year period, with the present time right in the middle.

■ For each phrase shown below, please place a check mark in *one* of the columns to indicate the degree to which you agree or disagree that the phrase describes this time in your life. For example, if you "Somewhat Agree" that this is a "time of exploration," then on the same line as the phrase, you would put a check mark in the column headed by "Somewhat Agree" (3).

Is This Period of Your Life a ...	Strongly Disagree (1)	Somewhat Disagree (2)	Somewhat Agree (3)	Strongly Agree (4)
1. Time of many possibilities?				
2. Time of exploration?				
3. Time of confusion?				
4. Time of experimentation?				
5. Time of personal freedom?				
6. Time of feeling restricted?				
7. Time of responsibility for yourself?				
8. Time of feeling stressed out?				
9. Time of instability?				
10. Time of optimism?				
11. Time of high pressure?				
12. Time of finding out who you are?				
13. Time of settling down?				
14. Time of responsibility for others?				
15. Time of independence?				
16. Time of open choices?				
17. Time of unpredictability?				
18. Time of commitments to others?				
19. Time of self-sufficiency?				
20. Time of many worries?				
21. Time of trying out new things?				
22. Time of focusing on yourself?				
23. Time of separating from parents?				
24. Time of defining yourself?				
25. Time of planning for the future?				
26. Time of seeking a sense of meaning?				
27. Time of deciding on your own beliefs and values?				
28. Time of learning to think for yourself?				

29. Time of feeling adult in some ways but not others?

30. Time of gradually becoming an adult?

31. Time of being not sure whether you have reached full
   adulthood?

To convert the 31 items (above) into the five core subscales of emerging adulthood (plus an extra sixth one described below), you need to compute the averages of sets of items. For example, to obtain your score for identity exploration, you would take the average of the response scores you gave for items 12, 23, 24, 25, 26, 27, and 28.

Subscale	Take the Average of Your Responses to These Items:	Your Average Score	Average for Previous College Students
Identity Exploration	12, 23, 24, 25, 26, 27, 28		3.30
Experimentation/Possibilities	1, 2, 4, 16, 21		3.25
Negativity/Instability	3, 6, 8, 9, 11, 17, 20		2.90
Self-Focused	5, 7, 10, 15, 19, 22		3.30
Feeling "In-Between"	29, 30, 31		3.25
Other-Focused (This is an extra subscale to assess the degree to which people become more focused on other people, such as a spouse or children, as they age out of emerging adulthood.)	13, 14, 18		2.55

2. Interview a friend or family member who fits Osgood and colleagues' (2005) types of transitions. For example, you could interview a "fast starter" who has married, had one or more children, works full time, or has moved out of their parents' home by age 24 (or so). I assign my students to interview a fast-starter for one mini-paper and someone going more slowly (e.g., educated single) for another. Possible questions include: Did you plan to follow the life path you're following, or did circumstances intervene? Did you marry at a much younger or much older age than your peers? If so, do you feel out of sync with them? If you took on adult roles at a young age, do you feel you've missed out on things such as socializing with friends? For privacy, you should ask the interviewee if it is OK to use their real name or if they would prefer a pseudonym. These papers should relate the interviewee's experience to the course material.

Notes

1 "I'm Not a Girl, Not Yet a Woman" (written by Max Martin, Rami Yacoub, and Dido Armstrong, produced by Martin and Yacoub, Jive Records, 2002); "This One's for the Girls"

(written by Chris Lindsey, Hillary Lindsey, and Aimee Mayo, produced by Martina McBride and Paul Worley, RCA Nashville, 2003); "Big Girls Don't Cry"(written by Fergie [Stacy Ferguson] and Toby Gad, produced by will.i.am [William Adams, Jr.], A&M Records/will.i.am/Interscope).

2 *Friends* (created by David Crane and Marta Kauffman, Warner Brothers, 1994–2004); *Atypical* (created by Robia Rashid, Exhibit A/Sony Pictures, 2017–2021); *Sex Education* (created by Laurie Nunn, Eleven, 2019–2021); *Failure to Launch* (Produced by Scott Aversano and Scott Rudin; Paramount Pictures, 2006); *Juno* (Produced by Lianne Halforn, John Malkovich, Mason Novick, and Russell Smith; Fox Searchlight, Mandate Pictures, and Mr. Mudd, 2007); *Pride and Prejudice* (written by Jane Austen, originally published by Thomas Egerton, 1813); *On the Road* (written by Jack Kerouac, Viking Press, 1957). See also Barmak (2010) for literary references to the transition to adulthood.

3 Greenwood and colleagues (2019) present a history of contraception going back to the 1800s and a mathematical analysis of how the availability of contraceptives may have affected people's decision to marry. It is the only article I am aware of that contains both photos of some of the earliest condoms and equations using calculus!

4 Greenwood and colleagues (2019) did not report the percentage of women born in the 1980s who had engaged in premarital sex by age 30, perhaps because women born late in the 1980s would only have been reaching age 30 in the late 2010s.

5 The 1964 Civil Rights Act's ban on sex discrimination in employment actually has a strange history. Representative Howard Smith, who wanted to sink the overall bill, thought the prospect of women's employment rights would turn off some members of Congress who otherwise were leaning toward supporting the overall legislation. Smith therefore proposed an amendment protecting against sex discrimination. The ban on sex discrimination in the workforce passed, but contrary to the object of Smith's ploy, the overall Civil Rights Act passed as well (Menand, 2014; Zelizer, 2015).

6 Dr. Colwell mainly studies child development, but also occasionally studies other ages, with the rationale that children eventually do become adolescents and adults.

7 As will be discussed later, people can be emerging adults whether they attend college or not. College attendance is not required to be considered an emerging adult. However, because most people who study emerging adulthood are professors and have ready access to survey students at their universities, most of the research on EA involves college students.

Cultural and Demographic Variation

You can take the guy out of the neighborhood but you can't take the neighborhood out of the guy.

— Frankie Valli

The play *Jersey Boys* (later made into a motion picture[1]) chronicles the history of the pop-music group The Four Seasons, with Frankie Valli as lead singer. It focuses on the importance to the members of their heritage growing up in the US state of New Jersey. As the opening quote suggests, where you come from – encompassing the traditions you learn, the people you meet, and so forth – affects the kind of person you become. At least for some people. Other people, upon moving into a new environment, quickly absorb the culture of their new setting and behave more like people in their new surroundings than like those from their original home. Physical locations are not the only source of culture, traditions, and societal expectations for how we should act. Our race–ethnicity,[2] gender, and social class may also affect our life opportunities and behavior. These ideas certainly apply to the steps of becoming an adult, as we'll discuss in this chapter. Here, we examine differences in the forms and timing of individuals' attainment of adult milestones, comparing different countries, different subgroups within the US, and different immigrant groups to the US.

Transition to Adulthood around the World

Researchers predominantly have studied the transition to adulthood (and most other issues in social science research) in the US, Europe, and other "WEIRD" (Western, Educated, Industrialized, Rich, Democratic) societies (Henrich et al., 2010) such as Canada and Australia. What about other parts of the world, such as Africa, Asia, and South America? As we'll see there's a growing body of research on the transition to adulthood in different corners of the world, using different approaches. These include studying parental socialization of grown children as they move toward full-fledged adulthood, the different features of Arnett's (2015a) theory of emerging adulthood, and people's criteria for considering someone an adult.

DOI: 10.4324/9781003156567-3

Parental Socialization of Grown Children

A great source of information on the transition to adulthood around the world, in general and from a parental-socialization perspective, is the book *The Accordion Family* (Newman, 2012). The book's title refers to how households can expand and contract with the arrival or departure of family members, the same way one stretches or compresses an accordion to play music. The book features interviews with emerging adults and parents in the US, Japan, and several European countries on people's attitudes toward grown children living at home until their thirties or moving back home with their parents after having lived elsewhere (such as college) for a time ("Boomerang Kids"). According to Newman, parents around the world fall into three camps when it comes to their feelings about grown children living in the family house: vehement opposition; grudging acceptance, as long as their child is working at a job or receiving some kind of training or apprenticeship that holds the promise of future employment; and complete and unconditional support. Take a moment to think of where you would place your home country on this spectrum. In addition, if you have visited other countries or know people from them, how supportive do families in those countries seem to be of grown children living at home?

Among the nations studied by Newman (2012), opposition to grown children living at home is greatest in Japan, where the issue is said to exasperate parents to "almost hysterical proportions" (p. 83). Key to Japanese parents' thinking is the concern that the grown children are missing many of the challenges (e.g., finding a job, managing their finances, and maintaining their own household) that the parents believe are necessary to develop a proper work ethic and maturity for adulthood in general. (US Senator Ben Sasse, cited in the first chapter, would certainly agree.) Further, Japanese parents believe, the failure of so many grown children to take on these challenges will result in the society as a whole declining. The marriage rate in Japan is also declining, one apparent reason being that many young women have been rebelling against traditional Japanese caregiving norms (that women devote themselves to caring for their husbands and that the wives of eldest sons devote themselves to caring for their husbands' parents). According to one Japanese mother quoted in Newman (2012), "because of increasing information and work, women can see different worlds, and they are challenging such things, and that is why marriage is delayed" (p. 94).

Let's look at the other end of the spectrum of countries studied by Newman (2012). In the southern European nations of Italy and Spain, parents are, for the most part, very happy to have their grown children with them at home.[3] According to research cited by Newman, "Italian parents benefit from the companionship and other services their children provide … [and] importantly, from the opportunity they have to get their children to 'conform' to their precepts when they live together" (p. 98).[4] As for Spain,

> The older generation remembers their relations with their fathers as emotionally distant … Today, Spanish parents want nothing to do with that old-fashioned model of parent-child relations. They want to feel close and affectionate, even as their children become in-house adults. No one seems to fear any loss of independence.
>
> *(p. 114)*

Interestingly, while the percentage of grown children living at home is noticeably different between Japan, on the one hand, and Italy and Spain, on the other, the differences are not extremely huge. Whereas "80% of Spaniards under thirty still live at home with parents" (*The Local*, 2016) and 76.4% of 20–29-year-olds in Italy live with their parents, 60.0% of 20–24-year-olds and 43.2% of 25–29-year-olds do so in Japan (Crocetti et al., 2015). One factor that likely contributes to the different parental attitudes is Japan's low youth (15–24) unemployment rate of 8%, compared to 29.1% in Italy (Crocetti et al., 2015) and the mid-fifties to the mid-thirties percentage range between 2012 and 2019 in Spain (Statista, 2021a). Many a Japanese parent has probably wondered: *Why, when my grown children are working, must they remain at home?* Newman (2012) also notes that parents in Spain tend to see their children's current economic difficulties as due to structural factors – the actions of government and businesses – rather than the shortcomings of their grown children.

What about the country in which parents grudgingly accept their grown children living at home? That country is the US, where 15.9% of men and 9.7% of women ages 25–34 live at home (Crocetti et al., 2015). Newman (2012) elaborates that

> In the American context, as long as a young man or woman appears to be making headway toward a profession or a meaningful career, the family can take heart and understand its role as facilitating an honorable future that is just harder to come by than it once was … It wouldn't be the same if Junior were holed up in his room practicing air guitar.
>
> *(pp. 82–83)*

The US unemployment rate for 15–24-year-olds is 17.3%, roughly halfway between Japan and Italy (Crocetti et al., 2015).

In addition to the US and Italy, greater frequency of young adults living in their family home and increasing average ages of moving out over the past 30–40 years have been reported in Australia, Belgium, Canada, France, the Netherlands, and Sweden (Seiffge-Krenke, 2016).[5] In England, where "One in five working 20 to 34-year-olds … has moved back in with their parents or grandparents in the last year," the phenomenon is known as the "Clipped Wing Generation," which can't fly away (Shaw, 2015). Data on the extent and timing of home-leaving behavior in non-WEIRD countries are hard to come by. I did find one reference to the Clipped Wing Generation in Nigeria, however, pertaining to the high cost of housing in the large city of Lagos (Sofola, 2019). To examine non-WEIRD countries, we look next at other measures of the transition to adulthood.

Features of Arnett's Emerging Adulthood Theory

Crocetti and colleagues (2015) administered a modified version of the Inventory of the Dimensions of Emerging Adulthood (the questionnaire you encountered at the end of Chapter 1) to 18–30-year-olds in Japan and Italy. As you will recall, this questionnaire measures features of EA such as feeling one is experiencing a time of exploration, and open possibilities. Take a moment to consider which of these countries – Italy, with its high rates of unemployment and grown children living at home, or Japan, with its lower unemployment and moderately high rate of grown children living at home – you think would have higher scores for the features of emerging adulthood. I initially thought it would be Italy, as its young adults might feel in more of an exploratory mood with their parents' blessing than in Japan. Naturally, the country that scored higher was Japan! Japanese respondents exceeded their Italian counterparts by a large margin on sense of open possibilities and by smaller margins on identity-seeking, self-focus, stress-instability, and feeling in-between. Crocetti et al. (2015) suggested that the low sense of possibility exhibited by Italian youth could reflect economic and employment difficulties in their country, pessimism over whether increased education could increase their life opportunities, and a general sense of uncertainty.

Researchers have also examined the features of emerging adulthood in Latin America, a large region of the world consisting of Mexico (North America), the nations of Central America and the Caribbean (e.g., Dominican Republic, Grenada, Nicaragua), and the continent of South America (Facio et al. 2017). Most EA research in Latin America has occurred in the South American nations of Argentina (Facio et al., 2007) and Brazil (Dutra-Thomé, 2013). Facio et al. (2007) reported that, whereas the average scores of Argentinian youth (18–21 years old) on identity exploration, open possibilities, and self-focus matched closely with those obtained in the US (see Activity 1 at the end of Chapter 1), participants in Argentina scored lower on stress-instability than did their US counterparts. In Brazil, Dutra-Thomé (2013) recruited a sample of 18–29-year-olds through institutions offering various instructional levels such as adult education on basic skills and universities. As with Argentina, average scores on most of the EA facets were similar between Brazil and the US (Dutra-Thomé, 2013). One exception involved the sense of open possibilities, on which Brazilian participants scored higher than those in the US.

Criteria and Choices for Adulthood

As you will recall from Chapter 1, assessing criteria for adulthood entails asking respondents which of a set of actions such as getting married and taking responsibility for oneself they would require of people to consider them adults. Some studies ask participants to answer "yes" or "no" whether they think each criterion is necessary for adulthood, in which case researchers report the percentage of respondents who say "yes" (e.g., Obidoa et al., 2019). In other studies (e.g., Mitra & Arnett, 2021; Wider et al., in press), researchers ask participants to rate how important they believe each criterion is, on a scale from 1 ("not at all important") to 4 ("very important").

Africa contains over 50 nations, two of the most populated being Nigeria (1st, 206 million people) and Ghana (13th, 31 million; Worldometer, 2021). Obidoa et al. (2019) surveyed university students in these two nations to assess their criteria for adulthood. Traditionally, marriage was a key marker of adulthood in at least some parts of both Ghana and Nigeria (e.g., Igbo society in Nigeria), along with economic independence, family togetherness, and childbearing. As in other countries, however, individuals are delaying marriage in Africa until their mid-late twenties, in part due to increasing education for girls and women (Obidoa et al., 2019). Further, as Obidoa and colleagues note, "as a result of globalization, young people are being increasingly exposed to Western ideas and popular culture that introduce new ideas that are different from beliefs and practices found in their traditional cultures" (p. 271); this exposure could also contribute to delayed marriage in Africa.

So what kinds of accomplishments did the respondents in Ghana and Nigeria say they considered important for considering someone an adult? Unlike in the US, where it has been rare to find 90% agreement on anything, many criteria garnered 90% (or higher) support in these two nations (the researchers combined the categories "agree" and "strongly agree" to constitute an affirmative response). The most agreed-upon criterion for adulthood was "Decide on personal beliefs and values independently of parents or other influences" (99.1% in Ghana, 96.7% in Nigeria). This kind of independence-related standard resembles what we have seen in the US and other countries (Chapter 1). Along the same lines, becoming "Financially independent from parents" and "Accept[ing] responsibility for the consequences of your actions" exceeded 90% endorsement in both nations. Another widely endorsed set of items fell within the domain of family responsibilities, such as "becom[ing] capable of supporting a family financially" and "becom[ing] capable of caring for children." Respondents expected both men and women to possess these abilities, with over 90% consensus. Finally, the third set of highly endorsed items pertained to personal restraint and conduct. These included "Learn[ing] always to have good control of your emotions" (97.2% in Ghana, 98.8% in Nigeria), "Avoid[ing] use of profanity/vulgar language" (89.2%, 92.4%), and "Avoid[ing] drunk driving" (87.4%, 92.4%).

The continent of Asia includes many countries comprising regions such as East or Northeast Asia (e.g., China, Japan, South Korea), Southeast Asia (e.g., Malaysia, Philippines, Vietnam), and South Asia (e.g., Afghanistan, India, Pakistan). Researchers have conducted studies on the transition to adulthood in many of these countries. Nelson et al. (2004) surveyed university students in China to determine their criteria for adulthood. Three items – accepting responsibility for the consequences of one's actions, becoming financially independent, and deciding on one's own beliefs and values – received endorsement from 89% to 97% of respondents as being necessary for adulthood, a result resembling those from many nations. The item about controlling one's emotions garnered 95% endorsement, revealing a parallel between the African nations described above and China. Finally, 93% of Chinese respondents endorsed the item "Become less self-oriented, develop greater consideration for others," which may provide a balance to the self-oriented criteria endorsed there.

Wider et al. (in press) surveyed 18–29-year-olds in Sabah, East Malaysia, the second largest state in Malaysia, on how important they considered various behaviors for adulthood (1–4 ratings). The items rated highest, on average, in importance for considering someone an adult were having control over one's emotions, avoiding drunk driving, avoiding illegal drugs, and refraining from petty crimes such as vandalism and shoplifting. These items are conceptually similar to the self-restraint items noted above as being important in Ghana and Nigeria. Note that, in the Malaysia study, the kinds of items about establishing independence and acting for oneself showed some statistical difficulties and were not included in the final analyses.

Lastly, among the Asian studies, Mitra and Arnett (2021) conducted a study in India, examining the transition to adulthood from a somewhat different angle than whether participants considered certain behaviors essential to becoming an adult. Mitra and Arnett gathered data from university-based samples of 18–29-year-olds via focus-group discussions and measures completed by individuals. These respondents came mostly from large cities (e.g., Mumbai and Delhi, each with over 10 million population; Worldometer, 2020). Instead of investigating the students' criteria for adulthood, Mitra and Arnett looked at what they considered the most important decisions they would have to make in becoming an adult. Mitra and Arnett suggested that the cultural characteristics of India might lead to different personal choices than would likely be seen in the US and other Western countries. As they noted, "While emerging adulthood is often seen as a time of self-focus in individualistic cultures, it may be different in other cultures, such as India, where interests of the community are placed higher than the interests of the self" (p. 229).

Choices the Indian students considered most important (average rating of 3.50 or higher, where 4 was the maximum) fell into three domains (Mitra & Arnett, 2021). These involved *responsibility toward family* ("Being responsible for the well-being of my parents," "Maintaining a healthy lifestyle"); *independence/autonomy* ("Choosing my own hobbies and interests," "Becoming financially secure before getting married"); and *exploring education and career* ("Pursuing a job that complements my skills and interests"). As many of you probably know, a feature of Indian society that is different from the US is arranged marriage (for some couples). For the record, though, participants' importance rating for "Selecting a spouse by myself" was a relatively high 3.35. Mitra and Arnett concluded from their overall findings that individuals going through emerging adulthood in India face a balancing act between "establishing continuity of family values and traditions while seeking and exploring identities to enhance their sense of their individual self" (p. 235).

Let's return to Latin America to close out this section. Within Argentina, the most highly rated criteria for adulthood match those typically found in the US, namely taking responsibility for one's actions, deciding on beliefs and values, and becoming financially independent, all with over 90% endorsement (Facio et al., 2007). Controlling one's emotions and showing consideration for others, which have frequently emerged as important criteria in Africa and Asia, exceeded 90% endorsement in Argentina, as well. Researchers have also investigated the criteria for adulthood in Brazil. Using the same respondents as those in the aforementioned study of features of EA in Brazil, Dutra-Thomé (2013) likewise found taking responsibility and becoming financially independent to be the two most commonly cited criteria. The third-highest criterion was completing one's studies, which the author attributed to "difficulty of access to higher education throughout the country" (p. 39). One way in which the results for Brazil differed from all the other countries studied was the relative lack of consensus characteristic of other places. Whereas 90% or more of respondents in most countries agreed on the top criteria for adulthood, the most commonly cited one in Brazil – that is, taking responsibility for oneself – drew support from only slightly above 40% of participants.

Before we leave the topic of emerging adulthood around the world, here is an important warning. Although research is branching out into many understudied areas (i.e., Africa, Asia, South America), often the research participants in these parts of the world are university students. In many countries, individuals who go to "Uni" (a British shorthand) are likely to be more privileged than are their non-student counterparts and therefore are not totally representative of a given nation or continent. Now that we are done with our international tour, there is a memento for you, a map of the world, highlighting the countries from which we have seen research results (Figure 2.1).

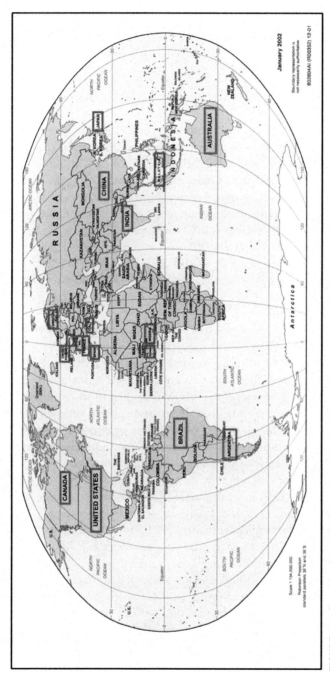

FIGURE 2.1 Countries from which this chapter has cited research on the transition to adulthood (country names boxed in red).

Source: Map from Wikimedia Commons; produced by US government, so in the public domain (red boxes added by A. Reifman).

Differences within the US in Attaining Adult Milestones

As the sociologist Andrew Cherlin (2009) says, race–ethnicity, gender, and social class comprise the "holy trinity of social science" (p. 159). We will cover these three areas within US society in this new section. Many people are simply curious about similarities and differences in the attitudes, behaviors, and life circumstances of people of different races and ethnicities; men, women, and those with other gender identities; and those of different social classes. Others see the examination of group differences as a way to test claims of universality. Do most people in all social groups in the US go through the stage of emerging adulthood (or something like it), or do members of some groups largely miss EA and chart out a different path for themselves to adulthood?

Race–Ethnicity

There are several reasons for supposing that, on average, members of different racial–ethnic groups might experience their transitions differently. One way to approach this question is through the lens of ethnic minority psychology, which posits that "In many societies … minorities have restricted access to power and resources that give rise to a unique psychological experience and perspective" (Syed & Mitchell, 2016, p. 89). For one thing, growing up as a member of a minority group may create a greater obligation to help one's family rather than being so concerned with independence (Syed & Mitchell, 2016). Again, not every Black, Hispanic, Asian, or Native American young adult would be family-oriented, but on average these groups might exhibit greater family affinity than Whites. Also, racial–ethnic minorities in the US, on average, have lower income than Whites, which could intensify the sense of family obligation.

To examine some of the similarities and differences in the experiences of members of racial–ethnic majority and minority groups in the US, we will start with an in-depth examination of an older study (Furstenberg & Kmec, 2000) that illustrates some of the issues researchers need to consider. We will then evaluate a couple of more recent studies. Furstenberg and Kmec sought to study "how race and gender segregation might affect the social mobility of minority and white men and women differently" (p. 6). To do so, they analyzed data originally collected in 1991 from "poor, working-class, and lower-middle class communities in inner-city areas of Philadelphia" (p. 3). Nearly 500 families with children ages 11–15 participated, most of whom were White or Black, with a smaller number of Puerto Ricans. As of 1990, Philadelphia was the fifth most populated US city, with roughly 1.5 million people (Fernández Águeda, 2009). It was also at that time deemed a highly segregated city (Othering and Belonging Institute, 2021). Twenty years later (in 2010), Whites (depicted in red) and Blacks (depicted in blue) were still living largely in different parts of Philadelphia, as shown in Figure 2.2.

Furstenberg and Kmec (2000) then re-contacted as many of the originally participating youths as possible several years later (1998 or 1999) when they were 18–23, securing cooperation from all but around 100 of the original youth to complete another round of measures. As you may recall from Chapter 1, attainment of traditional roles is one marker of whether someone has successfully reached adulthood. Furstenberg and Kmec focused only on education and paid labor as markers of

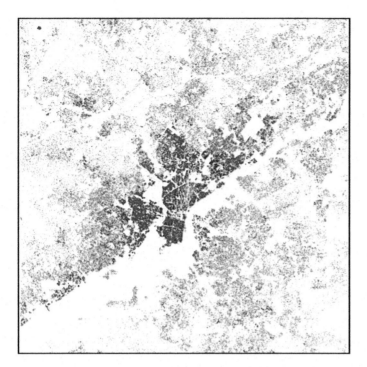

FIGURE 2.2 Race and ethnicity 2010: Philadelphia by Eric Fischer. Red is White, blue is Black, green is Asian, orange is Hispanic, and yellow is Other. Each dot is 25 residents. Maps of racial and ethnic divisions in US cities, inspired by Bill Rankin's map of Chicago, updated for Census 2010.
Source: Data from Census 2010. Base map © OpenStreetMap, CC-BY-SA. https://commons.wikimedia .org/wiki/File:Race_and_ethnicity_2010-_Philadelphia_(5559907949).png

adulthood, creating a system to define whether each young adult in their study had been on-track or off-track en route to adulthood. For example, if someone pursued some type of post-high school education (technical, community college, bachelor's degree, or postgraduate) and/or obtained full-time employment, they would be considered on-track. On the other hand, if they dropped out of high school or went no further than a high school diploma, as well as working no more than part-time, they were considered off-track. Furstenberg and Kmec also classified their partici-pants into low, medium, and high socioeconomic status (SES) in 1999. (Remember that we need precise definitions to conduct scientific research so that other scholars could try to reproduce Furstenberg and Kmec's findings in a different year or city.)

What percentage of these Philadelphia-based White and minority men and women had achieved success (were on-track) in the educational–occupational sphere by age 23? White and minority women were just about equally likely to have stayed on track. In fact, by 1999, 41.3% of White women and 40.0% of minority women had achieved high SES. It was a different story among men, however, as White men (31%) were more likely than their minority counterparts (22.3%) to have achieved high SES. Why might this be the case? First, although the researchers sought out comparably disadvantaged White and minority communities,

it [was] not possible to find equivalently bad conditions in white neighborhoods though we did manage to include the poorest white areas of Philadelphia. Even so, none of these completely matched the poorest black and Puerto Rican areas in the study.

(Furstenberg & Kmec, 2000, p. 3)[6]

Second, note Furstenberg and Kmec, "Possibly the risk of living in poor neighborhoods takes a higher toll on minority males who are less likely to find employment, more likely to hang out on the streets, and more likely to suffer discrimination" (p. 28). Of course, not all minority men did poorly in the educational–occupational sphere. According to Furstenberg and Kmec, "increased frequency of parent religious service attendance reduce[d] the odds of minority men being off track in early adulthood by 35%" (p. 23). This does not prove that having your parents take you to religious services improves your educational and economic attainment, although it's possible. It could also be the case, however, that families in which the children work hard at school also are drawn to organized religion.

Note that it was the *combination or intersection* of race–ethnicity and gender (in terms of minority women, White women, minority men, and White men) that really delineated between those groups in the Philadelphia study that did well or poorly in their school and work lives in early adulthood. With this finding, we have our first encounter with the term *intersectionality*, which currently is one of the hottest concepts within the social sciences. Introduced by law professor Kimberlé Crenshaw (1989), intersectionality has taken 30 years to reach large segments of academic and general audiences (Coaston, 2019). Simply stated, the way individuals are treated in society – sometimes with discriminatory effect – often depends on *combinations* of their characteristics. A working-class Latino man, for example, may be treated differently than a wealthy Latino man or a Latina woman.

Two studies, both more recent than the Philadelphia study, have examined the transition to adulthood through the lens of intersectionality. Lee and Waithaka (2017), noting that "extant studies fail to simultaneously consider the intersection of multiple marginalized social statuses" (pp. 151–152), used 2010 data from the American Community Survey to examine how various intersectional statuses were associated with adult attainments. Specifically, these researchers investigated the extent to which people with different combinations of gender, race–ethnicity, immigrant status, income level,[7] and age achieved the traditional adulthood milestones of marriage, parenting, completing (or pursuing advanced) education, working in the labor force, and establishing an independent household. Considering all of the possible combinations of statuses, the results naturally were complex. Some examples, to give a flavor to the findings, are as follows. Whereas 35-year-old White women exhibited very different rates of marriage depending upon whether they were poor (34%) or not poor (61%), Hispanic men of that age had similar marriage rates whether they were poor (57%) or not (61%). In addition, at age 35, non-poor individuals were working in the labor force in substantially higher numbers than were poor individuals (usually by margins of around 20%) for nearly all intersections of gender and race–ethnicity (White, Black, Hispanic, Asian/Pacific Islander, and Native American). However, immigrant men were almost entirely in the labor force whether they were poor (88%) or not (97%). As can be seen, it is not easy to stay on top of all the results with intersectionality, but real life indeed appears to be intersectional. One other study alluded to above, by Sironi and Furstenberg (2012), looked at the attainment of economic independence in young adulthood. This outcome is an important one because, not only is it a traditional adult milestone, but as you will recall from Chapter 1, achieving economic independence is one of the "Big Three" criteria laypersons around the world use to judge if they think someone has reached adulthood (Beck, 2016). Sironi and Furstenberg's primary finding, based on National Longitudinal Survey of Youth data from respondents born in the early 1980s, is that the combination of being a woman and having highly educated parents was associated with a higher probability of being able to support themselves financially by their mid-twenties (observed in 2007).

With most research on the transition to adulthood having been conducted on White youth, but also some on African Americans, one of our Texas Tech graduate students, Ali Luempert, decided to conduct her dissertation study (a big project necessary to complete one's PhD) on Hispanic participants (Luempert, 2021). Ali (now officially Dr. Luempert) recruited 342 Hispanic/Latinx students at the university (80% Mexican, Mexican American, Chicano, or Mestizo; 8% South American, 7% Central American, and 5% Other) and administered several questionnaires pertaining to emerging adulthood, criteria for adulthood, economic status, their families, and cultural attitudes. One of the questionnaires she administered was the Inventory of the Dimensions of Emerging Adulthood (Reifman et al., 2007a), which you saw at the end of Chapter 1. Whereas US college students (who are predominantly White) typically score around 3.25–3.30 on average (maximum = 4.00) on the IDEA subscales of identity exploration, open possibilities, self-focus, and feeling in-between, participants in Dr. Luempert's study had mean scores around 3.50 on these measures. We will need to see more results from Hispanic/Latinx populations to rule out that there was something unique about her sample, but for now at least, it seems possible that Hispanic/Latinx college students have a stronger sense than do other groups that they are experiencing a time of exploration, open possibilities, and so forth.

Gender

As promised near the end of Chapter 1 (Table 1.1), we now take up gender. Probably the most visible treatise on gender and the transition to adulthood is the book *Guyland: The Perilous World Where Boys Become Men* by sociologist Michael Kimmel (2008). "Guyland" is a venue replete with "drinking, sex, and video games. It's watching sports. It's television – cartoons, reality shows, music videos, shoot-em-up movies, sports, and porn – pizza, and beer" (p. 9). Its inhabitants are "mostly white, middle-class kids; they are college-bound, in college, or have recently graduated; they're unmarried. They live communally with other guys, in dorms, apartments, or fraternities. Or they live with their parents (even after college)" (p. 8). One young man who took a class from me several years ago claimed not to live in Guyland but admitted that he had "made occasional excursions" there! Though many examples in Kimmel's writings link Guyland to college, he also says that non-college guys can express their male bonding in the military, certain kinds of traditionally male worksites (e.g., construction, firehouses), bowling alleys, and bars. Kimmel assures that "most young men will eventually outgrow many of the more unattractive aspects of Guy culture" (p. 259), but the sexual hookup aspect of the lifestyle may last for many more years.

What about women's lives while men are in Guyland? Kimmel (2008) considers young women, for the most part, to be "preparing for adult life" educationally, occupationally, and in terms of relationships (p. 259). However, many of those women seeking relationships with men are left only with "the hope of more responsible and serious relationships later" (p. 260). Other women join in the Guyland activities themselves ("matching [guys] drink for drink or sexual hookup for hookup," p. 14). Finally, Kimmel discerns a third group of young women, those "searching for ways both to stop playing by men's rules and to find their own voices, their own sense of agency that can guide them into adulthood" (p. 263). Doing so requires full gender equality and the social changes necessary to make it happen, says Kimmel, so how soon and to what extent gender egalitarianism will arrive remains to be seen.

Kimmel's (2008) ideas are lively and interesting, as I think many of you would agree. Many of his characterizations of young adult men and women come from qualitative interviews, in which participants describe their experiences, feelings, and perceptions in their own words. One form of qualitative inquiry, phenomenology, is a valuable research technique for describing "the essence of a phenomenon by exploring it from the perspective of those who have experienced it" (Neubauer et al., 2019, p. 91). Hence, to learn what it feels like to be a young man or woman approaching adulthood within a certain cultural context (that of Guyland or some other one), qualitative interviews are a good way to go. These interviews are also likely to expose scholars and consumers of their research to ideas they may not otherwise have encountered. However, we lack precise estimates of how common the different behavioral patterns described by Kimmel really are. Now that we have some ideas percolating in our minds, let's examine the available research further.

Three behaviors Kimmel (2008) considers central to Guyland are heavy drinking, watching pornography, and engaging in hookup sexual encounters. We will cover substance use and abuse later, in Chapter 10, but for now we can briefly summarize evidence showing young men to engage in heavier drinking than do young women. On a national (US) survey item asking 19–30-year-olds about times they had consumed 10 or more drinks in a row (i.e., in one sitting or occasion), 16.6% of men reported drinking this amount at least once in the past two weeks, compared to 9.1% of women (Schulenberg et al., 2021). The authors of this study refer to this amount of alcohol intake as "high-intensity drinking." If we define heavy drinking in terms of five-drink (rather than 10-drink) episodes, 34.3% of men report at least one of these, whereas 23.7% of women do. Regarding pornography viewing, Cooper and Klein (2018) surveyed students at one university on their frequency of visiting online porn sites (the question did not define "porn" further in terms of photos vs. videos or the type of content depicted) in the past six months. Results showed that men clearly consumed porn more frequently than did women. Roughly 75% of men reported some degree of porn watching (vs. 25% who said "never"), with 21% claiming weekly viewing and another 20% watching more than four times per week (i.e., more days than not). Thirty-five percent of women reported some degree of viewing (vs. 65% saying "never"); very few women reported viewing porn at the highest frequencies, however (3% weekly and 2% more than four times per week). Finally, in the hookup arena, Olmstead and colleagues (2015) examined the behavior of male students at one university. The majority of first-year undergraduate men (58%) reported at least one hookup during the first semester. None of these studies is definitive, as all were based on self-reported behavior (which is not always truthful) and two of the studies were conducted in only one location. Still, even taking these studies as just approximations, there seems to be a lot of Guyland-type behavior going on!

What about Kimmel's (2008) general claim that women do more than men to prepare for a responsible, successful adulthood? A study of 18–30-year-olds who had grown up in high-crime neighborhoods of Seattle found a lot of similarities between men and women in their attainment of traditional adult roles (Oesterle et al., 2010). One difference, however, was that a somewhat higher percentage of women than men appeared to combine postgraduate education with marriage between ages 24 and 30 (Oesterle et al., 2010), similar to Osgood and colleagues' (2005) notion of educated partners described in Chapter 1. Kimmel's assertion seems to have been borne out in this study, but only to a moderate extent.

To conclude our consideration of gender and the transition to adulthood, let's look at the IDEA questionnaire, on which young adult men and women have been compared in many studies. As shown in Figure 2.3, on all five features of Arnett's (2015a) theory of emerging adulthood, but especially identity-seeking and feeling in-between, women have tended to score higher on average than have men. Note that the studies depicted in Figure 2.3 were conducted in many nations – Italy (Crocetti et al. 2015); Japan (Crocetti et al. 2015); Austria (Duris, 2009; Sirsch et al., 2009); Greece (Galanaki & Leontopoulou 2017); Macedonia (Kolevska, 2017) – along with predominantly White (Reifman et al., 2007a, 2007b; Schnyders & Lane 2018) and Hispanic (Luempert, 2021) US samples.

Social Class

Silva (2013) conducted an extensive qualitative study of working-class young adults in the US. One of Silva's central findings was that, even though personal responsibility and independence are almost universally important criteria for judging whether someone has reached adulthood, the working-class people she interviewed had taken these traits to an extreme level of individualism. Many linked self-reliance to their own self-worth and dignity, believing that "if they had to survive on their own, then everyone else should too" and "draw[ing] harsh boundaries against those who cannot make it on their own" (p. 84). We will revisit additional ideas from Silva (2013) when we discuss identity, work, and parenting in later chapters.

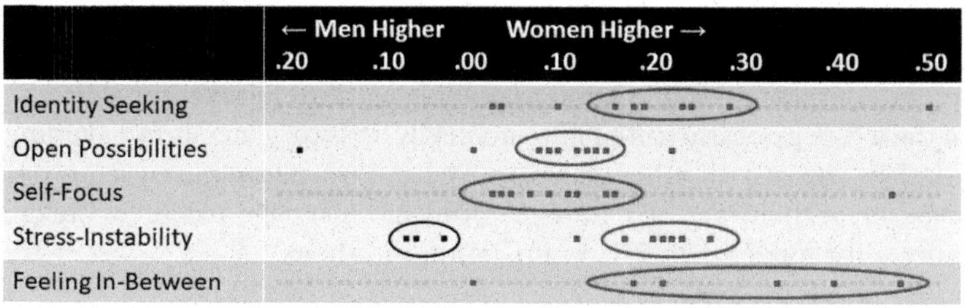

FIGURE 2.3 Gender differences on the Inventory of the Dimensions of Emerging Adulthood in 10 studies conducted in several different countries and in predominantly White and Hispanic US samples. Each dot represents the difference between women's and men's means in one study (red = women higher, black = men higher, blue = equal). Clusters of similar findings are circled to highlight the major trends.

Region of the Country

Whereas the US is sometimes viewed as a single entity, there are considerable differences within the country. Different regions of the US, reflecting different political, cultural, and religious traditions, differ (on average) in behaviors pertinent to emerging adulthood. Cahn and Carbone (2010) extended the terminology of "red" (Republican-leaning, conservative, more rural and religious) and "blue" (Democratic-leaning, liberal, more urban and secular) states to red and blue *family development*. Citing some statistics from Cahn and Carbone, whereas the median US ages of the first marriage were around 28 for men and 26 for women when their book came out, marriage ages were notably younger in red states such as Utah, Arkansas, and Oklahoma (roughly 25–26 in men and 23–25 in women) and older in blue states such as New York, New Jersey, and Massachusetts (roughly 29–30 in men and 27–28 in women). Thus, it is not just what country you grew up in (and currently live in) that may influence your decisions, but also where within the country you are from.

Immigrants to the US

The study of immigration raises the perpetual question of how much immigrants to a new country retain the culture (e.g., language, music, foods, political and religious views) of their country of origin and how much they adopt the culture of their new host country. In terms of youthful immigrants to the US, the answer appears to depend on where these immigrants came from. A study by Rumbaut and Komaie (2010) nicely illustrates this fact regarding Latin American and Asian immigrants to the US. First, though, it is helpful to review what we mean by first generation, second generation, etc. when referring to immigrants' family histories in a new country. Higher numbers (e.g., third generation) indicate more generations (e.g., grandparents, parents, and oneself) being US-born and thus having more exposure to US culture. Conversely, low generation numbers represent less exposure to US culture. Rumbaut and Komaie use the terminology of the 1.0 generation representing a relatively late, post-childhood, arrival in the US, whereas the 1.5 generation arrived during childhood and thus has had more time in the new country than the 1.0 generation. Findings showed that, among immigrants from Latin American countries to the US, only if these youths' families had spent many generations in the US did the youth immigrants' behaviors start to resemble an emerging-adult type of lifestyle (e.g., higher rate of living with parents, lower marriage rate). Youth immigrants from some Asian countries, in contrast, exhibited emerging-adult patterns almost immediately upon arrival in the US (e.g., nearly half of Filipino newly arrived, generation 1.0 immigrants lived with their parents). In other words, many Latin American immigrants to the US appeared to retain their (perhaps more religious and marriage-oriented; Lipka, 2014) origin culture for longer than Asian immigrants did theirs.

Review

As we did at the end of Chapter 1, let's make a numerical list of the important concepts in Chapter 2. We have:

FIVE characteristics of the kinds of people who have tended to be studied in social science research: "WEIRD" (Western, Educated, Industrialized, Rich, Democratic; Henrich et al., 2010).

THREE types of stances parents appear to take toward their grown children living at home into their twenties or thirties: vehement opposition, grudging acceptance, and open arms (Newman, 2012).

TWO additional criteria (beyond the common ones of taking responsibility for one's actions and becoming independent) for considering someone an adult – controlling one's emotions and actions and caring for one's family (both one's parents and future children) – emerged in studies within African and Asian countries.

ONE concept, intersectionality, that ties together different demographic and sociological statuses (e.g., race, ethnicity, social class) to study how individuals' combinations of characteristics affect their life chances (Crenshaw, 1989).

Possible Class Activities

1. Many classrooms have international students. If these students are willing to speak on the topic, the instructor can begin a class discussion of cross-national and cross-cultural issues by asking one or more of them if their experiences in their home countries match what research studies about their respective countries have shown.

2. Salisbury University (2021) maintains an online collection of resources for teaching about intersectionality (available at https://libraryguides.salisbury.edu /c.php?g=903753&p=6507941).

Notes

1 For the play, music by Bob Gaudio, lyrics by Bob Crewe, book by Marshall Brickman and Rick Elice, 2005. For the movie, produced by Clint Eastwood; Ratpac-Dune Entertainment, GK Films, and Malpaso Productions, 2014.

2 According to the American Psychological Association (APA Style, 2019): "Race refers to physical differences that groups and cultures consider socially significant. For example, people might identify their race as Aboriginal, African American or Black, Asian, European American or White, Native American, Native Hawaiian or Pacific Islander, Māori, or some other race. Ethnicity refers to shared cultural characteristics such as language, ancestry, practices, and beliefs." Hispanic or Latinx would thus be considered an ethnicity rather than a race.

3 Note that these are only general trends, not claims that everyone in a given culture feels the exact same way. One can find some parents in Japan (albeit in the minority) who are happy to have their grown children living with them or some in Italy who are not.

4 One of my Texas Tech colleagues, historian Aliza Wong, was on a research trip many years ago in Italy, when she met a young Italian man with whom she developed a romantic relationship and eventually married. My friend had one condition before moving forward with the relationship, however, namely that the fellow needed to move out of his parents' home! Dr. Wong recently clarified for me that "Stefano was 29 when I met him and 30 when he finally moved out of his parents' house on my insistence."

5 Sweden and other Northern European nations provide financial assistance to help young adults obtain their own housing, which likely helps them leave home earlier than they

otherwise would (Newman, 2012; Swedish Social Insurance Agency, 2021). We will cover this topic in greater depth in Chapter 12 on public policies to assist young people in their transition to adulthood.

6 Criminology scholar Thomas Abt (2019) echoes this point in a more recent context: "As a consequence of discrimination, deindustrialization, and out-migration, poor African Americans live in neighborhoods far more segregated and disadvantaged than those occupied by similarly situated whites ... There is simply no large American city where black and white people live in 'ecological equality'" (p. 20).

7 Income was defined in terms of the US Federal Poverty Level (US Department of Health and Human Services, 2021). Depending on a family's size, a certain annual income would be considered to place the family in poverty. For example, if a family of three had total annual income of US$21,960 or lower, it would officially be in poverty. For their study, Lee and Waithaka (2017) classified families as being "poor" (if their income fell below double the poverty level, e.g., US$43,920 for a family of three) or "non-poor" (if their income exceeded double the poverty threshold). For context, with even a one-bedroom apartment carrying an average monthly rent of US$1,800 in large US cities such as Chicago (per apartmentlist .com), a family making US$44,000 may have to pay half of its income for housing.

PART

II

Developmental Processes

Relations with Parents, "Boomerang Kids," and "Helicopter Parents"

The present chapter on how individuals who are transitioning to adulthood interact with their parents and the next two chapters, on identity development and on the brain and cognitive development, comprise Part II of the book on "Developmental Processes." What is human development? It is a question faculty love to ask on the doctoral qualifying exams of graduate students studying the topic (just sayin'). Definitions of human development typically encompass several themes. These include *ongoing changes*; processes of *growth*, as changes in our physical, cognitive, emotional, and social characteristics move in certain directions (e.g., we grow taller up to a point); and the *interaction* of genetics, biology, life experiences, and environments in driving and regulating these developments (Srivastava & Rani, 2014). How do these aspects of our lives change between the ages of 18 and 30 specifically?

> *The day the child realizes that all adults are imperfect, he becomes an adolescent; the day he forgives them, he becomes an adult; the day he forgives himself, he becomes wise.*
> – *Alden Nowlan*

Gaining independence from parents is a key developmental task in emerging adulthood (Arnett, 2015a). Yet, that does not mean relations between grown children and their parents are entirely distant, as they perhaps were during periods of adolescent rebelliousness. In many families, grown children and their parents are able to strike a balance between forces pushing them apart (i.e., the children's desire for independence) and drawing them together ("the mutual affection and attachment they have for one another on the basis of many years of shared experience," Arnett, 2015a, p. 81). The above quote from Alden Nowlan, a Canadian author of poetry and prose who lived from 1933 to 1983, captures how children's views of their parents likely evolve. Parents' views of their children likely do, as well.

As Arnett (2015a) concluded from extensive interviews with young Americans going through emerging adulthood, parent–child relations generally grow more harmonious as children progress from adolescence to young adulthood. This mainly seems to happen when grown children are not living in their parents' house. Fingerman et al. (2017) showed, in fact, that among 18–30-year-old children,

DOI: 10.4324/9781003156567-5

"[a]pproximately two thirds of coresident offspring and a third of noncoresident offspring had an irritating encounter with parents or the parents got on their nerves" in the past week (p. 341). In Arnett's view, at least three developments tend to improve emerging adults' relations with their parents. First, relations between grown children and their parents become more egalitarian and less hierarchical. Parents and grown children "learn to see each other as persons, as individuals, rather than being defined for each other strictly by their roles as parent and child" (p. 81). Second, when living apart, grown children can "edit" what aspects of their personal lives they tell their parents about. Third, parents and their grown children learn to enjoy each other's company when they do visit. Even when grown children live away from their parents, nearly all still communicate regularly with their parents via electronic means (Fingerman et al., 2020). Interestingly, as Fingerman et al. (2020) pointed out, trends toward increasing contact between parents and grown children actually began *before* cell phones became widely available; these authors suggest that greater affordability and access to long-distance telephone plans and air travel in the 1990s may have spurred the increase in parent–child contact.

We know from the previous chapter, however, that countries differ in how common it is for grown children to live at home continuously into their twenties and beyond (from 10–15% in the US to 76% in Italy; Crocetti et al., 2015) and in parents' attitudes about their children remaining home. Part of what seems to smooth the way for good parent–child relations, in Arnett's (2015a) view, is the element of *selectivity* (e.g., grown children being able to select when to see their parents and what to tell them about their personal lives). Living with parents greatly reduces grown children's selectivity, so they cannot avoid contentious topics so easily.

Along with grown children who never leave in the first place until their late twenties or thirties, there are also young-adult children who leave the family home to attend college or strike out on their own in some other way but then return to live at home. In reference to the V-shaped Australian device that you can throw in the air and, after spinning around, flies right back at you, these returning family members are known as "boomerang kids." Boomeranging may create more tension between parents and grown children than if the latter never left, as the children will have enjoyed a taste of independence on their own, which their return threatens (Sassler et al., 2008). In the next section, we examine life for boomerang kids in greater depth.

"Boomerang Kids"

Let's start out with some basic statistics on boomeranging in the US. Sandberg-Thoma and colleagues (2015) examined data from roughly 8,000 young adults in the National Longitudinal Survey of Youth. The sample of participants was nationally representative, so the results are applicable to the entire nation. By 2011 (when respondents were aged 27–31), 83% had left the parental home. Thirty-six percent returned home (boomeranged). Sandberg-Thoma et al. also constructed profiles of typical leavers and returnees (Table 3.1)

Sometimes, the same characteristic that led young adults to leave also led them to return (Sandberg-Thoma et al., 2015). For example, feeling distressed (sad and anxious) was an impetus both to leave the family home and to return. The same was

TABLE 3.1 Characteristics Associated with Leaving the Family Home and with Returning to It

Characteristics (Before Leaving) of Young Adults Who Left the Family Home and Did So Sooner Rather Than Later	Characteristics of Those Who Returned to the Family Home and Did So Sooner Rather Than Later
■ Relatively high sadness and anxiety	■ Relatively high sadness and anxiety
■ Family in poverty	■ Alcohol problems
■ Employed	■ Not in poverty
■ Low education	■ Employed
■ Female	■ Low education
■ White	■ Male
■ Non-marital pregnancy	■ Non-marital pregnancy

Based on results reported by Sandberg-Thoma et al. (2015).

true for being employed but with relatively low educational attainment and having a non-marital pregnancy. In other instances, opposite characteristics predicted leaving and returning. For example, women were more likely to leave their family home than were men, but men were more likely to return home. Sandberg-Thoma and colleagues speculated that daughters may be more closely monitored than sons by their parents about where they are going, who they are spending time with, etc., and this perceived intrusion on freedom may lead young women to leave (and perhaps keep them away, as well). It might have crossed some of your minds that young women may leave earlier because women tend to marry at younger ages than do men. The authors ruled out this explanation through statistical techniques, but if you thought of this, it is great that you are spontaneously trying to understand the findings! Results pertaining to socioeconomic status were complex, but the authors suggested that relative lack of education (and the associated difficulties obtaining high-paying work) may make it hard for young adults to sustain independent housing and lead them to boomerang. Finally, experiencing alcohol problems while living outside the family home was associated with returning home, perhaps as a way for the individual to reduce their heavy drinking.

What about the quality of the parent–adult child relationship as a possible determinant of whether and when the child leaves the family home and returns? A fractious relationship might hasten the grown child's departure. This variable was not available in the dataset used by Sandberg-Thoma et al. (2015) but is in other datasets. Ward and Spitze (2007) studied 765 parent–adult child (ages 18–25) dyads in the National Survey of Families and Households, using parents' rating of their relationship with each of their children on a scale from "very poor" to "excellent." Most (57%) of the grown children had moved out and not moved back in, 26% had never left, and 17% had left and moved back (boomeranged). Results showed that the quality of the parent–child relationship was better when the parent and child lived under the same roof than when they did not, but the difference was small and unlikely to be a major factor in determining why adult children move out.

As I've noted previously, qualitative studies allow participants to describe aspects of their lives from their own perspectives, which typically yields information not available from large statistical studies. Based on qualitative interviews with 30 grown children ages 21–36 who returned home after living away, Sassler and colleagues

(2008) identified some key issues that created a major challenge for both parents and children in many families. Note that, not only was this a small sample, but also not typical of the entire US (e.g., from only the New England region, mostly White, and higher than average in education). Sources of tension in the families studied included whether the returnees felt that their parents perceived them as a child or an adult, whether returning children contributed to household expenses, and whether they felt they received sufficient independence and privacy from their parents. As Sassler et al. previewed the findings in their article, "the return home was not always smooth or conflict free" (p. 679). Most of the returning children did not contribute to household expenses despite a median income of $17,500 (a few over $30,000). This is not a lavish income, but it might have allowed the grown children to help pay some amount of rent or utilities. The grown children did pay for most or all of their personal expenses (e.g., credit card bills, clothes, car maintenance). Wrote Sassler and colleagues:

> Although parents may not have demanded that children pay rent, many apparently did suggest various contributions … Some ignored parental suggestions; others resisted such requests, or framed them as a possibility in the future. A third group contributed to the family coffers.
>
> *(p. 681)*

Most who resisted paying were young men, some of whom were adamant about using their time at their parents' house to improve their material well-being or save money for the future. In contrast, the authors noted, making financial contributions, for those who did, "gave them a greater sense of their own maturity" (p. 682). Contributions in the form of housework were also rare among the full sample of returning grown children.[1]

Parents tried to influence their returning children in ways other than monetary contributions, at least in the children's eyes (Sassler et al., 2008). Curfews and attempts by parents to monitor their grown children via cell phone when they were out – restrictions mainly directed at daughters rather than sons – often provoked tension. Parents' disagreements with sons are more often centered on job-related issues. Interestingly, disagreeing with parents was precisely the event many returnees felt *allowed them to feel like adults*. This dynamic was more common among sons than daughters. Another way in which the grown children felt they benefited from moving home was through opportunities to develop their negotiating skills with their parents. Overall, some may interpret the interviews conducted by Arnett (2015a) and by Sassler and colleagues (2008) as suggesting that it is better for young adults to move out of the family home and begin their journey toward independence. Even with parents and grown children having some areas of conflict under the same roof (Sassler et al., 2008), however, the children did feel they benefited in some ways. The Italian scholar Marco Tosi (Tosi, 2020; Tosi & Grundy, 2018) has looked at boomeranging kids from the parents' perspective and generated several interesting findings. Parents tend to respond most favorably to the return of grown children when it comes after a positive development (e.g., graduation from college) and less well when the child is returning after a setback (e.g., divorce, unemployment; Fingerman et al., 2020; Tosi & Grundy, 2018). Tosi (2020) has found a modest rise in parents' depressive symptoms after the return of an adult child, but these depressive symptoms go back down to their pre-boomerang levels over the next several months. Also, boomerang kids' return home only tends to affect parents if there had not been any children living at home (an "empty nest"). If one or more siblings were still living at home when the boomerang kid returned, the return would tend to have little impact on parents.

COVID-19 and Boomerang Kids

The coronavirus (COVID-19) pandemic has altered life in many different domains (e.g., schooling, work, health precautions) around the world, and the boomeranging of young adults is no exception. In the spring of 2020 universities across the US, UK, Germany, Japan, and elsewhere closed down their in-person instruction and switched to online course delivery. Many businesses either closed or operated under restrictions (e.g., only outdoor dining or takeaway service at restaurants). Either as a matter of necessity (e.g., university residence halls closing), economics (e.g., job loss and inability to pay rent on apartments), or safety (parents wanting their grown children to move back home to monitor their actions during COVID-19), there was a lot of boomeranging.[2] In fact, according to a report from the Pew Research Center, as of July 2020, 52% of 18–29-year-olds in the US were living with one or both parents, the highest percentage since the Great Depression of the 1930s (Fry et al., 2020). Pew provided some interesting demographic breakdowns in the change in percent living with their parents between February 2020 (when Italy became a "hot spot" for COVID-19 and government warnings were beginning in the US; CDC, 2021) and July 2020. Between these two months, the percentage of 18–24-year-olds living at home rose by 8 percentage points (63–71%), whereas the percentage among 25–29-year-olds rose only 2 points (26–28%). Increases ranged from 3 to 7 percentage points in different racial–ethnic groups: White (42–49%), Hispanic (55–58%), Black (50–55%), and Asian (46–52%). The Pew article did not provide specific figures by gender but reported that "Young men are more likely than young women to live with their parents, and both groups experienced increases in the number and share residing with mom, dad or both parents since the beginning of the coronavirus outbreak."

Evidence on how the return of increased numbers of young adults to their parents' homes during COVID-19 has affected family dynamics and the returnees' emotional well-being is still very new. Preetz and colleagues (in press) had begun a longitudinal survey of German university students in 2017, which continued into June–July 2020. Hence, the study had a pre-to-post COVID element. Ten percent of the participants had moved back home with their parents. Participants who returned to the parental home experienced a greater reduction in life satisfaction during COVID than those who did not come back home. Returnees and non-returnees did not differ in mental-health changes pre-to-post COVID, however. The authors suggested that returnees' diminished life satisfaction likely stemmed from their loss of independence.

In conclusion, some might consider boomerang kids' return home to be an intrusion on the lifestyles to which parents had become accustomed without the grown child living at home. Parents can and do intrude on their grown children's lives, as well, which we will cover next in our section on "helicopter parents."

"Helicopter Parents"

Many parents, understandably, want to help their children as they transition to adulthood. Sometimes, though, the extent of assistance goes too far, in many observers' eyes (including sometimes the children's). The best-known term for this phenomenon is "helicopter parents," who figuratively hover over their children and rush in at the slightest sign of trouble. LeMoyne and Buchanan (2011) succinctly define helicopter parenting as "appropriate parenting characteristics taken to an inappropriate degree" (p. 405). Similar terms to helicopter parents include "bulldozer parents" and "lawnmower parents," both of which clear obstacles out of their children's way.[3] The big question is whether these types of parenting help or harm children on their way to adulthood.

"Old Wine with a New Label"?

Before addressing whether helicopter parenting is helpful, harmful, or neutral for young adults, we first need to test whether helicopter parenting is really a new, unique style of parenting or merely a new name for parenting styles that have already been studied for years (Padilla-Walker & Nelson, 2012). To quote an old saying, is helicopter parenting something exciting and new or just "old wine with a new label"? Padilla-Walker and Nelson administered a set of questionnaires to over 400 university students and most of their parents, measuring helicopter parenting (e.g., making important decisions and solving disputes for their grown children) and four older, potentially similar parenting concepts (behavioral control, psychological control, autonomy support, and availability as a confidante). Figure 3.1 briefly defines these concepts. Some degree of correlation between helicopter parenting and the other concepts – that is, people who score high on helicopter parenting also score moderately high on the other concepts – is OK. Helicopter parenting and behavioral control, for example, both pertain to parents making decisions for their children, so some degree of overlap is to be expected. In fact, we call this property *convergent validity*. However, we do not want the correlation or similarity to be so

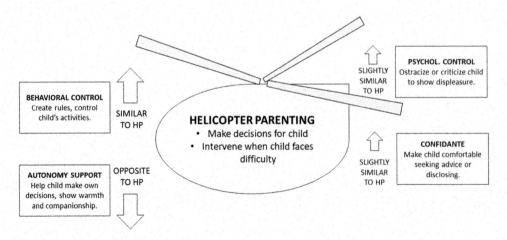

FIGURE 3.1 Helicopter parenting and potentially similar parenting concepts.
Source: Graphic by A. Reifman, based on findings in Padilla-Walker and Nelson (2012).

high as to render helicopter parenting redundant with any of the other concepts (we call a lack of complete overlap *discriminant validity*). If the newer concept (helicopter parenting) yields the same information that an older one does, the newer concept is unnecessary.

We gauge the similarity, overlap, or redundancy of measures of different concepts via the correlation statistic (which some of you would have covered if you've had a statistics course). Suffice it that a correlation of +1.00 represents total redundancy between two variables, whereas −1.00 signifies a perfect opposite relationship (as someone's score on one variable rises, their score on the other variable falls). Padilla-Walker and Nelson (2012) showed behavioral control to be most similar to helicopter parenting. When the same person reported on both behavioral control and helicopter parenting (e.g., mothers reporting on both their behavioral control and helicopter parenting; college students reporting on both behavioral control and helicopter parenting received from their mother), behavioral control and helicopter parenting correlated in the .50s. That's fairly sizable (indicated by the large upward arrow in Figure 3.1). Psychological control and availability as a confidante also positively correlated with helicopter parenting but not as highly as was behavioral control. Autonomy support, which involves parents creating a context for their grown children to make their own decisions (Deci & Ryan, 1987), correlated in the opposite direction with helicopter parenting (downward arrow in Figure 3.1), suggesting that helicopter parenting works *against* grown children learning how to make their own decisions. We can conclude therefore that the concept of helicopter parenting has something new to offer, but it is moderately similar to the older concept of behavioral control.

Healthy, Harmful, or Neutral?

We can now return to the question of whether helicopter parenting seems to promote healthy youth development. Padilla-Walker and Nelson (2012) suggest that

> if parents repeatedly make decisions and solve problems (with roommates, employers, professors) for their children, it would limit the children's opportunities to practice the skills needed to flourish in emerging adulthood, successfully take on adult roles, and in general, become a self-reliant individual.
>
> *(p. 1187)*

Several studies have examined the extent to which receipt of helicopter parenting is associated with favorable or unfavorable developmental markers (Cui et al., 2019; Darlow et al., 2017; Jung et al., 2020; Kouros et al., 2017; Padilla-Walker & Nelson, 2012; Schiffrin et al., 2014). Four studies examined helicopter parenting and depressive symptoms (feelings of sadness, lack of energy, etc., not full clinical diagnoses). These revealed correlations between .14 and .28, suggesting a modest link. These correlations do not tell us, however, whether helicopter parenting increases young adults' depressive symptoms or seeing depressive symptoms in one's grown child spurs a parent to intrude more heavily into the child's life. Correlations between helicopter parenting and young adults' anxiety symptoms, also addressed in four studies, were weaker, between .04 and .21. Two studies showed greater helicopter parenting to go along with diminished academic engagement and adjustment

(−.22 and −.19), although again, we cannot tell if helicopter parenting diminishes students' enthusiasm for college or parents intervene when they see their grown children unmotivated academically. Padilla–Walker and Nelson concluded from their own findings that "while it may not be directly *destructive* …, helicopter parenting may not be *conducive* to growth during emerging adulthood" (p. 1187). This characterization seems to fit the other studies, as well.

One study frequently cited as evidence that helicopter parenting may benefit college students is one year's version of the National Survey of Student Engagement (NSSE, 2007). The NSSE (2007) report noted,

> 13% of first-year and 8% of senior students reported their parent or guardian frequently intervened on their behalf to help them solve problems they were having at the college. Another quarter of first-year and 21% of senior students said their parent or guardian sometimes intervened.
>
> *(p. 25)*

The report also stated that "Students with 'helicopter' parents (those in frequent contact and frequently intervening on their student's behalf)" experienced "[h]igher levels of engagement and more frequent use of deep learning activities" and "[g]reater gains on a host of desired college outcomes, and greater satisfaction with the college experience" (p. 25). There are at least two reasons to interpret the NSSE report with caution. First, it does not say how large these differences were. Did students who experienced greater helicopter parenting exhibit average campus-engagement, deep-learning, and other scores that were slightly higher than those who experienced lesser helicopter parenting or average scores that were substantially higher? Second, the NSSE report notes that students whose parents were highly involved on their behalf showed a lower mean GPA than did students with less-involved parents. The report acknowledges that some parents may have intervened specifically to help their students when they were having academic difficulties and were not the type of parents to intervene in all areas of their students' lives.

Parents' and Grown Children's Views on Specific Forms of Helicopter Parenting

So far, we have examined helicopter parenting as an overall, general type of parenting. In reality, however, many specific actions in specific domains constitute helicopter parenting. I began studying helicopter parenting in 2010. By that time, I had heard about parents contacting instructors to inquire about their students' class performance (which violates US educational privacy laws[4]) and intervening to help get their children a job. When I asked my students for additional examples, I discovered that I didn't know the half of it! Students shared examples of parents deciding which university their children would attend or which major they would study (linked to parents paying for college). Parents reportedly also asked their children's friends and roommates for information on their child, asked for their children's passwords to check on their credit card and other financial accounts, and looked up syllabi and academic calendars online to remind their children of upcoming exams and assignments.

Knowing about different types of helicopter parenting can be useful, as parents and their grown children can discuss them and avoid a situation in which a parent, thinking that a given helicoptering act was appropriate, goes ahead with it, unaware that the grown child considers the act highly inappropriate. Parent–child agreement or disagreement was therefore one of the key issues animating the studies my students and I conducted (Reifman & Oblad, 2012). In a study conducted during the Summer 2010 New Student Orientation at Texas Tech University, we presented the following five items to incoming students and their fathers and mothers,[5] asking them to indicate whether they thought the action depicted in each item "falls within the scope of proper support" or "may take away from the student's development of self-sufficiency."

- Going with their child on job or school-related interviews or appointments.
- Expressing a strong preference for what child should major in.
- Checking up on child's course requirements (e.g., via online syllabi/calendar) to remind child about upcoming tests.
- Making calls to set up child's appointments or take care of other errands.
- Assist with cleaning child's dorm room, doing laundry, etc.

Before reading on, think about how you would respond to each item. As it turned out, only small percentage of our orientation respondents considered these "helicoptering" actions to be proper. Parents checking online for their students' course requirements so they could remind their students received the greatest endorsement as being proper, but still well below 50% (30% of students, 33% of fathers, and 17% of mothers). Many universities make academic calendars and syllabi publicly available, which may be why endorsement was relatively high. Parents and students were in relative agreement regarding parents expressing a "strong preference" for their child's major (16% of students, 11% of fathers, and 21% of mothers deeming this action proper). The other three actions revealed interesting differences of opinion between students, fathers, and mothers. Students seemed absolutely repelled by the idea of their parents accompanying them on job- or school-related interviews, with a microscopic 2% saying this was proper. Fathers (22%) and mothers (12%) were a little warmer to this idea. As for parents setting up students' appointments and helping clean up the student's dormitory room, zero fathers thought either was proper, but 11–18% of students and mothers did. We repeated this survey with a new set of fathers and mothers at the Fall 2010 Family Weekend, and most results were fairly similar to those from the summer orientation. One difference was that 47% of fathers at Family Weekend thought strongly urging a major for their child was proper, a far higher figure than for fathers (and mothers and students) at the summer orientation.

Helicopter Parenting around the World

Helicopter parenting is evident internationally, leading authors in other countries to address the phenomenon. Han and Dong (2009) suggest that Chinese helicopter parents take on large roles in their children's college education. Early on parents gather information on colleges and majors. Ultimately, "[r]egardless of their children's intentions, these parents decide which college their children will attend and which major they will declare" (p. 75). Parents in China also carry their children's luggage and help them with college entrance procedures. Han and Dong offer possible reasons for these parents' heavy involvement, one being China's one-child policy: "The parents of these children have cared for and taken pride in their children for eighteen years and more. It is not strange that we should often see helicopter parents and feel their influence on the college campus" (p. 76). Another country in which there have been sightings of helicopter parenting is Germany. Wilhelm et al. (2014), hoping to launch helicopter-parenting research in this country, developed a German-language questionnaire to assess this behavior. Themes assessed in Wilhelm and colleagues' measure include some that are commonly found in other helicopter-parenting questionnaires, such as parental over-involvement (*Überinvolviertheit*), over-protection (*Überbehütung*), and restriction of their children's autonomy (*Autonomieeinschränkung*). Two other less common and perhaps more complex themes identified by these authors involve parents casting external blame (i.e., blaming parties other than their child when something goes wrong) and seeing their child as a "project" or work in progress. Another interesting suggestion by Wilhelm and colleagues is to see if helicopter parenting differs depending on where grown children are in the family's birth order. In a follow-up study, Wilhelm and Esdar (2014) estimated, based on cut-offs they established, that 2.4% of university students had helicopter parents. This may not sound like a lot, but with millions of students attending universities, helicopter parents would number in the tens of thousands. Finally, Yilmaz (2020) investigated helicopter parenting in Turkey, among a younger group of participants (11–22 years old) than typically studied. This study examined helicopter parenting in four domains (basic life skills, academics, emotional and private life, and ethical and moral issues). Yilmaz deemed 30% of mothers and 14% of fathers to have the characteristics of helicopter parents. The higher percentage of helicopter parents observed in the Turkish study compared to the German study likely stems in part from the younger ages examined in Turkey.

Extreme Helicopter Parenting

In an era of *Extreme Makeover, Extreme Cheapskates,* and the *X Games* (extreme sports) showing up on our television screens,[6] why wouldn't there also be extreme helicopter parenting (non-televised)? Back in 2008, I received an e-mail from *New York Times* reporter Louise Tutelian, asking me about a new phenomenon among parents whose children had gone to college far from home. A few days later, Tutelian's (2008) article came out, announcing this new parenting phenomenon to the world: "From South Bend, Ind., to Oxford, Miss., from Hanover, N.H., to Knoxville, Tenn., they are buying second homes for themselves near campuses where their children are enrolled." Part of parents' motivation may be a real-estate investment, she wrote, but if that was parents' only reason, they could buy property in places where their children were not going to college. Staying close to their children clearly had to be foremost in parents' minds. And, not surprisingly, not all students in this situation were thrilled, at least at first. Tutelian quoted one as saying, "This seemed like the ultimate hovering ... I fought it. But my mom has done a really good job of making her own friends and doing her own things when she is out here." Another student remarked, "Are you kidding me? You're following me across the country?" As I told the writer, "We've heard about boomerang kids who return home after college, but this is kind of like boomerang parents." DenYelle

Kenyon, another researcher quoted in the article, mentioned that "Research has found that the parent–child relationship grows better once the child has left the house," as we learned earlier in this chapter. Accordingly, Kenyon added, "Parents should be careful not to interrupt that process." I have to think this phenomenon is pretty rare; after all, how many people can afford $600,000 second homes? The article did not state or estimate how many parents buy homes in their students' college towns, but it did quote a real estate expert to the effect that it was a growing trend.

Concluding Thoughts on Helicopter Parenting

"Helicopter parenting" is one of the more colorful concepts to come around in the social sciences in recent decades. The accumulated research suggests four tentative conclusions regarding helicopter parenting. It (1) mostly represents something not already assessed by existing parenting measures, and (2) shows a modest link to poor functioning in young adults (e.g., higher depressive symptoms). Parents and college students (3) largely hold similar views regarding what types of parental actions are appropriate; and existing work on helicopter parenting (4) is increasingly inspiring new research around the world. And if you have wealthy parents, look out. They may buy a second home where you are attending college! (Just kidding.)

Other Forms of Parental Assistance to Grown Children

If you were to ask 100 people with interests in parenting (parents, grown children, researchers, therapists, etc.) where they would draw the line between ordinary parenting and helicopter parenting, you would probably get 100 different answers. In my view, the key distinguishing factor would be whether a parent can expect the grown child to accomplish a given task by him- or herself, without parental intervention. Grown children should be able to clean their own room or apartment, do their own laundry, schedule their own classes (if they go to college), stay on top of assignments (at work or school), and do other similar things by themselves. Parental intervention in these areas (beyond limited advice) constitutes helicopter parenting, in my view. Grown children may face other kinds of tasks, however, that would be more difficult for them to handle effectively on their own. These would include making a deposit on an apartment, caring for themselves during a serious illness, or dealing with a challenging interpersonal situation (e.g., a dispute with a work supervisor, professor, or romantic partner). In these cases, parents might be able to offer financial assistance or the wisdom of their greater life experience, which would exceed what coping resources grown children could muster on their own. These latter forms of assistance (as long as they are limited to advice or emergency funding) are what I would consider ordinary parenting help.

A leading researcher of what I call "ordinary" parenting assistance, whose research I have already drawn upon in this chapter, is Karen Fingerman. She and her colleagues (Fingerman et al., 2009) have conducted various studies on parents' provision to their grown children with emotional, practical, and financial support, and spending time with them socializing, offering advice, and listening to them talk. These supportive acts might include trying to cheer their grown child up after a setback, going to a sporting event with them, or discussing a problem. Fingerman and colleagues (2009) found that parents provided the greatest support to two different subsets of grown children: those who were doing well in the domains of relationships, education, and career; and those who had experienced some type of hardship (e.g., health problem, financial difficulty). Grown children who were doing OK, but neither extremely well nor poorly, received less assistance. Giving more aid to children having difficulties is understandable. Giving more aid to those already doing well, Fingerman and colleagues speculated, may stem from parents wanting to share in the glory of their grown children's achievements or to lay the groundwork for their successful children to reciprocate the assistance back to the parents at a later time.[7]

Other researchers have studied specific kinds of ordinary parenting assistance to their grown children, attempting to gauge the extent to which parents offer the support and how grown children react to it. Wang and colleagues (in press) focused on advice given from parents to adult children, with reference to whether the advice was wanted or unwanted. The vast majority of grown children in this study reported receiving advice from parents in the past week (62% received support from their fathers and 76% from their mothers), with unwanted advice relatively rare (16% of adult children reported unwanted advice from their fathers, whereas 24% reported receiving it from their mothers). Grown children were likeliest to perceive advice as unwanted when the parent–child relationship had already been strained. Finally, Kornrich and Furstenberg (2013) used decades of US consumer spending data to probe financial assistance from parents to grown children. They discovered a fascinating trend:

> In the early 1970s … spending was lowest in households with very young children or those of college age. In the early 1980s … spending declined after age 18. *In the 1990s and 2000s*, spending was highest for young children and *for children over age 18.*
>
> *(p. 12)*

In other words, around the same time that various trends – delayed median age of marriage, increased need for education, etc. – were inspiring Arnett (2000, 2004) to call for research on the life stage he termed "emerging adulthood," parents were starting to reallocate more of their financial assistance to children in the EA age range.

Review

Here's your countdown chapter review:

FOUR conclusions regarding helicopter parenting: it is not overly redundant with parenting concepts that had existed previously, it is correlated with somewhat lesser well-being, parents and their college-student children tend to agree on the appropriateness of specific kinds of parental assistance, and helicopter-parenting research is spreading throughout the world.

THREE reasons parent–child relations improve during emerging adulthood: parents and grown children relate more as equals than during childhood and adolescence, grown children can be selective in what they reveal of their personal lives, and as interactions between parents and grown children become less frequent, both come to enjoy the time they do spend together (Arnett, 2015a). Also, THREE main sources of contention when grown children boomerang: degree to which parents see boomerang kids as adults vs. children, returnees' contributions to household expenses and housework, and returnees' sense their independence and privacy are respected (Sassler et al., 2008).

TWO homes on the part of extreme helicopter parents who buy a house where their grown child is attending college (Tutelian, 2008).

ONE basis (in your author's view) for distinguishing helicopter from ordinary parenting: is the task in question something the grown child can do by him- or herself?

Possible Class Activity

1. How would you rate the quality of your relationship with your parents in the years since you have been attending college? Take the Parent Adult Relationship Questionnaire (PARQ), a brief questionnaire developed by Pitzer et al. (2011; online appendix). One interesting angle might be for your instructor to help the class compare the average scores of those of you who live at home while attending college to those of you living apart from your parents.

Notes

1 The Pew Research Center (2012; cited in Fingerman et al., 2020), reported from a national (US) survey that, "Young adults who live with their parents contribute to the household in various ways. Nearly all of the 18- to 34-year-olds surveyed (96%) say that they do chores around their parents' house. And fully 75% say they contribute to household expenses such as groceries or utility bills. More than a third (35%) pay rent to their parents." Hence, Sassler et al.'s (2008) participants appeared to be less inclined to contribute to household expenses and maintenance than the general population of young adult children who lived with their parents.

2 As of this writing (April 28, 2022), the worldwide death toll has reached 6,255,184, including 1,019,804 in the US and 174,696 in the UK (https://www.worldometers.info/coronavirus/). Even with the discovery of effective vaccines against COVID-19, new cases, hospitalizations, and deaths continue to climb periodically due to lack of vaccine access in poorer countries (https://www.worldbank.org/en/news/podcast/2021/07/30/-absolutely-unacceptable -vaccination-rates-in-developing-countries-the-development-podcast), unwillingness to be vaccinated on the part of some in wealthier countries, and new, more dangerous variations of the virus. How things go in the next few years is anybody's guess.

3 Another similar term, referring to childhood and adolescence, is "indulgent parenting," in which parents show excessive responsiveness to their children via material gifts and over-protectiveness, while not expecting much from them (Cui et al., 2019). Cui et al. argue that, "Indulgent parenting and helicopter parenting are related … because both demonstrate high parental responsiveness. They are, however, also distinct in that indulgent parenting reflects a broader range of parental high responsiveness and low demandingness … whereas helicopter parenting focuses mostly on the relational aspects of parental overinvolvement" (pp. 860–861). Indulgent and helicopter parenting correlate positively, as parents who engage

in one also engage in the other (Cui et al., 2019). In this study, however, parents of college students answered items on their *current* helicopter parenting and *retrospective* impressions of their indulgent parenting when their students were younger. A longitudinal study in which indulgent parenting was assessed when parents' kids were perhaps in their early teens, and helicopter parenting was assessed when their children were in college, would be great, but would take several years to conduct!

4 According to one university website's explanation of the Family Educational Rights and Privacy Act (FERPA), faculty "may not discuss anything about a student with a parent or spouse, unless [instructors] have advance written consent from the student" (Arizona State University, University Registrar Services, https://students.asu.edu/faq/154#t104n11163).

5 I certainly don't recall any parents attending New Student Orientation with my fellow incoming UCLA students and me in the summer of 1980.

6 *Extreme Makeover* (created by Howard Schultz, Lighthearted Entertainment and Greengrass Productions, 2002–2007), *Extreme Cheapskates* (TLC [The Learning Channel], Sharp Entertainment, 2012–2014), and *X Games* (ESPN Sports, 1995–present).

7 Fingerman et al. (2012) examined a phenomenon they called "intense support," based on how many of the six types of support the grown child received "several times a week." In other words, receiving emotional support several times a week *and* practical support several times a week *and* socialization opportunities several times a week, and so forth would constitute intense support. Intense support has some similarity to helicopter parenting, to which Fingerman and colleagues alluded. Fingerman and colleagues found that the greater the amount of intense support grown children received, the higher was their reported life satisfaction. In addition, however, "grown children who received intense support were more likely to report that they received more support than they would like" (p. 888).

CHAPTER

4

Identity

In the social jungle of human existence, there is no feeling of being alive without a sense of identity.

– Erik Erikson

Identity – who you believe you are, what is important to you, what you stand for, etc. – is a rich and prominent topic in the study of human development.[1] In Erikson's theory of lifespan development, individuals face different challenges at different parts of their lives. Identity formation (vs. role confusion) is the central challenge of adolescence in Erikson's (1968) theory. However, because most people do not finalize their identity during adolescence (Steinberg & Morris, 2001), Arnett (2004) included the continued pursuit of identity as one of the five features of emerging adulthood (see Chapter 1).

Identity formation is not simply a binary matter (yes or no) of someone having adopted an identity. Identities pertain to many different areas of life such as religion, occupation, politics, and family, and someone's identity may be more developed in one domain than in another. Here is an admittedly unusual example of how an identity may encompass several domains: in her 1997 hit song "Bitch," Meredith Brooks sings, "I'm a bitch, I'm a lover, I'm a child, I'm a mother, I'm a sinner, I'm a saint, And I do not feel ashamed"[2] (whether Brooks really is all of those things or is voicing a character, I do not know). Some researchers assign people an overall score based on an average of how developed their identities are in multiple domains. A prominent team of identity researchers (Schwartz et al., 2014) discourages this approach, however. At best, I would say, averaging might be OK for people who are consistent across domains in their identity development (either well developed in many domains or poorly developed in many domains). How to characterize someone who, for example, had a well-developed career (or career aspiration) identity but only a slightly developed political identity would be trickier. Schwartz and colleagues raise the idea of a domain-free identity measure, assessing the extent to which people generally have a good sense of who they are, putting aside specific domains. As I envision things, someone with a well-developed general identity would have good self-definition in many domains and, even in domains

DOI: 10.4324/9781003156567-6

in which this was missing, they could be expected to approach their self-definition thoughtfully.

As we'll see, exploration is a key element in theories of identity formation. Young people can do all sorts of things to explore possible careers and other aspects of their identity. Growing up, I thought that I might like to become a sportswriter, so I covered sports for my high school and college newspapers.[3] I also volunteered during one summer in the local district office of a US Congressperson. My wife volunteered at a veterinary clinic when she was exploring careers. Other young people volunteer at hospitals and community organizations or join pre-professional associations such as Future Farmers of America or Boys and Girls Clubs.

How does someone develop their identity? How, if at all, do they explore options? How long do people take to form an identity and in what domain(s)? These are but some of the questions we will tackle. The following sections do just that.

Theories of Identity

Erikson/Marcia Perspective on Identity Formation

James Marcia (1966, 1980), whom Arnett (2018) describes as "[o]ne of Erikson's most influential interpreters" (p. 178), developed a framework for understanding how individuals pursue and reach a sense of identity.[4] This framework appears in Table 4.1. "Seek and ye shall find," states a biblical passage. Identity formation sometimes works this way, but not always. If you seek an identity – via exploration of different possible careers, political and religious beliefs, etc. – and ultimately find one, Marcia's framework deems it identity *achievement*. One can also find an identity *without* seeking or exploring extensively for one, through the adoption of significant others' identities. For example, grown children often go into the same career field as one or both parents. This method of adopting an identity is known as *foreclosure*, as in closing off further exploration.

Another possibility is that one seeks or explores different possible identities but never finds one (or not for a long time, at least). This state of affairs goes by the term *moratorium*. The ordinary meaning of the word moratorium is a stoppage or suspension of something. In the case of identity-seeking, Erikson (1968) defines a moratorium as

TABLE 4.1 Marcia's Framework of Exploration and Commitment Leading to Four Possible Identity Statuses

		Commitment to Identity	
		No	Yes
Exploration	Yes	**Moratorium** (Exploring, but No Commitment Yet)	**Achievement** (Commitment after Exploration)
	No	**Diffusion** (Neither Exploring nor Committing to Identity)	**Foreclosure** (Reach Identity Not through Exploration, but by Following in Parents' Footsteps)

a period of delay granted to somebody who is not ready to meet an obligation or forced on somebody who should give himself time … It is a period that is characterized by a selective permissiveness on the part of society … For the most part, these moratoria coincide with apprenticeships and adventures that are in line with the society's values.

(p. 157)

Although some may read negative connotations in Erikson's definition of moratorium (e.g., that it applies to those "not ready" to meet obligations), many would consider engaging in moratorium-based exploration to be completely natural in today's times. As covered in Chapter 1, you will recall, Arnett's (2015a) theory of emerging adulthood places exploration front and center. Finally, some people neither engage in identity-relevant exploration nor find an identity. This situation is called *identity diffusion*, which bears some resemblance to the idea of "slow starters" (Osgood et al., 2005) we learned about in Chapter 1.

Classifying a person's identity-related activity as achieved, foreclosed, in moratorium, or diffused does not mean that the person will remain in that status for all time or even for just a few years. According to research by Meeus and colleagues in the Netherlands (Meeus, 2011; Meeus et al., 2010), a considerable change in identity statuses takes place between ages 12 (early adolescence) and 20 (young adulthood).[5] Highlights of these changes over a four-year period (12–16 or 16–20) are as follows:

- Of those adolescents initially categorized as having a diffuse identity (neither searching nor finding an identity), four years later 39% were still diffuse and 45% had shifted to foreclosure (adopting an identity from a significant other).
- Of those initially in moratorium (exploring), four years later 39% were still in moratorium, 30% were in what the authors called "closure" (like foreclosure, but not identical because individuals coming from moratorium would have done some exploration), and 22% had achieved identity.
- Of those initially considered to have reached an identity via foreclosure, four years later a whopping 80% still had foreclosed identities and 11% had achieved identity (finding an identity after exploring, i.e., seeking and finding). These results show the persistence of a foreclosed identity, either through foreclosed individuals lacking opportunities to explore or showing no interest in doing so.
- Finally, of those considered to have achieved an identity at the beginning of the study, 62% were still considered to have achieved an identity four years later, 11% had shifted to closure, and 22% had gone back to exploration in a moratorium state.

Going from achievement to the less-advanced states of closure or moratorium is considered a "regressive" change. All of the other kinds of changes discussed above, leading away from diffusion or toward achievement or closure, are "progressive."

Newer Identity Frameworks

Schwartz and colleagues (2014) noted that, as Marcia's (1966) identity status model approached its 35th birthday, Schwartz and other identity scholars were beginning to question whether Marcia's model was still useful. Were achievement, foreclosure, moratorium, and diffusion the best ways to conceptualize identity? Did they capture a developmental process, or were they too static? As a result of this questioning, newer models of identity formation began to emerge. Many of them are not all that different from Marcia's vision, still encompassing exploration and commitment as central concepts. The new models differ from Marcia's in several ways (Schwartz et al., 2014). First, they take more of a dynamic, process-oriented perspective, recognizing that identity formation is an ongoing endeavor and that people change over time. We already got a hint of this above, with Meeus's findings (Meeus, 2011; Meeus et al., 2010) that sizable proportions of youth moved around from one identity status to another (e.g., from diffusion to foreclosure, or moratorium to achievement). Second, they look at *gradations* of exploration and commitment (e.g., where does someone fall on a 1–10 scale from no exploration at all to extremely active exploration?) rather than placing people in one of four boxes (achieved, foreclosed, moratorium, or diffuse). Third, they explicitly recognize that people *reconsider* the identities they have adopted.[6]

One of the newer models, Crocetti and colleagues' (2008) three-factor model, specifies the concepts of in-depth exploration, commitment, and reconsideration (a link to take this questionnaire yourself as a class activity appears at the end of the chapter). Luyckx (pronounced "Luikes") and colleagues' (2006) dual-cycle model covers similar ground but is a little more elaborate. The first cycle consists of *commitment formation*, in which the individual engages in exploration in breadth (looking at many options) and then, when seriously considering one of the options, switches to commitment making. This first cycle is thus very similar to Marcia's (1966, 1980) identity status model; even though exploration and commitment are part of the dual-cycle model, however, respondents are not assigned to categories of achieved, foreclosure, moratorium, and diffuse. Once the individual commits to an identity, they move to the second cycle, known as *commitment evaluation*. Here, they engage in exploration in depth (reconsidering the selected identity) and, if they feel it is a good fit, they identify with the commitment and consider the identity part of their sense of self (Schwartz et al., 2014). In other words, the second cycle involves challenging oneself on one's identity and either deciding to keep it or look for other ones. The dual-cycle model also includes a fifth component (along with the four of exploration in breadth, commitment making, exploration in depth, and identification with commitment), namely ruminative exploration. To ruminate is to think constantly about something, in this case because one is frustrated at failing to find the perfect identity and feels "stuck" (Schwartz et al., 2014). Hence, ruminative exploration hinders the other, forward-moving steps of identity formation. Luyckx et al. (2013) showed that average levels of commitment making and identification with commitment among Belgian youth were progressively higher from age 14 to 30. Mean exploration in breadth was progressively higher from 14- to 19 years old, peaked between 19 and 22, and then became progressively lower. Exploration in depth showed a similar pattern, but the peak lasted from 17 to 28. Hence, the mechanisms of commitment rise steadily (at least to age 30), whereas the mechanisms of exploration peak in people's twenties.

The theories discussed above only scratch the surface of all those that have been proposed. If you would like to "explore" these additional theories of identity, see Schwartz et al. (2014).

Identity and Well-Being

Identity researchers have debated whether identity *achievement* (through exploration) is healthier than attaining identity by emulating one's parents or other significant others (i.e., foreclosure). The evidence suggests not. Hofer et al. (2007) summarized the research available at the time, with reference to European and American populations, as follows: "individuals in the Moratorium status seem to be the least happy, individuals in the identity Achievement and Foreclosure (high commitment statuses), respectively, are the happiest, and those categorized as Identity Diffusion seem to hold a position in between" (pp. 268–269). Results from 2007 and thereafter are mixed. A study of roughly 9,000 students at 30 US universities (Schwartz et al., 2011) yielded results largely in line with Hofer's characterization. On measures of positive psychological well-being (e.g., self-esteem, life satisfaction), the achieved and foreclosed groups had similar average scores to each other, which were the highest among the identity-status groups. However, unlike the pattern described by Hofer, the moratorium group had slightly higher well-being than the diffused groups.[7] On measures of negative well-being (e.g., depression, anxiety), the achieved and foreclosed groups were similar to each other and lower than other groups. Consistent with Hofer's characterization of pre-2007 studies, the moratorium group showed the highest average depression and anxiety. Hofer and colleagues (2007) also conducted a new study of university students in Cameroon and Germany. In both nations, identity achievement was correlated with greater life satisfaction, high levels of positive emotions, and low levels of negative emotions. Foreclosure was not linked to any of these emotional states in Cameroon but was linked to lower positive emotions in Germany. What makes the study in Cameroon valuable is that the nation's characteristics resemble the African continent as a whole; according to the BBC (2018), Cameroon "is often known as 'Africa in miniature' because of its geographical and cultural diversity." Cakir (2014) conducted a similar study in Turkey. In this study, as well, only identity achievement was associated with good psychological well-being.

Let's sum up this section. Achieving an identity after exploring several possible ones is generally associated with good psychological well-being. Adopting a significant other's identity without extensive exploration, namely foreclosure, has been shown in some, but not all, studies to yield as high a level of psychological well-being as identity achievement. Moratorium and diffusion are linked to poorer well-being. Interestingly, although individuals going through exploration during moratorium may not enjoy it at the time, many wise observers argue that exploration can be as or more fulfilling than what you find at the end of the journey.[8]

Frequencies of the Different Identity Statuses

According to James Côté (2006), we should expect identity achievement to occur frequently, perhaps more than any of the other identity statuses (foreclosure, moratorium, or diffusion). He writes that "surely exploration-based identity formation must be commonplace among those of emerging adult age – especially college students – and most students must graduate with a strong sense of themselves and where they are going in the world, especially occupationally" (p. 96).

At Texas Tech University, where I teach, there is a daily e-mail bulletin called "TechAnnounce," which informs all in the university community of entertainment events, club meetings, prominent visiting speakers, and so forth taking place on campus. Figure 4.1 presents a screenshot of cultural-event listings for a two-day period (October 25–26, 2021). This seems to me like a typical two-day listing of events at Texas Tech. Whether it is fine arts, a talent show, undergraduate research, a film series, a Halloween party with the History Club, or a workshop on applying to graduate school, there is something to meet the interests of many students. In fact, I challenge anyone to come up with any location that offers more cultural activity than a college campus! All of this is to say that Côté's (2006) argument that college students should be especially likely to explore different areas, adopt an identity, and move on to a carefully planned postgraduation endeavor (e.g., work or graduate school) seems pretty compelling.

He concludes, however, that when it comes to emerging adults' and college graduates' exploration-based identity achievement, "In fact, there is little evidence for this" (Côté, 2006, p. 96). For whatever reason, whether it's that many students are working long hours at jobs to pay their college expenses or they just lack the interest, identity achievement in emerging adulthood just isn't that common.

According to figures available as of 2006 for Western nations, roughly 25% of college students and 10–20% of adults in general were in diffusion, whereas 30–40% of adults had arrived at an identity via foreclosure. The percentages of young adults in moratorium (10–30%) and achievement (20–30%) were smaller than for foreclosure (Côté, 2006). What about more recent estimates? Fadjukoff et al. (2016) conducted an adult development study in Finland, beginning when participants were 27 years old (toward the latter part of emerging adulthood). These participants were followed up until age 50, but only the age-27 results are within the scope of our subject matter. The researchers classified participants into the Marcia (1966, 1980) identity statuses in the five areas of religion, politics, occupation, intimate relationships, and lifestyle. Some of you readers are probably only a few years away from being 27 years old. In which of the five domains do you think 27-year-olds would be most likely to have achieved an identity? Do you think individuals in the early to mid-twenties would spend more time exploring their religious beliefs, political views, occupational choice, relationship and marriage possibilities, or lifestyle (e.g., hobbies, exercising)? In which of these domains do you think it would be easiest to form an identity? After you have thought about these questions for a while, go ahead and look at Table 4.2. It shows the percentages of 27-year-old Finnish adults who achieved an identity and adopted one through foreclosure.

As shown in Table 4.2, identity achievement (seeking and finding) was most common in the area of intimate relationships, for both women (51%) and men (34%). Note that forming an identity in the relationships domain was not simply a matter of finding a spouse or partner. The interviews also probed participants' ideas about what they expected from a close relationship. Identity achievement was much less common in the other domains, ranging from 16% for men's occupational identity to 31% for men's political and women's lifestyle identities. Foreclosure was most common in the lifestyle domain (41% in women, 32% in men). For most of the other domains, roughly 20–25% of women and men adopted an identity through foreclosure. The rest of the participants were in either moratorium or diffusion in the various domains (not shown in Table 4.2).

AZIZA ABDDIEVA: Human Being and Being a Human

TTU School of Art MFA Lecture
Wednesday. November 10th 7:00 PM, MCoM Building Room #153

Originator: Dani Marshall   Posted On: 10/26/2021
Lectures & Seminars

- -

Red Raider Showcase Applications are open!

Apply and audition for Red Raider Showcase! Compete in our annual talent show to win fa

Originator: Loni Crosby   Posted On: 10/26/2021
Arts & Entertainment * Student Organization

- -

Undergraduate Research Conference 2022 Abstract Call

URC ABSTRACT SUBMISSION IS NOW OPEN!

Originator: Ryan M Bain   Posted On: 10/26/2021
Research *Lectures & Seminars *Academic

- -

Sexism|Cinema presents FISH TANK

Join us on 11/3 at 7:30pm for a screening and discussion of Andrea Arnold's FISH TANK.

Originator: Allison Whitney   Posted On: 10/26/2021
Arts & Entertainment *Lectures & Seminars

- -

Doing History with the Dead

Just in time for Halloween! History Club Presents: Doing History with the Dead with Dr. Eri
p.m. in Holden Hall 130. New Members Welcome! History Club t-shirts for sale, and free p

Originator: Amanda Chattin   Posted On: 10/25/2021
Lectures & Seminars *Student Organization

- -

Pathways to Graduate School

The Department of History is holding an infromation session on applying to graduate program
- 4 p.m. outside Holden Hall in the SW corner.

Originator: Amanda Chattin   Posted On: 10/25/2021
Lectures & Seminars *Academic

- -

FIGURE 4.1 TechAnnounce listing of campus cultural events in a two-day period.

Eriksson et al. (2020)[9] followed the same Swedish residents at ages 25, 29, and 33, examining Marcia's identity statuses pertaining to occupation, romantic relationships, parenthood, and work/family priorities. These researchers studied overall identity (combining the different domains). In other words, participants were classified as having achieved identity in general (taking into account all the domains studied) or attained identities via foreclosure in general, with no differentiation between occupation, romantic relationships, and the other domains. Identity

TABLE 4.2 Percent of 27-Year-Olds in Identity Achievement (Bold) and Foreclosure (Italics), Finnish Adults Studied by Fadjukoff et al. (2016)

	Religion	Politics	Occupation	Intimate Relationships	Lifestyle
Women	**26**/*26*	**19**/*26*	**17**/*24*	**51**/*23*	**31**/*41*
Men	**23**/*11*	**31**/*18*	**16**/*21*	**34**/*21*	**24**/*32*

Source: Compiled by A. Reifman based on graphs in Fadjukoff et al. (2016).

achievement was more common at age 33 than at 25 or 29, whereas moratorium (still exploring) was less common at 33. At ages 25 and 29, women tended to be disproportionately in achievement and men in diffusion, but these sex differences disappeared by age 33.

Topolewska-Siedzik and Cieciuch (2019) investigated age differences in identity among 3,000 Polish participants ranging from 18 to 65, but we will look only at 18–35-year-olds. The authors created a modified version of Marcia's (1966, 1980) model. A form of identity status called *consolidation* (an exploration-based stable identity with openness to reconsideration of one's identity) rose steadily from 18–19 years old to 32–35.

Special Focus: Identity in Working-Class American Young Adults

Silva (2013), while not presenting a formal theory of identity, offers some interesting observations from her qualitative interviews with 100 working-class Americans in their mid-twenties to the early thirties. She writes that many of her interviewees who had a child "construct a coming of age narrative in which their previously unsettled and nebulous lives take shape and direction only after they embrace the *identity and ongoing work of parenting*" (p. 76; my emphasis). Silva quotes a 30-year-old woman as saying that "I didn't have any dreams until I had my daughter" (p. 76). Having (or expecting) a child can lead some to aspire to certain careers that will help provide a good standard of living for their child. Relating this topic to the identity theories we've covered, one can see how having a child could spur identity explorations and achievement to a greater extent than before in these young adults' lives.

What Is Identity Good For?

Tremendous effort clearly has gone into developing theories of identity and ways to measure identity and the processes leading to it. A question I always pose to my classes when the topic comes up is: Why do we need the concept of identity? In other words, could individuals get by in life, feeling reasonably happy, if they just lived in the moment, responded to events as they happened, and never tried to develop a larger concept of who they were? I don't know if it is even possible to live an identity-free life, but I think it is worth exploring the possibility so that we can understand identity more deeply.

Researchers have proposed several ideas for why identity is indeed useful and valuable, and how our lives would not be as meaningful and productive without a sense of identity. The following five benefits are said to follow from having an identity (Serafini & Adams, 2002; Serafini et al., 2006). An identity

- Gives individuals a sense of structure in their lives.
- Brings their values, beliefs, and commitments into harmony and consistency.
- Gives them a future orientation toward pursuing their goals.
- Aligns individuals' goals with their sense of self and identity.
- Promotes an internal sense of control (i.e., that accomplishing goals is within one's power to achieve).

Serafini and colleagues showed that, among Canadian university students, those who were classified not only as achieved, but also moratorium, also tended to endorse self-descriptive items reflecting these benefits, such as "I feel I have a consistent sense of self from one day to the next" and "Learning what I am capable of doing provides the basis for deciding what I will become." Foreclosed individuals, who, as we saw earlier, tend to be fairly happy in their lives, nevertheless scored as low on the benefits of identity (as did diffused individuals). Hence, it appears that the benefits Serafini and colleagues ascribed to having an identity also accrue to those who are currently exploring one.

A study of 150 adolescents and emerging adults (15–24 years old) from "deeply disadvantaged origins" (p. 3; nearly half had parents who had been incarcerated or had alcohol/drug problems; parental education generally low) in Baltimore, Maryland, also illustrates the apparent benefits of having a certain kind of identity (DeLuca et al., 2016). These researchers set out to address a very straightforward question: What characteristics in these youths seemed to distinguish those who stayed "on track" (in school or working), were "disconnected" (not in school or working, but not in serious trouble, either), or were "in the street" (criminal activities and drug use; quoted terms from pp. 40, 65–66)? As the authors summarized:

> we explored a variety of possibilities ... such as childhood trauma ..., direct exposure to violence, the presence of adult role models, and whether a parent or primary caregiver was employed, struggled with a substance abuse problem, or was in jail. Each of these factors turned out to be important ... None ... was as powerful, however, as what we call an identity project.
>
> *(p. 66)*

An identity project, in DeLuca and colleagues' (2016) words, "is a source of meaning that provides a strong sense of self and is linked to concrete activities to which youth commit themselves" (p. 66). Examples of identity projects among the Baltimore youth included arts/music, poetry, making rap beats and putting them on the internet, tending to a flock of birds, and working with learning-disabled children. The results were clear. After ruling out statistically any effects of age, gender, and neighborhood poverty, "those with an identity project were only 15 percent as likely as those without an identity project to engage in illegal activities" (p. 244). Another way to look at this finding is that, for every 10 youths without a project who engaged in crime, only 1.5 youths with a project acted criminally. Another finding from this research was that identity projects appear to be most effective when pursued in conjunction with some kind of community organization, rather than just personally in isolation. Such broader involvement connects youth to like-minded others, gives them a sense of belonging, and draws upon the resources of the organization (e.g., the Junior Reserve Officer Training Corps for someone considering a military career).

The best description I've seen of something that sounds like an identity project comes from the award-winning writer Ta-Nehisi Coates (2009), who recalls his love of djembe drumming in his youth. Wrote Coates, "All year, I'd been working toward better drumming, showing up early for classes, teaching young children, and tinkering with the threading and tightness of my own djembe" (p. 210). Ability was second to intrinsic interest, at least in Coates's case, as he claims that "My talent was second tier and I knew I would always be a workman, a support player for someone else's glorious show. But I was so in love, and so of the spirit, that I just did not care" (p. 216).

Ethnic Identity

A topic that has attracted a great deal of attention over the past 30 years or so, but which, in my view, goes back more like 75 years, is that of ethnic identity. In a classic psychology study, Kenneth and Mamie Clark (1947) showed some dolls to 253 African American children between 3 and 7 years old, asking them to respond to prompts such as "Give me the doll that is a nice doll" and "Give me the doll that looks bad." The key element of the experiment was that some of the dolls looked like Black children, whereas others resembled White children. This was, of course, before the landmark US Supreme Court case of *Brown v. Board of Education* ended official segregation in public schools, and the 1964 Civil Rights Act outlawed segregation of public accommodations such as restaurants and hotels. Some of the participating children were from Massachusetts, where schools were racially mixed, whereas others were from Arkansas, where they "had had no experience in racially mixed school situations" (p. 170). On the question of who was the nice doll, 59% of these African American children said the White doll, 38% the Black doll, and the remaining 3% were undecided. On the question of which doll looks bad, 59% of these Black children said the Black doll, 17% said the White doll, and 24% were undecided. African American children in both locations selected the White doll over the Black doll as being nice and the Black doll over the White doll as looking bad. Black children's self-denigration was actually stronger in the integrated northern location than in the segregated southern one, suggesting the likely presence of racism throughout the country. Demonstrating the impact of Clark and Clark's study, it was cited by the Supreme Court in its *Brown* decision. CNN (2010) revisited the doll study with a smaller-scale replication. The CNN study found that, as described by Professor Margaret Beale Spencer, an expert hired to conduct the new study, "even black children, as a whole, have some bias toward whiteness, but far less than white children." Hence, Black children's self-denigration has not disappeared, at least as of 2010.

How do we get from children's racial–ethnic identity in the 1940s to modern-day emerging adulthood? Summarizing a large body of research from recent decades on ethnic identity and psychological well-being, Nguyen and Benet-Martínez (2013) found that the ethnic identities relate to psychological well-being in the same way in emerging adulthood as in any other life stage. Hence, ethnic identity remains an important issue in emerging adulthood. Let's review some basics of ethnic-identity research before looking at the research findings. First, as immigration to the US and other countries[10] has increased in recent decades (immigrants comprising 13.7% of the US population in 2018, compared to 4.8% in 1970; Budiman, 2020), the focus has shifted from own-race denigration in the 1940s to the consequences of different types of ethnic identities for immigrants and others who potentially have multiple sources of ethnic identity. These include "immigrants, refugees, sojourners (e.g., international students, expatriates), indigenous people, ethnic minorities, those in interethnic relationships, and mixed-ethnic individuals" (Nguyen & Benet-Martínez, 2013, p. 122). There are many ways to measure identification, such as preferences for language, media, foods, and cultural traditions (e.g., holidays).

Second, as described by Nguyen and Benet-Martínez (2013), researchers have developed a typology to represent the four types of ethnic identification (Table 4.3). Historically, many immigrants to the US changed their first and last names to sound more like the dominant culture. Wikipedia has a page on "Anglicisation of Names" (https://en.wikipedia.org/wiki/Anglicisation_of_names), which provides numerous examples. Just a few are the Italian surname "Rossellini" being converted to "Russell" and the Scandinavian "Nilsson" to "Nelson." This would illustrate *assimilation*, a stronger identification with the host or dominant country. More recently, however, some individuals have sought to preserve aspects of their heritage cultures in their names. For example, Major League Baseball player Adrián González in 2016 had an accent mark added to his name on the back of his jersey (Gonzalez, 2016). Allegiance to one's heritage culture could represent a *bicultural* identity (if one identifies with the host/dominant culture and the heritage one) or a *separation* identity (if one identifies only with the heritage culture). Finally, identifying with neither one's host/dominant nor heritage culture is known as *marginalization*.

Nguyen and Benet-Martínez's (2013) main purpose was to see if one or more of the four ethnic-identity configurations were associated with particularly good or poor psychological well-being (e.g., depression, anxiety, life satisfaction) and other types of accomplishment (e.g., academic, career). Each person is different, but on average, which group would you expect to be the happiest and most successful – those with bicultural, assimilated, separated, or marginalized attitudes? Nguyen and Benet-Martínez's main finding, based on 141 studies they collected, was that of a "strong association between biculturalism and positive adjustment" (p. 131).

TABLE 4.3 Four Ways of Identifying with One's New Host (or Dominant) Culture and Heritage Culture (Nguyen & Benet-Martínez, 2013)

		Identification with Heritage Culture	
		Low	**High**
Identification with Host or Dominant Culture	High	**Assimilation** (Identification with host culture only)	**Bicultural** (Identification with both host and heritage cultures)
	Low	**Marginalization** (Identification with neither culture)	**Separation** (Identification with heritage culture only)

As noted, this was just as true in emerging adulthood as in any other part of the lifespan. Why might this be the case? The authors suggested several possibilities: holding a bicultural identity requires, and ultimately, may sharpen cognitive and social competencies in both cultures; a bicultural identity puts a person in contact with others from both cultures, potentially leading to a larger social network that can provide companionship and help the person cope with stress; and identifying with one or no cultures may limit one's social connections.

Review

You know the routine. There are:

FIVE identity dimensions included in Luyckx and colleagues' (2013) dual-cycle model: exploration in breadth, commitment making, exploration in depth, identification with commitment, and ruminative exploration. Also, FIVE benefits of having an identity: structure, harmony, future orientation, synchronizing one's goals and self-concept, and sense of control (Serafini & Adams, 2002).

FOUR identity statuses: achievement, foreclosure, moratorium, and diffused (Marcia, 1966, 1980). Also, FOUR types of ethnic identity: bicultural, assimilation, separation, and marginalization (Nguyen & Benet-Martínez, 2013).

THREE identity dimensions studied by Crocetti and colleagues (2008): exploration in depth, commitment, and reconsideration.

TWO dimensions studied by Marcia (to generate the four identity statuses): exploration and commitment.

ONE identity for Raymond's brother Robert: He's a cop.

Possible Class Activities

1. Elisabetta Crocetti has made available copies of the Utrecht-Management of Identity Commitments Scale (U-MICS) in 22 languages on her website: https://www.elisabettacrocetti.com/u-mics/ (Utrecht is a city and province in the Netherlands). The website instructs that:

   The U-MICS includes 13 items: 5 items measure commitment (items 1-5), 5 items tap in-depth exploration (items 6-10), and 3 items assess reconsideration of commitment (items 11-13). Each item is rated on a 5-point Likert scale ranging from 1 (completely untrue) to 5 (completely true).

2. Try to write a statement of your identity to the chorus of the song "Bitch," which was discussed in the chapter. Here's my attempt:

   I'm a prof, I'm a hubby,
   I'm for Tech, and the Cubbies,
   I'm an uncle, and a son,
   UCLA and Mich. Alum

Notes

1 A more traditional academic definition of identity is an "organization of self-understandings that define one's place in the world" (Schwartz et al., 2006, p. 5).

2 "Bitch" (written by Meredith Brooks and Shelly Peiken, produced by Geza X, Capitol Records, 1997).

3 Obviously, I never became a professional sportswriter. However, my love of writing about sports never went away, either. As a result, I still write for some sports websites and for publications of the Society for American Baseball Research (SABR).

4 I know that references from the *Brady Bunch* (created by Sherwood Schwartz; Redwood Productions; airing on ABC 1969–1974) are not exactly current, although reruns continue running to the present day. Some readers may be familiar with how Jan, the second-oldest sister, expressed frustration whenever she was compared to her seemingly perfect older sister: "Marcia, Marcia, Marcia!" If thinking of the Brady Bunch helps you remember Marcia's identity framework, more power to you!

5 Meeus et al. (2010) studied two separate cohorts of adolescents, one ranging in age from 12 to 16 years old and the other from 16 to 20. These authors reported results for both cohorts combined. Although the 12–20 age range is young for a book on emerging adulthood, the authors' clarity in depicting transitions between the four Marcia identity statuses makes their study worth looking at, in my view.

6 Another classic television comedy series, *Everybody Loves Raymond* (created by Philip Rosenthal; Where's Lunch, Worldwide Pants Incorporated, and HBO Independent Productions; airing on CBS 1996–2005) had an episode that nicely illustrates identity reconsideration ("Security," Season 8, Episode 16). Raymond's brother Robert, a New York City police officer for 27 years, has had a tough time lately, including being injured in a confrontation with a suspect. When a friend offers Robert a job selling home-security systems, he begins questioning whether he wants to remain on the police force. After a humorous heart-to-heart discussion with Raymond, in which Raymond forces the indecisive Robert to make a decision, Robert decides to stay with the police, declaring "I'm a cop."

7 Some researchers, including Schwartz and colleagues, distinguish between two types of diffusion, one in which individuals fail to explore or attain an identity due to worries over adopting the right identity and becoming "stuck," and the other consisting of individuals who do not care about or show any interest in developing an identity. In the Schwartz et al. (2011) study, the two diffusion groups scored similarly to each other on self-esteem, life satisfaction, depression, and anxiety.

8 Historians have attributed quotes embodying this idea to many people, but my favorite version is the following from tennis champion and civil rights legend Arthur Ashe: "Success is a journey, not a destination. The doing is often more important than the outcome."

9 Not the same Erikson (with one "s") as the one whose lifespan development theory we have discussed. That is Erik Erikson, who lived from 1902 to 1994.

10 Other countries with large numbers of immigrants (in raw numbers, rather than the percent of the population) include Russia, Saudi Arabia, Germany, and the UK (World Population Review, 2021).

5

Brain, Decision-Making, and Risk-Taking

People sometimes ask me when the brain stops developing – when does it "become adult"? This question might seem highly relevant to issues such as the age of consent, voting threshold, criminal responsibility, alcohol consumption, joining the army and so on. It might be quite useful if brain research could help us to inform these difficult and complex issues, and to pinpoint a precise age at which the brain suddenly becomes "adult". But it's not that simple.
— Sarah-Jayne Blakemore (2018, p. 87)

Brain Functioning in Young Adulthood

More Efficient and Mature Than at Younger Ages

Emerging adulthood represents a time of significant changes in both brain structure and functioning, especially in comparison to adolescence. Some of the key processes we'll discuss in this chapter, such as synaptic pruning and myelination, begin as far back as childhood, but EA is when these processes are completed, to put the finishing touches on your adult brain. Compared to adolescence, the EA brain is better able to say no to risky, impulsive actions that may have seemed like a good idea at the time, providing a little voice that says, *You know, sticking a lit firecracker or bottle-rocket in your rectum to try to propel yourself into flight may not be such a great idea …*[1] In some ways, also, mental operations are done more quickly during early EA than they ever will again. Get ready, as some highly cerebral discussion is headed your way!

Overview of Terminology

Brain research contains a number of complex and unfamiliar terms. Therefore, Table 5.1 provides definitions for several terms that will come up in this chapter.

The adult brain weighs about 3 pounds (1.4 kg; Blakemore, 2018). The brain's cerebral cortex (outer layer) contains four relatively large lobes (frontal, parietal, temporal, and occipital), each containing many different regions and structures (Blakemore, 2018). The frontal lobe is, as the name suggests, at the front of your

DOI: 10.4324/9781003156567-7

TABLE 5.1 Definitions of Key Terms in Brain Research

Term	Definition
Functional Magnetic Resonance Imaging (fMRI)	Brain scan showing changes in activated areas while the participant works on a task while lying down in the scanner. Readings are based on blood flow through the brain. Specifically, the "scanner detects the levels of oxygen in the blood, because oxygen has magnetic properties" (Blakemore, 2018, p. 72). Sometimes known as "Blood-oxygen-level-dependent" or BOLD imaging.
Structural Magnetic Resonance Imaging (sMRI)	Stationary picture of the size and shape of brain structures, often used as "an anatomical reference for visualization of activation patterns and regions of interest to extract functional signal information" (Center for Functional MRI, not dated).
Prefrontal Cortex (PFC)	Involved in "[i]mpulse regulation, planning, decision making, categorization, and application of rules and principles" (Niehuis et al., 2019, p. 212).
Cerebral Cortex	Outer layer of the brain (Dafny, 2020).
Subcortical	Below the cortex (Tunç & Gülsoy, 2010).
Limbic System or Regions	Involved in emotional and behavioral responses. Includes the hippocampus (processes episodic memory), amygdala (detects threatening and other emotionally significant stimuli), nucleus accumbens/ventral striatum (reward prediction and anticipation) (Blakemore, 2018; Haber, 2011; Niehuis et al., 2019; Queensland Brain Institute, 2019). Most of these structures are considered subcortical (Catani et al., 2013).
Corpus Callosum	Connects the right and left sides (hemispheres) of the brain, so that the hemispheres can share information to aid in complex problem-solving (Seymour, 2017).
Anterior Cingulate	Involved in "[p]rocessing conflicting information and monitoring task performance" (Niehuis et al., 2019, p. 212).
Functional Connectivity	Statistical/correlational linkage between signals of different brain regions (i.e., one activates and then another) (Rogers et al., 2007).
Structural Connectivity	Physical connections of fibers between brain regions (Park et al., 2015).
Neuron	"the fundamental units of the brain and nervous system, the cells responsible for receiving sensory input from the external world, for sending motor commands to our muscles, and for transforming and relaying the electrical signals at every step in between" (Queensland Brain Institute, 2019). The brain contains an estimated 86 billion neurons (Blakemore, 2018).
Axon	Cable running down most of neuron, which sends electrical signals (Figure 5.2).
Myelin	A fatty coating that develops on axons to make them faster, like electrical cords you have at home (Figure 5.1).
Synapse	A gap (or cleft) between one neuron and another (Figure 5.1). The terminal buttons of one neuron release a chemical neurotransmitter into the gap, which is picked up by the next neuron's treelike dendrites. Adult brain has a quadrillion synapses, which is one million billion (Blakemore, 2018).

head, along with the prefrontal cortex (PFC). These are perhaps the most important brain structures for emerging adulthood, in terms of reasoning and executive control. The temporal lobes (on the lower half of both sides of the head) contain the auditory cortex and are involved with hearing (Blakemore, 2018). The occipital lobes (at the back of the head) contain the visual cortex allowing us to see (Johnson, 2020a), whereas the parietal lobes (top of the head toward the back) work with our senses of touch, taste, and temperature and are involved in visuo-spatial perception (Johnson, 2020b). Below the cortex are smaller subcortical regions and structures, including the limbic system, which contain structures such as the hippocampus (involved in memory) and the amygdala (involved in emotions, particularly fear processing). Blakemore (2018) notes, based on her own cutting into a brain during anatomy lab, that "The cortex is fairly uniform, vast and folded. The subcortical regions, however, are distinct" (p. 54), meaning that subcortical structures are like separate little statues (the amygdala appearing like an almond and the hippocampus like a seahorse). Note that these linkages between a given brain region and some kind of mental function (e.g., that the amygdala processes emotions) represent only plausible interpretations of previous research findings and are listed for simplicity. The idea of strict one-to-one correspondence – that a given brain region performs only one function and that function is performed by no other brain region – has been "abandoned" by many theorists and researchers (Kragel & LaBar, 2016, p. 444). For example, the visual cortex also responds to touch in blind people and can even respond to sounds under certain circumstances (Blakemore, 2018). Researchers now emphasize connectivity between structures and among regions to carry out brain functions. Still, we're on firm ground saying that the visual cortex deals *primarily* with vision, even if there are some exceptions. Also, I am highlighting only a few brain areas that are thought to undergo important changes during emerging adulthood. A comprehensive overview of all brain features is beyond the scope of this book and can be obtained elsewhere (e.g., Borden et al., 2015; Mai et al., 2016; Woolsey et al., 2017). Below is the famous "hand-brain" model developed by Daniel Siegel (2021) in which simply inserting one's thumb beneath rolled-up fingers forms a crude model of the brain (Figure 5.1). The cerebral cortex ends up on the outer layer of the brain, the prefrontal is at the front of the cortex (behind the forehead), and the limbic system fits in underneath the fingers (subcortical).

At a micro level within the brain, neurons communicate with each other across synapses (gaps). An extremely simplified neuron appears in Figure 5.2. Within a neuron, a signal travels from dendrite to cell body to axon to terminal buttons. Communication across the axon is electro-chemical, such that when the signal leaves the neuron's terminal body and enters the synaptic gap before the next neuron, the communication is conducted via neurotransmitters (chemicals). The dendrite of the next neuron absorbs the neurotransmitter, and we're off to the races![2] Anytime you have a thought, feel an emotion, meet a friend, or do anything else, millions of neurons kick into action (Blakemore, 2018). Neurons and their axons are everywhere in the brain, traveling to the top layer of the cortex, away from the top layer, and to every additional part of the nervous system, including the spinal cord; these neurons and axons make a good part of the volume of the two brain hemispheres, left and right (Blakemore, 2018).

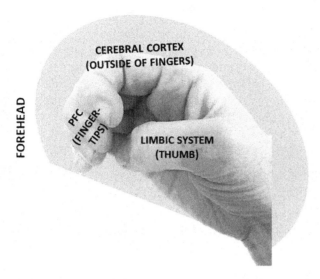

FIGURE 5.1 Siegel hand model of the brain (hand courtesy of A. Reifman).

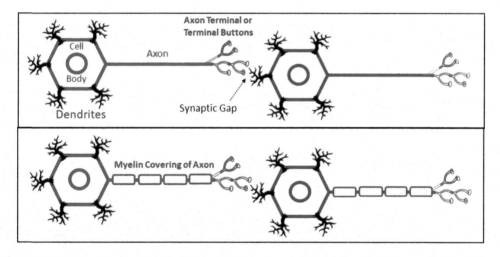

FIGURE 5.2 Simplified version of a neuron (one in red, one in blue) before and after myelination of the axons. Parts of real neurons are curvier and more jagged.

Three Major Changes: Pruning, Myelination, and Increasing Role of the Prefrontal Cortex

Pruning

When a neuron communicates frequently with another neuron, the connection between them grows stronger through complex biological processes (Munno & Syed, 2003; Trafton, 2015). The building of synapses takes place during childhood and proliferates to a very high density. A large, dense network of synaptic connections is not optimal for brain functioning, so synaptic connections that are not heavily active are pruned away (Cafasso, 2018), just like we trim trees or bushes in our yard. Pruning thus makes the surviving synaptic connections stronger. A 2011 study of postmortem brains summarized by Blakemore (2018) found that "the number of synapses in the prefrontal cortex is highest during childhood, starts to decline around puberty, continues to decrease throughout adolescence and the twenties, and eventually stabilizes in the early to mid-thirties" (p. 86). Indeed, most pruning during the early twenties occurs in the prefrontal cortex (Cafasso, 2018). This results in more efficient connectivity networks and is the hallmark of "development" (in this case, less not more reflects enhanced development).

Myelination

Myelin is a white fatty substance that coats the axons of our neurons like the electrical cords we plug into outlets at home, making the axons super-speedy (Blakemore, 2018). Blakemore adds that "Relatively large myelinated fibres in human beings, such as those from the cortex to the spinal cord, can conduct impulses faster than 100 metres per second" (pp. 83–84). Let's think about the speed of myelinated axons for a little bit. Fans of the major international sporting events may know that the world record in the men's 100-meter dash belongs to Usain Bolt of Jamaica, who ran it in 9.58 seconds at the 2009 track and field world championships. To dramatize the speed of an axon vs. Bolt over 100 meters, I created a humorous scoreboard graphic (Figure 5.3). Axons that have been coated in myelin (myelinization) are known as "white matter," whereas parts of the brain not so covered are known as "gray matter."

Prefrontal Cortex

Finally, in terms of brain areas, we have the prefrontal cortex. Blakemore notes that

> one of the brain regions that undergoes the most striking and protracted change during adolescence and early adulthood is the prefrontal cortex … [which is] involved in a wide variety of high-level cognitive and executive functions including decision-making, planning, inhibition of inappropriate or risk-taking behaviour.
>
> (p. 73)

As we'll see shortly, the PFC is thought to hold the limbic system (which involves reward impulses and other emotions) in check so that emerging adults exhibit less risk-taking than do adolescents.

FIGURE 5.3 Results of a hypothetical race between a myelinated axon in the brain and men's 100-meter dash world-record holder Usain Bolt.

Gender Differences

Some tentative findings have emerged on gender differences, though some of the authors acknowledge that these conclusions are controversial (NeuroRelay, 2012). First, young women's PFC is larger than and matures around two years before men's. In terms of myelination, which speeds up axons and makes the brain operate (figuratively) like "high-speed internet," women may have ten times the white matter (myelin coating) than men, which gives them greater efficiency at multi-tasking (connectivity difference as well). Lastly, the amygdala, which gives rise to the "flight or fight" response, is larger in men than in women, potentially hastening men's anger reactions (NeuroRelay, 2012). Koolschijn and Crone (2013) also found white matter to increase more readily in women than in men. However, male/female differences were relatively small.

Risk-Taking

According to two similar conceptions, the dual-system (Steinberg, 2010; not to be confused with the dual-cycles model of identity) and imbalance (Casey et al., 2011) theories explain why risk-taking declines from adolescence to emerging adulthood (Blakemore, 2018). These theories are both grounded in the different rates at which the limbic system (including reward sensitivity) and prefrontal cortex (cognitive controls that keep the limbic system in check) mature. During adolescence, the limbic system has already matured, whereas the PFC does not fully do so until emerging adulthood – hence, an imbalance. Also, the corpus callosum and other aspects of connectivity between/among regions have not yet fully developed and are often not completely myelinated until late adolescence. Once the PFC catches up to the earlier-developing limbic system, however, and the two areas form connections (Bos et al., 2018; Taber-Thomas & Pérez-Edgar, 2015), the PFC can regulate the limbic system via "dynamic interplay between subcortical [limbic, particularly the striatum] and cortical [PFC] brain regions" (p. 21). Casey et al. (2011) reported research findings that stronger connections between the PFC and limbic (striatal) areas predicted impulse control performance on a go/no-go task (like a red–yellow–green stoplight system). In addition, Taber-Thomas and Pérez-Edgar (2015) argue that "Postmortem evidence also suggests ongoing EA neurodevelopment in the frontolimbic system, which connects the brain's affective (limbic) and executive (frontal) networks and is critical for integrating emotional information into cognitive processing" (p. 128).[3]

Blakemore and her colleagues (described in Blakemore, 2018) set out to see for themselves whether (and potentially to what degree) the limbic system – specifically the reward-focused nucleus accumbens/ventral striatum and emotion-processing amygdala – matured earlier than the executive-control PFC. They examined brain images from participants who had been scanned three times – in late childhood, mid-adolescence, and early adulthood. Participants' PFC changes lasted, on average, until a later age than did changes in the two limbic structures (indicative of later maturation), but not by a lot. Blakemore and colleagues then took a different approach, looking at the brain scans of each individual separately. In other words, how did Participant A's scans differ across the three time-points, how did Participant

B's scans differ, etc. These results were much clearer. Out of 33 participants,[4] 15 showed the sharpest developmental gap, in which the two limbic areas (amygdala and nucleus accumbens) matured clearly before the PFC. In another 12 participants, only the amygdala matured before the PFC, whereas in 2 people, only the nucleus accumbens matured before the PFC. The remaining four individuals showed no mismatch of any kind; in each of them, the amygdala, nucleus accumbens, and PFC matured around the same time. This is a small study, but it suggests that the kind of imbalance envisioned by the theory – the limbic system's amygdala and nucleus accumbens maturing before the PFC – is not universal. The imbalance may characterize most people, but not all. The next question was whether those participants whose limbic systems (associated with rewards and emotions) matured before the PFC actually engaged in more risk-taking in adolescence than in emerging adulthood.

A few studies offer some information on this question. McIlvain et al. (2020) used a technique called *viscoelasticity* in the brain, rather than MRI, to study 40 adolescents around 13 years old. According to these researchers, elasticity-based measures of "regional brain stiffness reflect brain health and development via myelin content and glial [physical support structure] matrix makeup, and have been shown to be highly sensitive to cognitive processes" compared to other brain research techniques. McIlvain and colleagues measured risk-taking via two virtual games, one pertaining to driving through yellow lights and the other to blowing up balloons, with greater balloon inflation earning more rewards, but popping it would lead to a penalty. Results showed that the stronger the nucleus accumbens (limbic system) was than two areas of the frontal cortex, the more risk-taking participants exhibited. Weinstein (2017) took a very different approach, reviewing many studies that compared brain-region connectivity in individuals who had been diagnosed with internet gaming disorder vs. control participants who had not. Functional (statistical) connectivity between the PFC and striatal (reward) area of the limbic system was decreased in a study of adolescents with the disorder. Finally, Jung et al. (2018) studied the risk tolerance of young-adult participants in relation to structural (fiber-based) and functional (statistical) connectivity. They found that the stronger the structural connectivity (physical connection of fibers) between areas of the PFC and the amygdala (limbic system), the lower the young adults' risk tolerance tended to be. This finding supports the idea that the PFC keeps the emotion centers of the limbic system in check. However, greater functional connectivity (statistical correlation or being "in sync") between the PFC and amygdala was linked to higher risk tolerance. Overall, the evidence that, once the PFC grows to maturity, it can keep the limbic system's emotional and reward centers in check is not fully conclusive (Blakemore, 2018).

Because brain-scanning research is complicated and difficult and expensive to do, others have used "lower-tech" methods to study executive function. One such method is the Stroop test, dating back to Stroop (1935). You may have seen Stroop materials on poster boards with color markers (I'm dating myself as an undergraduate in the early 1980s) or on a computer monitor, if you have taken some psychology classes. A Stroop display shows color names written out as words in an ink or font color different from the word's name. Examples include: **BLUE**, **GREEN**, and **YELLOW**. Our eyes and brain are used to reading words, so to offer a greater challenge, the Stroop test asks the participant to yell out the ink or font color of a large number of words (PsyToolKit, 2021). For the three words above, the correct answers would be "red," "purple," and "brown." The technical term for the difficulty of trying to distinguish between the colors spelled out by the letters and the colors of the ink or font is *response interference*. Overcoming response interference to name the ink rather than the written word takes the kind of executive control stemming from the prefrontal cortex.

Pharo et al. (2011) exemplify the study of the brain and risk-taking via low-tech methods. These researchers studied two samples of participants, one from 13 to 17 and the other from 18 to 22 years old, who reported their own risk-taking in the domains of alcohol, smoking, drugs, sex, driving, and antisocial behavior. Participants also completed several neuropsychological tests requiring executive control, including the Stroop test and other tests thought to assess similar brain capabilities (e.g., listening to a random sequence of perhaps four digits and then repeating them back in reverse order). The researchers combined scores from the various measures into an overall neuropsychological/executive-functioning score and an overall risk-taking score. These two scores correlated at −.33 (a moderate negative correlation), indicating that the greater one's executive function, the lower one's risk-taking. This result is consistent with much of the neuropsychological research, but a correlation cannot definitively prove causation. For example, perhaps engaging in a lot of risk-taking (including substance use) damages the kinds of brain functions studied by Pharo and colleagues.

Young Adult Behavior during the COVID-19 Pandemic

During the COVID-19 pandemic (still ongoing at this writing), the leading safety recommendations initially (during most of 2020) were to wear masks, maintain social distancing (at least six feet) from other people, and wash one's hands frequently. Once vaccines to minimize COVID-19 contagion and symptoms came along in early 2021, people were encouraged to get it. Though things turned in a positive direction when daily deaths fell in March 2021, the later emergence of the "delta" (Crist, 2021) and "omicron" (World Health Organization, WHO, 2021) variants of COVID and less than complete vaccination compliance launched additional waves of COVID cases, hospitalizations, and deaths as 2021 transitioned into 2022 (see https://www.worldometers.info/coronavirus/ for updates).

Of relevance to this book, a large share of COVID cases (although not as many deaths) affected young adults. In mid-summer 2020, a graph from the South Carolina Department of Health and Environmental Control (2020), which I found online, caught my eye. The graph showed the state's COVID-19 cases per 100,000 population by age group from March 7 to June 20, 2020, documenting that many cases during that time were among young adults. According to the South Carolina report, "Since April 4, data from the agency shows that there has been a 413.9% increase in newly reported COVID-19 cases among the 21–30 age group." Let me repeat that: a 413.9% increase! In early March 2020, there were few COVID cases in South Carolina among any age group, but by June, 21–30-year-olds topped the graph with roughly 150 new cases per 100,000 population (translating into over 4,000 cases overall). Scott (2020) noted that "Young people, who account for a bigger share of the recent cases, aren't at nearly as high a risk of dying from the virus, but some small number of them will still die and a larger number will end up in the hospital." Even if young adults' fatality rate is low overall, however, yet another manifestation of societal health disparities is a finding that "Black people with COVID-19 in the 25–34 age group had a mortality rate 7.3 times that of non-Hispanic white people." Hispanic-to-White mortality ratios were only slightly less pronounced.

Why did the COVID count surge among those in the emerging adulthood range, not only during 2020, but even into the Fall 2021 semester?[5] Three partially overlapping theories seemed to receive the most attention during 2020. Relative to their older counterparts, on average, adolescents and young adults are thought to see themselves as more immune to certain dangers, earning them the nickname "Young Invincibles." Research has indeed shown a greater sense of invulnerability to correlate with some risky behaviors. Also, as we have discussed, the brain's prefrontal cortex does not appear to mature fully until well into one's twenties. Hence, the lack of a fully developed PFC among many in the emerging-adulthood age range – combined with a brain-based attunement to rewards such as opportunities to socialize – may have left them susceptible to risky behaviors. These risk-taking tendencies are more pronounced among adolescents but not completely absent among emerging adults. Related to the previous two ideas, teens and young adults like to socialize, pure and simple. In Minnesota, four bars were identified as COVID "hot spots" for young adults in June 2020 (Olson, 2020). One of these bars is in the Dinkytown district by the University of Minnesota-Twin Cities, another is not too far away in downtown Minneapolis, and two are in Mankato, home to a Minnesota State University campus. College-area bars have also been linked to COVID in other states, as well.

How do young adults, themselves, view the situation? The *Huffington Post* (Edwards-Levy, 2020) teamed up with the polling organization YouGov to survey US adults of all ages between June 17 and 19, 2020, on their behaviors and attitudes regarding COVID. A key item concerned respondents' self-reported mask-wearing in public, near other people. Indeed, fewer respondents under 30 years old (40%) reported "always" wearing a mask than was the case in any of the other age groups. One of the attitude items asked respondents if they believed wearing a mask was more a matter of public health or of personal choice. Interestingly, in each of the four age groups (under 30, 30–44, 45–64, and 65+), far more people cited public health (roughly 60%) than personal choice (roughly 30%). Young adults, therefore, are seemingly on the same page attitudinally with their older peers, but they simply don't follow through in wearing masks.

Intelligence (Fluid and Crystallized)

Most discussions of brain functioning in emerging adulthood are framed in comparison to behavioral and brain characteristics of adolescents. How does the emerging-adult brain (on average) compare to its functioning at older stages of adulthood? Researchers who study lifespan trends in cognition focus on two types of intelligence: fluid and crystallized. Fluid intelligence refers to "perceptual speed, reasoning, spatial ability or memory. These are [assessed through] the deciphering of letter, word or number series; the comparisons of symbols or patterns; and, memory recall" (Desjardins & Warnke, 2012, p. 9). As we'll explore in a little more depth below, emerging adulthood is around the time that individuals are at their peak in fluid intelligence. Crystallized intelligence refers to knowledge and skills acquired over a lifetime, such as general knowledge and one's vocabulary (Desjardins & Warnke, 2012). To use an example from Hagerty (2016), a young-adult chess player would likely be good at noticing things and making moves quickly, but an older player will have observed a plethora of chess-board situations over their lives and can call upon the best moves for a given scenario.

Two ways to conduct age-comparison research on not only intelligence but other characteristics are longitudinal studies (inviting the same people back over and over again to detect a change in their performance) and cross-sectional studies (comparing, for example, people who are 20, 30, 40, and 50 years old at the same time, e.g., in 2021). Longitudinal methods are generally thought to be better than cross-sectional ones, but many of the age-difference results summarized in Desjardins and Warnke's (2012) report are similar, regardless of research design. Several markers of fluid intelligence – reasoning, perceptual speed, and memory – peak in adulthood at age 20. The decline is gradual at first, so fluid intelligence will generally be strong throughout the twenties and perhaps into the thirties. However, by the forties, the decline will be more pronounced (Desjardins & Warnke, 2012). On the other hand, average scores on the *New York Times* crossword puzzle – a skill requiring extensive crystallized intelligence – are lowest among people in their twenties and rise steadily into the mid-seventies (Desjardins & Warnke, 2012).

In closing, you should always be careful when consuming research, especially on aging. For example, older generations may score lower on some measures than do younger generations, but not because aging diminishes our abilities. Rather, it was less common in earlier generations to attend college, so today's older people, through no fault of their own, likely have less education than do today's younger adults.

Decision-Making

One of the central aspects of emerging adulthood we learned about in Chapter 1 was that, for many in their late teens and early twenties, it is a time when many possibilities appear open. Do you want to teach, start a small business, join the corporate world, go into law or law enforcement, enter the health care industry, or become an artist or musician? If you're in college, do you want to major in sociology, political science, biology, or business administration? Alexandra Robbins and Abby Wilner (2001), authors of the book *Quarterlife Crisis*, describe the situation of one young woman:

> With so many more alternatives available, it is more difficult to decide on one particular path. For Olivia, a 22-year-old in Raleigh, North Carolina, the proliferation of opportunities for her career, geographic location, and studies makes it more difficult for her to settle any one aspect of her life.
>
> *(p. 125)*

Choices, choices, and more choices!

Some might think that having a large number of choices is good, but as we'll see, it can be surprisingly counterproductive. Sheena Iyengar and Barry Schwartz are two prominent researchers in the study of choice. In a National Public Radio interview, Dr. Iyengar reflected on one of her first experiences with the abundance of choice in the kind of mega-supermarkets that are becoming increasingly common: "I mean, it had something like – well, it had over 300 different types of jams, and 250 different types of mustards" (Spiegel, 2006). At some point, it occurred to Iyengar that such a huge number of choices may not be empowering but actually demoralizing. As any good scientist would, she took this idea into the field and lab, conducting three experiments (Iyengar & Lepper, 2000). In the first, which she and Lepper set up at the very same supermarket she mentioned in her radio interview, they put out a table (presumably with the store's permission) for shoppers to taste different types of jam. During certain hours, they put out 6 kinds of jam to taste, whereas, during different hours, they put out 24 (the authors went to great pains to pre-test the jams to make sure the 6 were liked no better or no worse, on average, than the 24). There were three main findings. First, the table display with 24 attracted a higher percentage of passersby (60%) to sample the jams (possibly creating a traffic jam by the jams) than did the table with 6 jams (40%). Second, even though the 24-jam table offered much more opportunities to try out products than did the 6-jam table, there was no difference in the extent of the sample. Visitors to both kinds of displays tried an average of around 1.50 jams. Finally, which displays led to more purchases? It was the 6-display table, in which 30% of customers purchased the brand advertised at the table, in contrast to only 3% of those visiting the 24-display table.

The other two experiments Iyengar and Lepper (2000) conducted were similar to the first one but were done in different settings. In Experiment 2, students in a class were given the opportunity to write an essay for extra credit. Based on random assignments, students' instructions either gave them six possible topics on which they could write or 30. The difference between conditions in how many students chose to write was not as large as in the supermarket study but was still statistically significant: 74% of students who had received a limited number of topics turned in the assignment, whereas only 60% of those who had the extensive choice did so. Experiment 3 involved having students taste either 6 or 30 chocolates but added a "no choice" experimental condition in which the experimenter selected a chocolate for a participant to taste, as well as some other features. In the end, 48% of participants in the limited-choice condition purchased the chocolate, compared to 12% of those in the extensive-choice and 10% of those in the no-choice conditions. In a very real sense, the extensive choice was just as likely to turn people off from making a purchase as was no choice at all.

Note that the jam and chocolate displays, and list of essay topics, were purely a feature of the environment – either 6 or 24 or 30 options were laid out in front of you. The first two of the original experiments (jam and essays) did not take into account any characteristics of the shoppers or students themselves. An idea Iyengar and Lepper (2000) began exploring in their Experiment 3, and which Iyengar fleshed out in a later experiment, is that perhaps, when encountering numerous choices, some people really want to sample all or most of them (known as "maximizers"), whereas others are cool with just checking out a few choices and finding one that is "good enough" (known as "satisficers"). In other words, maximizers feel they need to check out all or most options before making a choice, whereas satisficers do not. There is a linked maximizer–satisficer questionnaire that you can take at the end of the chapter as a possible class activity. Before we get there, however, let's look at another of Dr. Iyengar's studies, conducted with Rachael Wells and Dr. Schwartz.

In this study, Iyengar et al. (2006) recruited graduating students who had sought career-services advice from 11 universities. Many of you who are reading this book are in the same boat regarding the need to find a postgraduation job, I would suspect. Iyengar and colleagues first administered a survey to measure maximizing tendencies, one sample item being, "When I am in the car listening to the radio, I often check other stations to see if something better is playing, even if I am relatively satisfied with what I'm listening to" (p. 144). The researchers also asked participants how many jobs they anticipated applying to (which yielded a range of answers from 1 to 1,000). Final results showed that, of those participants who had received and accepted job offers by the end of the school year in May, those who scored highly as maximizers received offers that were $7,430 larger on average than those received by staunch satisficers. These results remained significant, even when ruling out the impact of quality of the university, one's major, or grade point average on one's salary offer. That's not the end of the story, however. Maximizers not only had more cash on the way, but also likely more headaches. Compared to the more serene satisficers, maximizers reported a greater level of negative emotions (e.g., stressed, tired, anxious, overwhelmed) about their job search, as well as less satisfaction with their job offers.

I always enjoy discussing the maximizer–satisficer studies with my classes. For whatever reason, an example that has stuck with me for many years is one student who insisted on looking at every reasonable vacant apartment before every school year, to the horror of her roommates. If you'll recall from the previous chapter on identity formation, there's a concept known as ruminative exploration for someone who struggles to find identity in part because of perfectionistic tendencies. That's probably why, in addition to being a time of open possibilities, emerging adulthood is also a time of stress and anxiety!

Review

You know the drill. We have:

BILLIONS, TRILLIONS, and QUADRILLIONS of neurons and synaptic gaps between neurons (Blakemore, 2018).

FOUR main types of structures in the limbic system, which pertains to rewards and emotions: hippocampus, amygdala, nucleus accumbens, and ventral striatum, the latter two of which are sometimes used interchangeably (Blakemore, 2018; Haber, 2011; Niehuis et al., 2019; Queensland Brain Institute, 2019).

THREE ways in which brain functioning becomes more efficient and mature in young adulthood: excess connections (synapses) between neurons are pruned; axons receive myelination; and prefrontal cortex develops stronger connections with the limbic system, allowing PFC to exert greater control over emotions (Blakemore, 2018; Casey et al., 2011; Taber-Thomas & Pérez-Edgar, 2015).

TWO forms of intelligence: fluid, based on quickness and memory, on which emerging adults tend to score highly, and crystallized, based on accumulated knowledge, on which emerging adults do not do as well as their older counterparts (Desjardins & Warnke, 2012). Also, TWO styles of making decisions amid a large number of possible choices: maximizing and satisficing (Iyengar et al., 2006).

ONE structure for keeping risky or socially harmful impulses of the limbic system in check: the prefrontal cortex (Blakemore, 2018).

Possible Class Activities

1. It's always fun to have student volunteers (and the instructor) take the Stroop test for executive functioning. Examples of the color-word list are readily available over the internet. As people take the Stroop test, consider the mental processes they are engaging and what that tells us about the nature of executive functioning.

2. Are you a satisficer (who is content to examine a relatively small number of options and find something "good enough") or a maximizer (who wants to leave no stone unturned in the search for the ideal choice)? Take the questionnaire at: https://psychologisteurope.com/maximizer-vs-satisficer-quiz/

Notes

1 Someone really tried to launch himself in this manner (Flanagan, 2014).

2 A real-world example illustrating neurotransmitter chemicals and synapses between neurons involves the class of medications known as selective serotonin reuptake inhibitors (SSRI), such as Zoloft, Prozac, and Paxil for depression and other conditions. Reuptake refers to "cleaning away" extra neurotransmitter from the synapse after it has been used up. According to Griffin (2021) "A reuptake inhibitor prevents this from happening. Instead of getting reabsorbed, the neurotransmitter stays – at least temporarily – in the gap between the nerves, called the synapse. What's the benefit? The basic theory goes like this: keeping levels of the neurotransmitters higher could improve communication between the nerve cells – and that can strengthen circuits in the brain which regulate mood."

3 O'Boyle (2008) offers a concise discussion of how differences in the timing of different brain regions' maturation may be related to mood-related disturbances.

4 It is not easy to conduct brain scans, even once let alone three times on the same person. At my university, an hour of scanner time costs $550. Also, if the participant moves while in the scanner, the data may not be usable.

5 My university, Texas Tech, has shown tremendous transparency during COVID-19, maintaining a website with daily updates on COVID cases and other statistics among students and employees (https://www.depts.ttu.edu/communications/emergency/coronavirus/graph/). According to one graph, early in the Fall 2021 semester, 125–300 students were coming down with COVID per week.

Traditional Milestones

Education in Young Adulthood

We are now entering Part III of the book, entitled "Traditional Milestones." In the US, roughly 70 percent of high school graduates attend college, although only around half complete a bachelor's degree. Other high school graduates pursue career and technical education, which provides training to become a hairstylist, electrician, or mechanic. Accordingly, the first chapter in this section (Chapter 6) examines educational endeavors in emerging adulthood. Other common milestones, namely beginning a job or career, forming intimate relationships and perhaps marrying, and beginning a family, comprise Chapters 7, 8, and 9.

Typically, I begin each chapter with a quote. In the arena of post-high school education, however, I couldn't narrow the possible quotes down to one. So here goes …

> Once reserved for the elite, a college education is now a necessity for both men and women who want access to good jobs.
>
> *— Settersten and Ray (2010, p. 26)*

> College is a potentially transforming experience, a once-in-a-lifetime opportunity to challenge students to examine their previous ways of knowing, thinking, and behaving.
>
> *— George Kuh (2003, p. 28)*

College education

> is about expanding people's horizons and depths of understanding, engaging students with the big questions that matter most in life, giving them tools to think and learn and communicate well, and passing on the richness of scientific and humanistic inquiry and understanding.

DOI: 10.4324/9781003156567-9

But,

> What really matters to emerging adults is getting the credit, earning the diploma, and becoming certified as a college-educated person so that they can get a better job, [and] earn more money.
>
> — *Smith and colleagues (2011, p. 101)*

> I tested my limits freshman year. I drank too much and threw up too often. I joined crew and pushed myself harder physically than I ever imagined possible. I fell in love for the first time. I gained resilience when I had my heart broken. I met people from different economic backgrounds who gave me a sense of empathy.
>
> — *Scott Galloway (quoted in Walsh, 2020)*

Educational Attainment

The purpose of this chapter is to examine what impact, if any, college and career–technical education have on individuals during emerging adulthood. In other words, how would someone in their twenties be a different person – intellectually, socially, and attitudinally – having gone to college (or other forms of instruction) than if they did not go to college. Before addressing this question, however, let's look at educational attainment in the US and internationally to get an idea of how many people we're talking about at different levels of education.

Historical Trends

Historically, it is only over the past 80 years or so that high school graduation and college attendance have become widespread in the US. As of 1900, only 10% of 14–17-year-olds were enrolled in high school, a figure which rose to 30% in 1920 and 70% by 1940. Only 8% of 18–21-year-olds were attending college in 1920, rising to 16% in 1940 (Arnett & Taber, 1994). Something dramatic then happened in the 1940s, namely World War II. Then, a piece of legislation officially called the Serviceman's Readjustment Act (Public Law 346), but better known as the World War II (WWII) GI Bill was signed into law on June 22, 1944, by President Franklin Roosevelt (Bound & Turner, 2002), providing college educational benefits (tuition, books, and a cash allowance). Recipients' extent of the benefit depended in part on their length of military service, but "Most men would have been eligible for the maximum benefits" covering four years (Bound & Turner, p. 790). Among WWII veterans born between 1922 and 1928 (who were 16–22 years old when the GI Bill was enacted), roughly 50% or more (depending on specific birth year) used the benefit to attend college. Percentages were lower among veterans who were older or younger than those born during the middle seven years of the 1920s (Bound & Turner, 2002). The percentage of 20–24-year-old men enrolled in school (which for many would be college) more than doubled from 8% in 1940 to 18% around 1946 (Snyder, 1993). Of all men who enrolled in college in the immediate years after World War II, 70% of them were veterans (Bound & Turner, 2002). Interestingly, no more than 15% of veterans born between 1915 and 1929 who used the GI Bill attained a bachelor's degree (Bound & Turner, 2002). Large numbers of people attending college but without completing a bachelor's degree remain a feature of US higher education to this day, as we'll see.

Current US Higher Education Statistics

The rise in Americans' college enrollment, which was initially spurred by the GI Bill, has continued to this day. Whereas fewer than 10% of those in the relevant age group were attending college 100 years ago, 70% of high school graduates were as of 2016 (71.9% of women and 67.4% of men; Figure 6.1). Because college-attendance rates zigzag from year to year (that's the scientific term), I have included trendlines to make things easier to grasp.

Figure 6.2 presents data points and trendlines for US college attendance by race–ethnicity (data on Asian Americans were not reported until 2003). Current trendlines have White, Hispanic–Latinx, and Black/African American college-attendance rates around the mid-60% to low-70% range. Asian Americans' annual rates have fluctuated between the mid-70% and mid-90%, but this group's larger trend is currently approaching the upper-80s.

As noted, however, only about half of US college enrollees complete the bachelor's degree. As of 2018, 35.0% of Americans had a bachelor's degree or higher (Statista, 2019), compared to the 70% who were attending college around that time. Among racial–ethnic groups, 56.5% of Asian/Pacific Islander, 35.2% of White, 25.2% of Black, and 18.3% of Hispanic Americans were college graduates (Statista, 2019).

Minority enrollment has been rising steadily at some of America's highest-ranked universities. Reflecting population growth among the Hispanic–Latinx population

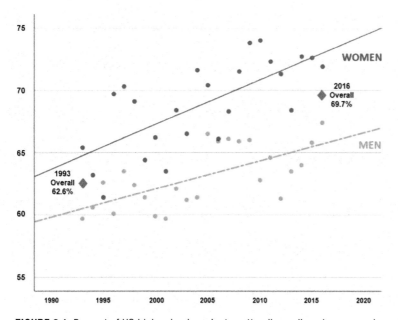

FIGURE 6.1 Percent of US high school graduates attending college by year and gender.
Source: Data from US Bureau of Labor Statistics (2017).

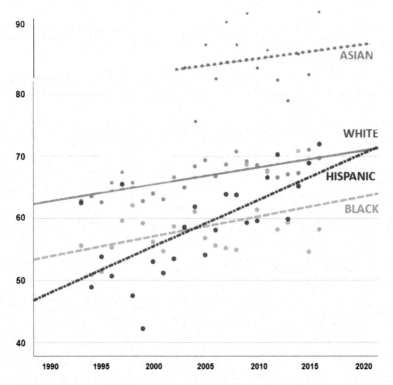

FIGURE 6.2 Percent of US high school graduates attending college by year and race–ethnicity.
Source: Data from US Bureau of Labor Statistics (2017).

in California (the state with the largest overall population) and outreach efforts by universities and high schools, the University of California system, which includes campuses such as UC Berkeley, UCLA, UC Santa Barbara, and UC Davis, recently reported dramatic rises in in-state admission of minorities, low-income students, and first-generation college students:

> Latinos slightly eclipsed Asian Americans for the first time, making up 36% of the 79,953 California students offered admission. Asians made up 35%, whites 21% and Black students 5%. The rest were American Indians, Pacific Islanders or those who declined to state their race or ethnicity. About 44% of admitted students were low-income while 45% were the first in their families to attend a four-year university.
>
> *(Watanabe, 2020)*

Attending a more selective university is associated with higher graduation rates (Mayhew et al., 2016). This may seem counterintuitive, as more competitive institutions likely have harder assignments, which should make it harder to graduate. However, other factors (e.g., students' motivation, campus academic climate) likely promote graduation (Mayhew et al., 2016).

Whereas most discussion of college attendance in the US centers on the roughly eight to nine million students attending four-year, bachelor's granting universities full time (US Census Bureau, 2021), students at two-year community colleges are often overlooked. According to the American Association of Community Colleges (AACC, 2021), 2.4 million students attend these institutions full time, whereas another 4.4 million matriculate part time. White students comprise 44% of community college students, whereas 27% are Hispanic–Latinx, 13% are Black, 6% are Asian/Pacific Islander, and 4% or fewer are multiracial or in other categories. Community college students tend to be older than their four-year counterparts (Fresquez & Rabinowitz, 2020). Specifically, community college students' average age is 28 years old, whereas the median age is 24[1] (AACC, 2021).

To the extent one sees community colleges as a conduit for transferring to four-year institutions and receiving a bachelor's degree, the results are disappointing. According to Fresquez and Rabinowitz (2020), "of the 80 percent of students entering community college each year who intend to earn a bachelor's degree, just 13 percent do so within six years." These authors advocate a "Transfer System for Tomorrow," which calls upon four-year colleges to make public commitments to welcoming community college transfers, establish working relationships with nearby community colleges, and minimize practical barriers to successful transfers (e.g., financial hardship, bureaucracies).

Current International Higher Education Statistics

International data on higher education come mainly from large organizations of multiple nations. One is the Organisation for Economic Co-operation and Development (OECD), a group of 38 countries containing "most of the world's highly developed economies" (Kenton, 2020). Another is the United Nations Educational, Scientific and Cultural Organization (UNESCO), which has over 200 member or associate member nations (UNESCO, not dated). According to UNESCO, "the number of students worldwide attending higher education institutions increased from 100 million to 207 million between 2000 and 2014" (Fish, 2021). With that rate of increase in just a 14-year period, the figure is likely much higher now. Still, there are large disparities in educational quality and attainment between countries with greater and lesser economic development (Fish, 2021). OECD data suggest that South Korea is the world's most educated nation, with 46% of its 25–34-year-olds holding a bachelor's degree and another 3% a master's (Fish, 2021; Institute of Education Sciences, 2021). One distinguishing feature of South Korean education is its high rate of early-childhood education (Fish, 2021), giving kids a good start. Other countries appearing on a list of "The 12 Most Educated Countries in the World" (from 2 to 12) are Canada, Russia, Japan, Ireland, Lithuania, Luxembourg, Switzerland, Austria, the UK, the US, and the Netherlands (Fish, 2021).

A country that one article calls an "Awakening Giant" in higher education is Nigeria (Tobenkin, 2019). Driven in part by its large youth population, "between 2012 and 2017, only 19 percent of applicants to Nigerian universities gained admission – excluding 6.3 million qualified applicants" (Tobenkin, 2019). Many Nigerian students come to study in the US and other nations. I personally have known several Nigerian undergraduate and graduate students who have come to study at Texas Tech (along with many graduate students from China, South Korea, and India). Nigeria faces many difficulties as a nation – including a large number of children without basic education (Ifedi, 2018) – but appears to be striving to increase access to higher education (Tobenkin, 2019) and schooling in general (Ifedi, 2018).

How Colleges May Shape Individuals

As we have now seen, in many countries the number of individuals with college experience (if not an actual bachelor's degree) is immense. So how does this experience change people's lives (if at all)? Presumably, completing college courses leaves students with greater knowledge of the subject area, on average, than before. Aside from the specific course material, does college attendance change individuals' personalities, values, outlook on life, and social interactions? We should expect to see that college's effects on emerging adult development are uneven. To have an impact, situations must command individuals' attention, get them to participate, and lead them to reflect. As Murray Sperber (2000), a critic of higher education in its current form and now-retired professor, pointed out, how can we expect college courses to have this kind of impact when classes at large, state-sponsored research universities (e.g., University of Illinois, University of Kansas, University of Michigan) often have hundreds of students in them. At large universities, such massive classes are almost guaranteed in introductory classes in popular fields (e.g., psychology, biology) and are pretty widespread for junior/senior-level required courses (as many readers know first-hand). Only with some advanced upper-level seminars are smaller classes likely. There is some movement to reduce the number of huge, amphitheater-type classes (Gordon, 2020), especially with COVID-19 having disrupted the usual forms of instruction, but I wouldn't hold my breath. In fact, a Kansas professor explains that smaller upper-level classes exist only because of large introductory ones, suggesting that the latter aren't going away anytime soon: "Course fees for big classes bring in enough money to have teachers for smaller classes" (Stingley, 2015).[2] On the other hand, there are also many universities – typically liberal arts colleges or private research universities (College Confidential, 2018) – that do offer small class sizes, with greater interaction between professors and students, and among students.

Evaluation Methods

In the field of evaluating college's impact on students, two names stand out: Ernest Pascarella and Patrick Terenzini. These two professors, both now retired, conducted a number of their own studies and also compiled the voluminous findings in this literature as a whole. The third volume of their roughly once-a-decade series on *How College Affects Students* came out in 2016, with the team now headed by Matthew Mayhew (Mayhew et al., 2016). One thing that jumps out about doing evaluation research in education is how challenging it is. The scientific experimental method would tell us to find a large number of high school graduates planning to enter college, flip a coin for each student, and then send the ones whose coin landed "heads" to college and prevent the ones whose coin landed "tails" from going to college, at least for a few years. The randomization aspect would ensure, as best as possible, that the experimental/program group (going to college) and control group (not going to college) had equal academic and social skills, on average, at the beginning of the study. Then, after four (or five, or six) years, any differences between the groups, such as the experimental/college group exhibiting greater concern with social issues than the control group, could only be attributed to the college experience. Such a research design would not be permissible, either ethically (i.e., banning half of the people from college) or practically.

With a true experiment out of the question, education researchers such as Pascarella, Terenzini, and Mayhew are forced to use methods that allow the soundest conclusions possible without depriving anyone of an education. In Figure 6.3, using the fictitious example of evaluating the wizarding education at the Hogwarts School (of Harry Potter fame), I illustrate one of the better research designs scientists could use, as well as some alternatives that would not be as good. The optimal design is shown on the left, in which a group of Hogwarts students and a comparison group of untrained young wizards (i.e., attending a "muggle" or non-wizard school) are observed in their wizarding skills at the end of their first, second, third, and fourth years of school (the Hogwarts curriculum is really seven years, but I'm just trying to simplify). For those not steeped in the Harry Potter canon, wizarding skills refer to flying on a broom, physically impersonating someone else using polyjuice potion, "apparating" oneself instantly from one location to another, and so forth. Because students were not randomly assigned to Hogwarts or a muggle school but were studied wherever they happen to be, the research design is a *quasi*-experimental one (i.e., similar to an experiment). In a quasi-experiment, the two groups are not guaranteed to be identical (on wizarding skills or other behaviors) at the study outset. That's OK. The Hogwarts group (solid-black line in Figure 6.3) turned out to exhibit better wizarding skills during the first year of school than did the untrained wizards (gray-dashed line). That's not surprising, as the Hogwarts students met the rigorous admissions criteria to get in. At this point, Hogwarts seemed to be looking good. As Harry Potter readers know, wizarding skills can emerge even without formal training, as in the example of pre-Hogwarts Harry escaping from dangerous situations (Wizarding World, 2021). However, after four years, we can see that the Hogwarts students and the muggle-school students showed the same degree of rise in their wizarding skills (i.e., the two lines had equal slope). Hogwarts students were still doing better, on average, than muggle-school wizards at the end of the fourth year, but the difference was no larger than at the end of the first year.

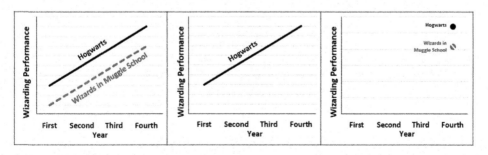

FIGURE 6.3 Quasi-experimental research methods for studying the hypothetical effect of attending Hogwarts School of Witchcraft and Wizardry on wizarding performance. From left to right, we see a non-equivalent program and comparison group design, a program-only design, and a post-test-only design.

The best (real) studies of college's impact on individuals use the design on the left of Figure 6.3. Sometimes, however, a researcher cannot find or afford to pay a comparison group (i.e., the non-Hogwarts students). In the middle square of Figure 6.3, therefore, we have a program-only design (if you consider education a program). It's useful to see that the Hogwarts students improved in their wizarding skills from Year 1 to Year 4, but we cannot put this finding in context the way we can with a comparison group. Finally, in the third square of Figure 6.3, we have a post-test-only (Year 4) design. We see that the Hogwarts students outperformed the comparison group in Year 4. However, this finding is not that informative without knowing that the Hogwarts group also outperformed the comparison group at Year 1 and thus that the Hogwarts group did not improve any more sharply in their slope within the first four years than did the control group.

How Does College Affect Individuals?

Cognitive Skills

Having reviewed the methodology, we now return to our regular programming. Mayhew et al. (2016) reviewed research conducted between 2002 and 2013, mostly from the US but also from Australia, Canada, and the UK. One important domain in which college may affect individuals is their cognitive and reasoning skills. Mayhew et al. reported that two large studies showed gains in students' critical thinking from the first to fourth year of college, without a non-college comparison group (program-only design, Figure 6.3, middle). A similar rise in moral reasoning was also reported. Studies have also shown higher reading, math, and problem-solving skills on the part of bachelor's degree holders than those who did not go beyond high school (post-test-only, Figure 6.3, right). Another research concept, from medicine, is a dose–response relationship (i.e., Does more of a treatment produce more improvement? Calabrese, 2016). Mayhew and colleagues note from this perspective that several studies found greater "dosages" of college exposure (e.g., years in college and completed credit hours) to go with a greater response, in terms of learning in math, reading, and writing. What about attending a more competitive university, one that is more difficult than average to get into? Mayhew and colleagues state that "Some evidence suggests that [greater] selectivity is … modestly related to cognitive gains and well-being, but other studies find no significant relationship" (p. 536).

Several studies have investigated how colleges' racial–ethnic composition is associated with cognitive and academic achievement (Mayhew et al., 2016). One important finding is that "institutions that are racially diverse or have high levels of diversity engagement tend to yield improvements in verbal, quantitative, and general education competence" (p. 541). However, diversity-related benefits may not accrue primarily to minority students. Mayhew and colleagues note that "When examining changes during four years of college, Black, Latino, and Asian American students have smaller cognitive gains than do White students," but also that "attending an institution with a sizable proportion of high-achieving, same-race peers may bolster the cognitive and intellectual outcomes of Black and Latino students" (p. 561).

Pascarella, Terenzini, and colleagues (Mayhew et al., 2016) generally seem to see college instruction and other aspects of the campus experience as improving students' cognitive skills. Another pair of education researchers, Richard Arum and Josipa Roksa (2011), reached a very different conclusion in their studies, publishing the pessimistically titled book *Academically Adrift: Limited Learning on College Campuses*. Arum and Roksa studied 2,362 undergraduates at 24 institutions nationally, who completed the Collegiate Learning Assessment (CLA) during their first semester of college (Fall 2005) and then again late in their sophomore year (Spring 2007). Their research method is thus like the program-only design shown in Figure 6.3 (middle panel), but with only two assessment points. Arum and Roksa explained that the CLA aims to assess "critical thinking, complex reasoning, and writing" (p. 36), as opposed to knowledge students would obtain in a specific course. During the 90-minute CLA, students would respond to hypothetical real-world scenarios, based on newspaper articles, statistical summaries, or other documents they received. According to Arum and Roksa, the CLA seeks to measure "how well the student assesses the quality and relevance of evidence, analyzes and synthesizes data and information, draws conclusions from his or her analysis, and considers alternative perspectives" (p. 22).

The average improvement from the first to the second year of college, taking the average of all students, was small. However, the average change in this context hides the fact that some students were showing considerable cognitive gain and others were not (the same way that the average of my professor's salary and LeBron James's basketball salary average out to around $20 million). Arum and Roksa (2011), in fact, revealed there were "no statistically significant gains … for at least 45 percent of the students in our study" (p. 36). In contrast, the highest 10% of students in their first year made huge gains in their second year. Rather than looking at cognitive gains among college students in average terms, therefore, it is probably best to think in terms of subgroups of students who do well. Mayhew et al.'s (2016) findings are consistent with this perspective, as well, such as their discovery (in at least some studies) that cognitive gains occur most often at highly selective universities.

Social Development

Individuals can change in many ways during college other than only their academic and cognitive skills. People can form close friendships, sometimes ones that endure a lifetime, as well as change their existing outlooks (or form new ones where none had previously existed) toward the environment, economic inequality, religion, or any number of other topics. I use the broad umbrella of "social development" to describe these kinds of changes. Fortunately, Mayhew, Pascarella, Terenzini, and their other colleagues (Mayhew et al., 2016) examined social development during college just as vigorously as they did cognitive development.

One form of social development is the acquisition and honing of leadership skills. Mayhew et al. (2016) report that students' leadership skills, on average, rose over their four years of college in one study (program-only design, Figure 6.3, middle). Mayhew et al. found that engagement in "interpersonal diversity interactions" (p. 553) is also linked to gains in leadership skills, as is participation in extracurricular activities through campus clubs and organizations. Finally, "larger effects among women [than among men] are apparent for socializing with friends and taking honors classes predicting leadership capacity" (Mayhew et al., p. 562).

Regarding cultural and political attitudes, Mayhew et al. (2016) concluded that changes occurring over the college years included "growing commitments to humanitarian values" and "[s]mall shifts toward liberalism" (p. 526). Greater liberalism was apparent only in some domains ("support for individual rights and freedoms"; gender equality; and LGBT rights) and not others ("endorsement of government intervention"; racial understanding and diversity, although for the latter issues, there had been gains in Pascarella and Terenzini's earlier volumes). Mayhew and colleagues also document a decline in materialism, which seems to contradict one of the chapter-opening quotes from Smith et al. (2011). One component of college life that one might expect to affect social development, but does not appear to, is living in residence halls. Mayhew et al. conjecture that

> Living on campus probably used to be a more immersive experience, with students within a residence hall communicating very frequently with one another and going home somewhat rarely. However, residents may be psychologically and physically less immersed on campuses today, given the proliferation and use of technology for communicating frequently with off-campus friends and family.
>
> *(p. 545)*

Fraternities and Sororities

Within universities, one social system that has been researched fairly extensively is that of fraternities and sororities (also known as Greek-letter organizations). Fraternities (to which men belong) and sororities (to which women belong) engage in a range of activities including parties, recreational sports, and philanthropic efforts, aside from the students' regular academic work. Fraternities and sororities participate jointly in many Greek-letter activities. An estimated one million US undergraduates are involved (Robbins, 2019). The same challenges noted earlier in studying the impact of college hold for researching the impact of Greek-letter organizations (e.g., lack of random assignment to participation vs. non-participation in these organizations; likely non-comparability in joiners' and non-joiners' personalities and attitudes; dearth of studies obtaining data over the four years of college from both Greek participants and non-participants; Reifman, 2011a).

An older, but still insightful, book on sororities is *Pledged*, in which author Alexandra Robbins (2004) combines information from multiple sources (member-informants, her own interviews and undercover observations, and research studies) to tell readers what goes on inside sorority houses and beyond. Robbins concludes harboring "deeply mixed feelings" about sororities. Many sorority members cited benefits of their experience, including a network of female friends, enhanced confidence, and community-service involvement (Texas Tech sororities have required their members to participate in at least two extracurricular activities; Lerma, 2011). As Robbins writes, however, "for every girl who emerges from a sorority with improved self-esteem, there are numerous others whose confidence has been crushed" (p. 320). Other concerning aspects of sororities, according to Robbins, are what some perceive as an atmosphere of conformity, intolerance, and "constantly being judged;" reliance on men for social validation; and heavy time and financial commitments (in conjunction with social functions, meetings, etc.).

Fifteen years after *Pledged*, Robbins (2019) was back with another book on Greek-letter life, this one aptly titled *Fraternity*. Robbins notes various negative aspects of fraternities: at least 72 fraternity-associated deaths from 2005 to 2017 and approximately 2,000 reported incidents involving sexual assault, hazing, racism, and other misconduct. Having seen fraternity men who entered the system vowing to refrain from antisocial conduct – some succeeding and some failing – Robbins concludes that there are both relatively bad and relatively good fraternities. She also offers advice for students and parents on how to tell the difference between them (e.g., reading campus safety reports, observing whether a given fraternity house is clean and well-maintained, observing whether the area around the fraternity houses appears safe and not awash in alcohol on party nights).

One of the key issues of fraternity life – if not *the* key issue – is masculinity. In Chapter 2, we learned about Kimmel's (2008) concept of Guyland, which referred to a lifestyle of heavy drinking, watching pornography, and sexual hookups. Underlying these and other behaviors, Kimmel argues, are young men's "struggles to prove masculinity," entailing "suppression of emotion, false bravado, and toughness" (p. 278). Kimmel states, as well, that "Nowhere is the brotherhood more intense, the bonding more intimate and powerful … than among athletes and fraternity members" (p. 233). Robbins (2019) likewise seizes upon exaggerated masculinity as a negative force in fraternity life. As she reports, "Experts say that one way to improve boys' mental and physical health … is to encourage friendships that defy masculine stereotypes by sharing thoughts and feelings" (p. 277).

I wrote a brief literature review on fraternity members' gender-related attitudes (Reifman, 2017). My general conclusions were as follows:

> fraternity members appear more likely than other male college students to exhibit degrading attitudes and sexually aggressive behavior toward women. Attitudes and behaviors linked to risk taking and self-perceived invincibility seem to be relatively common among fraternity members.
>
> *(p. 584)*

As noted, however, a correlation between fraternity membership and certain attitudes does not prove that one caused the other. Fraternities conceivably could have instilled or intensified these kinds of attitudes in their members, but it is also possible that individuals already holding these attitudes might have gravitated to fraternities (or that even other scenarios could undergird these findings).

Finally, one academically oriented recommendation made by both Robbins (2004) and researchers centers on the "rush" process of Greek-letter organizations' recruitment. In this process, new first-year undergraduates attend social functions at fraternity or sorority houses at the beginning of the fall term – when they are also trying to begin work in their classes – so that prospective and existing members can judge each other to find a mutually agreeable fit. To ease new students' transition to college-level academic work, Robbins and others urge fraternities and sororities to consider deferred or rolling admissions so that students could join during spring instead of fall. Spring joiners seem to do better academically. Also, slowing things down would, in Robbins's words, let those involved in rush "get to know each other naturally rather than through forced three-minute conversations" (p. 325).

Career and Technical Education

Another form of training for high school graduates is career and technical education (also known as trade or vocational school). These schools train individuals in practical (and, in my view, indispensable) occupations such as auto mechanic, electrician, cosmetologist, medical technician, and IT/computer technician, with instruction typically offered at free-standing facilities or at community colleges. According to St-Esprit (2019), "trade-school enrollment has ... risen, from 9.6 million students in 1999 to 16 million in 2014." An interesting concept within the context of career and technical education is that of "middle-skill" jobs (Holzer & Lerman, 2007). Middle-skill jobs are "those that require more than high-school, but less than a four-year degree" (Holzer & Lerman, 2007, p. 3). Middle-skill jobs have comprised roughly 50% of the US workforce for many years (Holzer & Lerman, 2007; Stephens, 2017).

In recent years, economists have claimed that the number of workers whose educational credentials fall in the middle-skill range (e.g., two-year college degree or career and technical certification) is falling short of the number of middle-skill job openings. According to Stephens (2017), "In 2015, 53% of [US] jobs were middle-skill, but only 43% of workers were trained at that level. This gap is reported by many states as well and is continuing to grow." However, certain factors may inhibit students who could do well in technical fields and would enjoy the work from entering them. One issue is that many parents want their children to attend college and may see technical education as an underachievement (St-Esprit, 2019). Another issue is the fear that one's technical credential will not lead to a job, a realistic concern given the less-than-optimal match between the fields in which students are trained and those in which jobs are available (Bolzman, 2019). A four-year college degree does not guarantee a job either, though.

Of course, individuals can obtain both career and technical education *and* a traditional four-year-college degree (Green & Kreamer, 2018). I have had a few students in my classes who had received cosmetology or medical technician training before coming to the university. As we have seen, there are many educational options in the US and internationally. All these carry potential benefits (e.g., preparation for your dream career, development of meaningful friendships) and risks (e.g., debt from tuition, lack of jobs in one's preferred career field). I wish you all as many of the beneficial aspects and as few of the risky aspects as possible.

Possible Educational Innovations

Given the potential difficulties on the road to an education, various academicians and policymakers have proposed innovations designed to increase access, hold costs in check, and enhance students' learning experience. I discuss several of these next.

- **Requiring a Personal Post-High School Plan**. As discussed in previous chapters, emerging adulthood is a time when individuals may perceive that they have numerous choices, which can be overwhelming. To get students to start narrowing their choices early on, the city of Chicago began requiring, as a condition for receiving a high school diploma, that students submit evidence of a postgraduation plan. This could include "a college acceptance letter, a job offer, military orders, or enrollment in a job training program" (Campbell, 2017). The first students to whom the requirement applied, the Class of 2020, fulfilled it in a spectacular fashion, with 97.5% submitting evidence of a plan (Chicago Public Schools, 2020). It will be interesting to see any follow-up research on whether these students made decisions more effectively into their twenties.

■ **"Gap Years."** A gap year is a year some students take off from school between high school and college. Students might do so for a variety of reasons, such as working to save money for college, using the time to reflect on one's priorities for college, taking a break to avoid burnout after 12 (or more) straight years of school, or traveling (Arnett, 2015a; Moody, 2020; Student Conservation Association, not dated). There is even a Gap Year Association (https://www .gapyearassociation.org/) that maintains a list of accredited gap-year programs students can join, as well as other resources. Gap years are probably most associated with the UK, but they occur in other countries, as well (Arnett, 2015a; Go Overseas, 2013). US college administrators' interest in gap years appears to be growing (Moody, 2020). Gap years have their advocates (Moody, 2020), with Arnett (2015a) deeming them "worth considering" (p. 164). Students who take a gap year overwhelmingly rate the experience positively (Student Conservation Association, not dated). However, research in Finland and Australia suggested there were no dramatic differences in developmental characteristics (e.g., goals, commitment, life satisfaction) between students who took vs. did not take a gap year (Parker et al., 2015). However, the topic seems ripe for additional research (e.g., in additional countries; types of students for whom gap years may be particularly beneficial).

■ **Service Learning**. Service learning augments a conventional course by including a field-placement component. For example, a course on youth development may involve placement at Boys and Girls Club centers or a nutrition course might partner with Meals on Wheels. Depending on the university, students are expected to spend two to three hours per week at the community organization, in addition to classroom hours. Professors of service-learning courses often require a reflection paper at the end of the field placement, sometimes along with a log sheet of field hours signed by an organization supervisor (Center for Community-Engaged Learning, 2011). (For a detailed overview of service-learning principles and examples of different universities' programs, see Center for Engaged Learning, not dated.) What does the evidence say about the potential benefits of service learning? According to Mayhew et al. (2016), "Service-learning appears to bolster learning, social skills, positive self-attitudes, personal insight (identity, self-awareness, self-efficacy), leadership, civic engagement and attitudes, political and social involvement, and diversity attitudes" (p. 552). Reflection in the form of the verbal discussion appears better than through a paper. Evidence is mixed on whether service learning promotes lifelong learning beyond the university years.

■ **Enhancing Online Instruction**. Online instruction (or distance learning) has been around even longer than widespread internet access has been, with some niche-based uses of it in the late 1980s and early 1990s (Kentnor, 2015).

Kentnor dates the "rapid growth of online education in traditional nonprofit institutions" to 1998 (p. 28). Online learning continued to expand in the following years, but not without growing pains. These difficulties stemmed from the hesitancy of traditional faculty to teach online and the slow realization that teaching methods needed to be different for online than in-person instruction (Kentnor, 2015). Many instructors appeared simply to transport the methods and materials they used with in-person classes to online contexts. As Kentnor states, "research has found that a well-designed, documented, and structured online course that facilitates active engagement with the students is essential for success" (p. 29). Accordingly, there have been increased efforts among online teaching experts to share their research and knowledge of the craft with other instructors. One example is the *Online Learning Journal*, which in 2021 published it 25th volume (https://onlinelearningconsortium.org/read/olc -online-learning-journal/). Widespread, albeit temporary, conversion to online instruction amidst the COVID-19 pandemic in early spring 2020 may (or may not) have served as a catalyst to improved distance instruction. Large numbers of professors (myself included) taught online for the first time in spring 2020.[3] I (and probably most other faculty) simply wanted to deliver a viable class for the rest of the semester and did not worry about whether I was using the best online teaching techniques. Having gotten a taste of online teaching, however, some of us have continued to instruct in this mode, have learned more about the technology for doing so (e.g., Zoom, Blackboard), and have tried to improve our online teaching by attending workshops. Whether the overall quality of online instruction will rise as a result of all this remains to be seen.

■ **Valuing People's College Training, Not Just the Credential**. Thomas Friedman (2016), a prolific book author and *New York Times* columnist, writes about a woman who studied computers in college for three and one-half years but had to drop out for financial reasons before finishing her degree. She continued to immerse herself in computer technology, working at a university help desk, as a back-up technician, and as a high school computer tutor. However, as she told Friedman, she was "blocked every time" from getting a more stable job, due to her lack of a college degree (p. 233). This story illustrates over-reliance on employers' part on a college degree as a *credential* and under-reliance on her actual skills and knowledge. Fortunately for her, some people directed her to some online training modules to fill in her missing technology skills. As of March 2016, she had been working for a major credit card company and had been promoted to systems engineer. As Friedman argued:

> there are about thirty-five million LaShana Lewises in America today who started college but never finished. Imagine how much more productive we could be as a country if we could find ways to value and capture the learning [of those people]. We simply cannot continue with this binary system of degree or no degree.
>
> *(p. 234)*

■ **College for All (or More Than Present Levels)**? Former President Barack Obama offered a variety of education goals and initiatives during his time in office. One aim, announced in 2009, was for 60% of Americans ages 25–34 to have an Associate's (community college) degree or higher by 2020. From the beginning of Obama's presidency in 2009 to its last full year in 2016, this percentage had risen from 41% to 48%. (Fry, 2017). The Lumina Foundation (2021) reported this percentage had continued upward, to 52% by 2019 (although this was among 25–64-year-old Americans rather than 25–34). Obama, in 2015, then called for tuition-free community colleges, a policy current President Joe Biden (who served as Obama's Vice President) is now pursuing. Spurred by Biden's plan, Cantwell (2021) provides a thoughtful overview of basic questions about expanding access to higher education (e.g., "Is free community college the best way to spend public money on higher education, or, what is the bang for the buck?"), whereas Nelson (2015) tackles similar issues. What kinds of policies (if any) are enacted in the near future to expand college access, and what effects they will have on students, remain to be seen.

- **Three-Year Bachelor's?** Finally, we have an idea that is more recent than some of the other innovations above: a three-year bachelor's degree (Whitford, 2021). Designed to reduce students' (and their families') expenses and accommodate students with unusual needs for a quicker degree (e.g., if their family is moving to another country), the proposed three-year bachelor's would likely eliminate some required courses rather than have students carry heavier loads to complete four years' worth of credits in three years. At this stage, a small number of universities are studying the issue; none will be enacting the "Degree in Three" anytime soon (Whitford, 2021). Also, the few times accelerated degrees have been offered, they have attracted little interest (Whitford, 2021).

Closing Note on Higher Education

I enjoy visiting and photographing college campuses. One of my favorite statues on any campus is the uncompleted "P" at Purdue University in West Lafayette, Indiana, which to many people symbolizes lifelong learning as a work in progress. This chapter has summarized several trends in higher education and their possible impact on emerging adult development. Ultimately, each of you pursues your own path to becoming an adult, a task that is always a work in progress! (Figure 6.4)

Review

We have:

FIFTY percent of US college attendees earning their bachelor's degree (Statista, 2019).

SEVEN higher-education innovations that were discussed.

FOUR types of outcomes of attending college that have been studied: cognitive, leadership, political attitudes, and masculinity (Kimmel, 2008; Mayhew et al., 2016; Robbins, 2019).

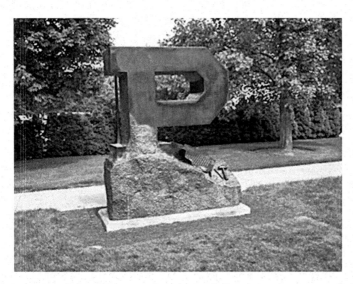

FIGURE 6.4 "Unfinished Block P" Statue at Purdue University.
Source: Photograph by author.

THREE types of post-high school education: four-year (bachelor's), two-year (community college, Associate's degree), and career and technical education (e.g., electrician, cosmetology).

TWO pioneering researchers on the impact college has on students: Pascarella and Terenzini (Mayhew et al., 2016).

ONE transformative event in expanding access to college in the US: The post-WWII GI Bill.

Possible Class Activities

1. Make a list of the educational experiences discussed in this chapter that you personally have been exposed to (e.g., service learning, online courses, fraternities, or sororities). Next to each, write 3 if you feel that experience had a big impact on your cognitive or social development, 2 if you feel it had a medium impact, and 1 if you feel it had little or no impact. Your instructor may wish to obtain averages of how impactful the class rated each type of experience.

Notes

1 That the mean (or average) of 28 is somewhat higher than the median (24) tells us that there are some older students attending community college who are raising the mean (8% of all community college students are 40 or older; AACC, 2021). The median of 24 tells us that half of community college students are younger than 24 and half are older, with the ages of the oldest students being irrelevant to the median.

2 Full disclosure: Most of the undergraduate courses I took at UCLA had hundreds of students and I turned out OK. I went to professors' and teaching assistants' office hours a lot, however,

which, in my mind, shrunk the university and allowed me to receive more individualized attention.

3 At Texas Tech, we taught our usual (mostly in-person) classes until the Friday before Spring Break in 2020. We were then given the one week of Spring Break plus the following week (during which classes were cancelled) to prepare to convert our classes to online format. Hardly enough time, especially for novice online instructors, to incorporate all the state-of-the-art online-teaching techniques into our classes.

7

Careers, Occupations, and Finances

Millennials want their dream job as early as possible, but entry-level positions are seldom dream jobs. As young people encounter the realities of the worka-day world, many are quickly disillusioned and want to continue exploring to get it right. In essence, the millennials operate as free agents who can bounce from one job to the next anytime they choose.
— Ron Alsop (2008, p. 32)

My goal is not to go back to having a boss.
— Cory Gabrielsen, 30 (quoted in Bruner, 2021)

Today's young adults – some of whom are in the millennial generation (born 1981–1996) and others in Generation Z or the iGen (born 1997–2012; Dimock, 2019) – are known for their distinctive attitudes toward work (Bruner, 2021; Chao & Gardner, 2007a).[1] By reputation, at least, they desire jobs that reflect their identi-ties and values, flexibility in both the time and location of their work and quick ascension up the corporate ladder (if they choose to work in a company setting at all) or to be self-employed so they can be their own boss. We will examine the evidence for these characterizations.

It is important to note that the work-related attributes of today's twenty-some-things, whatever they are, may well be specific to the present era. In other words, people who reach their twenties in 2030, 2040, and beyond may have totally differ-ent outlooks toward their jobs. This contrasts with other developmental processes discussed in earlier chapters, which are likely more intrinsic to the twenties. For example, brain wiring receiving its finishing touches or individuals zeroing in on their identities will likely still be taking place in people's twenties for the foresee-able future.

Still, today's young adults are who we have available to study, so we will look at this research. How do young people develop their career interests and find a good fit between their interests and the characteristics of their jobs? What kinds of jobs do they have? Is their reputation for job-hopping and wanting to be their own bosses warranted? And how well do they manage the money they earn from their jobs?

DOI: 10.4324/9781003156567-10

Development of Vocational Interests

Holland's (1959) conception of vocational interests or "personalities" has been highly influential for over 50 years (Nauta, 2010). Holland's theory posits six types of occupational domains that form the acronym RIASEC (Hoff et al., 2018; Nauta, 2010). These are Realistic ("getting one's hands dirty," building, repairing), Investigative (scientific, academic), Artistic, Social (working with people, helping professions), Enterprising (entrepreneurial, selling, marketing), and Conventional (administrative, office work). People do not neatly fall into only one category, but rather each person reflects some combination of the interests and motivations of the six domains. I see myself, for example, as mainly embodying the investigative dimension but also enjoying interaction with students (social) and (like any academician) trying to "sell" one's ideas (enterprising) to journal editors so I can get my research published. There's also a fair amount of form completion and record keeping in academia (conventional), which not everyone enjoys but everyone must do.

Research has documented how levels of interest in the six domains change between adolescence and young adulthood (Hoff et al., 2018). Judging from how your own and your friends' career interests may have shifted over time, which of the six domains do you think become more appealing as people enter adulthood and which become less appealing? Based on Hoff and colleagues' examination and statistical averaging of 49 studies (a meta-analysis), the two domains in which interest grows most dramatically from around age 20 onward are artistic and enterprising. As we'll see, the rising interest in enterprising endeavors fits with young adults' demonstrated attraction to self-employment. Interest in social careers grows, as well, but only modestly. Realistic (hands-on) work, after a slight dip and rebound during adolescence, maintains a stable level of interest in young adulthood. Finally, investigative and conventional careers decline in interest value, with an especially precipitous drop for conventional. Plenty of people work in offices with spreadsheets and strategic plans, but statistically speaking, it probably was not their primary aspiration during their twenties. Regarding the six RIASEC domains, Hoff et al. found that men's and women's career interests converge from late adolescence onward. However, "surprisingly little research has examined why interests change" (Hoff et al., p. 442).

In addition to the content area of one's work (i.e., RIASEC domains), there are many other dimensions on which jobseekers may have preferences. Michigan State University's Collegiate Employment Research Institute (CERI), in conjunction with the job-search firm MonsterTRAK, surveyed over 9,000 young adults (18–25), asking them to rank 15 job characteristics from most to least important to them (Chao & Gardner, 2007a). The top five most important to respondents were interesting work, good benefits (such as health insurance), job security, promotion opportunities, and chances to obtain new skills. Some characteristics commonly ascribed to young adults, namely the desire to work flexible hours (9th) and to work independently (11th), were not ranked particularly highly. Men gave significantly higher priority than did women to three job features that connote societal statute (chance for promotion, high income, and company prestige). The only feature on which women assigned greater value than did men was geographic location. A few racial–ethnic differences also emerged. Whereas African American, Asian American, and Hispanic respondents all ranked job security as their 1st or 2nd priority, White respondents had it as 4th. African Americans ranked work-hour flexibility higher (6th) than other racial–ethnic groups (all either 9th or 10th). Finally, Asian Americans valued working for a prestigious company higher (9th) than did the other groups (13th or 14th).

Finding One's "Match Quality" between Job and Interests/Abilities

Match quality, as Epstein (2019) explains, "is a term economists use to describe the degree of fit between the work someone does and who they are – their abilities and proclivities" (p. 128). Millennial and Gen Z young adults are said to put a high premium on match quality. Arnett (2015a) notes that "the ideal for emerging adults is finding a job that clicks with their developing identity" (p. 172). This raises an important question: What is the best way to achieve match quality?

Epstein (2019) discusses research by economist Ofer Malamud (2010) on how different nations' educational philosophies enhance or hinder students' likelihood of finding match quality. Within the UK, Malamud realized,

> English and Welsh students had to specialize before college so that they could apply to specific, narrow programs. In Scotland, on the other hand, students were actually required to study different fields for their first two years of college, and could keep sampling beyond that.
>
> (p. 129)[2]

In the terminology of emerging adulthood, then, Scotland was instilling a sense of *exploration*. What kinds of career trajectories did these students have after finishing college? As Epstein informs us, "college graduates in England and Wales were consistently more likely to leap entirely out of their [original] career fields than their later-specializing Scottish peers" (p. 130). Hence, greater opportunities to explore before and during college yielded better match quality.

Exploration before and during college may not be enough to ensure good match quality. Even if young workers who explored (like those in Scotland) arrive at a better idea of their ideal job than do those who specialized early (like those in England and Wales), they may still have to try out different companies before concluding that they have finally found their dream job. Another CERI/ MonsterTRAK report (Chao & Gardner, 2007b), this time with over 10,000 participants ages 18–28, examined young adults' willingness to make sacrifices and delay other aspects of their lives to pursue their desired jobs. Two key measures assessed Job Surfing (a sample item for which is "I would be willing to endure frequent job changes in order to find a job that fits my interests and abilities") and Delayed Marriage (e.g., "Marriage is not a high priority for me at this point"). Some slight differences emerged by gender (men a tad higher than women on willingness to delay marriage) and race–ethnicity (Asian American and White respondents being a little more inclined to job surf than were Hispanic and African American ones).

Descriptive Information on Young-Adult Workers

Now that we have examined some of the key elements of occupational preferences and how people search for jobs, let's look at the young-adult workforce as it currently is. The nationally representative 2015 Survey of Young Workers in the US (Federal Reserve Board, 2016) provides a good overview of the work (or non-work) experiences of those ages 18–30. Sixty-nine percent reported currently working for pay. Of those working for pay, nearly two-thirds worked full-time (defined in this study as at least 35 hours per week), whereas around one-third worked fewer hours. Nearly three-quarters of workers were employed at traditional for-profit companies, whereas the rest were divided between nonprofit organizations (14%) and government work (12%). Of those not currently working, 44% were currently looking. Of those not looking, 45% said that it was because they were currently in school. These are a lot of numbers, so I created a "treemap" chart of the key percentages (Figure 7.1).

What about earnings? The average salary in the US, before taxes, at young adults' main job (given that some people have more than one) was roughly $38,000, with roughly two-thirds earning between $3,500 and $73,000[3] (Federal Reserve Board, 2016). Four percent reported owning their own business, with a little under 2% running their own nonprofit. Even when people are doing similar work, one might think of it as part of a career (a long-term endeavor "with opportunities for growth, development, and purpose" Willkomm, 2020), whereas another might think of it as a job (mainly a means to earning a living). The Survey of Young Workers asked respondents how they would describe their own work, and they divided relatively evenly between "just a job" (40%), "stepping stone to a career" (33%), and "career" (27%). The sense of purpose that, according to Willkomm, helps people to view their work as a career also overlaps with a sense of identity (which we covered in Chapter 4). The OECD, an international economic and research organization described in Chapter 2, has compiled data on young adults' (20–29) self-employment internationally (OECD, 2021b). Many European countries are similar to the US figure of 4% of young adults owning their own business. However, the rate is much higher in some countries. In Greece, for example, roughly 16% of men and 8% of women in their twenties are self-employed (12% overall). In the Slovak Republic (which reported data only for men), the figure was 14%, whereas in South Africa, roughly 14% of men and 10% of women owned their own firms (12% overall). In countries that provided results separately by gender, men tend to have a higher rate than

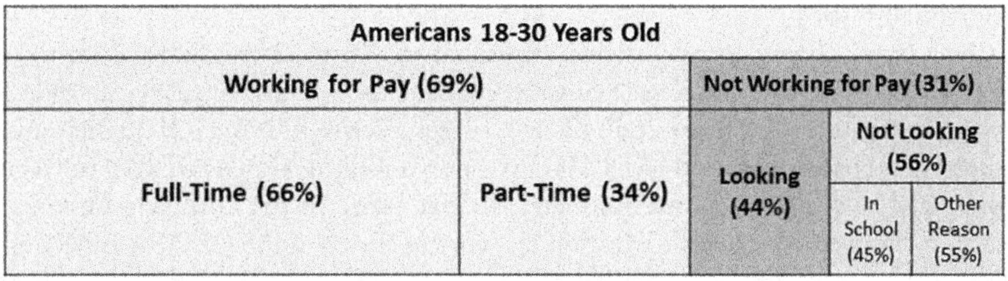

Americans 18-30 Years Old				
Working for Pay (69%)		Not Working for Pay (31%)		
Full-Time (66%)	Part-Time (34%)	Looking (44%)	Not Looking (56%)	
			In School (45%)	Other Reason (55%)

FIGURE 7.1 Treemap chart of divisions into different work statuses.
Source: Data from 2015 Survey of Young Workers, Federal Reserve Board, 2016.

women of owning their own business, but typically only by a few percentage points (OECD, 2021b). There was one nation in which a higher percentage of women (roughly 13%) than of men (12%) were self-employed, Mexico.

The *quality* of young adults' jobs is also of great interest. As discussed in Chapter 1, some observers consider the working world of young employees to be exploitative (Côté, 2014; Silva, 2013), involving frequent turnover, low wages, and limited benefits. Ross et al. (2018) probed the issue of job quality among young US workers from disadvantaged families, studying 29-year-olds. How did Ross and colleagues define their two central concepts, job quality and family disadvantage? I'm glad you asked! For job quality, they created a 0–8 scale, with 8 representing the highest quality. There were four dimensions (wages, benefits, hours, and workers' job satisfaction). Each worker could receive up to two points on each of the four dimensions. To receive the maximum two points for wages, a worker would have to have earned at least four times the federal poverty level in 2015 (roughly $47,000 for a person living alone, $64,000 for someone living in a two-person household, with higher thresholds for larger households). To receive the full two points on benefits, the worker had to receive paid leave, a retirement benefit, and health insurance. Employees who worked 31–50 hours per week received full points for hours (working fewer or greater hours than this would lose points), whereas choosing the survey option that one likes their job "very much" would receive full points for satisfaction. To be considered disadvantaged for purposes of the study, at least one of the following conditions had to hold when participants were between 12 and 18 years old: low family income, neither parent having a postsecondary (beyond high school) degree, participant's mother having her first child at age 19 or younger; and receipt of public assistance.

To put the above definition of adolescent disadvantage in context, only 79% of the disadvantaged youth were working for pay at age 29, whereas 90% of non-disadvantaged 29-year-olds were (Ross et al., 2018). Also, whereas 48% of workers who grew up without disadvantage had high-quality jobs (a job-quality score of 6 through 8), only 38% of those who grew up disadvantaged had high-quality jobs. Among only the employed disadvantaged participants, several variables were associated with the attainment of high-quality jobs. A larger percentage of men (40%) than women (35%) were in a high-quality job at age 29. Larger percentages of Hispanic (41%), White (40%), and "other" (39%) respondents had high-quality jobs than did African American respondents (26%). Prevalence of high-quality jobs differed markedly by educational attainment. Fifty-four percent of workers with a postsecondary degree (i.e., bachelor's or higher), 36% of those with a high school diploma, and 22% who dropped out of high school or obtained a GED found high-quality jobs.

To address the issue of possible exploitation (Côté, 2014; Silva, 2013), we also need to examine the prevalence of very low-quality jobs among 29-year-olds. In the rating system used by Ross et al. (2018), to get a score of 0 for job quality, someone would need to earn roughly $23,500 for a person living alone, $32,000 for someone living in a two-person household, etc.; receive none of the common benefits (paid leave, retirement, or health insurance); work either a light (1–20 hours) or heavy (61+ hours) schedule; and dislike their job or think that it is "OK." Even among the subsample who grew up in disadvantaged conditions, only 2% scored 0 on job quality, 4% scored 1 (meaning that things were going decently in one – but only one – domain out of wages, benefits, hours, or satisfaction), and 8% scored 2 (things

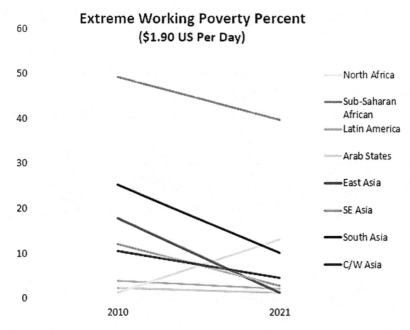

FIGURE 7.2 Percent of young workers (15–24 years old) making extremely low wages in different world regions.
Source: Data from International Labour Organization (2020).

going decently in two domains). The most common job-quality scores for those in the disadvantaged subsample were 4 (17%), 5 (21%), and 6 (20%). Only 4% of those who grew up disadvantaged had the very best jobs (score of 8). Twenty-one percent of African Americans who grew up disadvantaged had a low-quality job (defined by Ross et al. as 0–2), with either 13% or 14% of other racial–ethnic groups at the same low level. Also, 23% of high-school dropouts/GED recipients had low-quality jobs.

Wages for young workers vary extensively around the world. The International Labour Organization (2020) compiled a large number of statistics on this topic. According to this report, there are an estimated 429 million young (15–24 years old) workers worldwide (out of a world population of 7.8 billion; US Census website, 2021, November 22). Among these workers, 13% qualify as being in "extreme poverty" (daily income of below $1.90 in US currency). Figure 7.2 displays world regions' percentages of extreme poverty workers, in both 2010 and 2021, based on raw numbers presented by the International Labour Organization. In all the regions with available data except for the Arab States, extreme poverty work has declined. It is still very high, though, in sub-Saharan Africa (roughly 40%).

Social Challenges on the Job

In addition to the economic issues of wages, benefits, and hours, young workers may also have to deal with non-economic, social challenges on the job. In their book *Quarterlife Crisis*, Alexandra Robbins (the same person who wrote the books about sororities and fraternities) and Abby Wilner (2001) presented interviews with several new workers in their twenties. Three main social challenges were apparent from these interviews. First, perhaps the biggest shock to a young worker is that, unlike in college, where there are thousands of similar-aged peers around, most of one's coworkers may be several years older than you are. In extreme cases, you may be the *only* person in early twenties. According to a 24-year-old woman Robbins and Wilner interviewed,

> After college, you're no longer surrounded by people your age to go out and party with. I'm trying at work, but the truth is that most of my colleagues are at least five years older than me and mostly married. But I've found that with some prodding, even a few of the old fuddy-duddy ones will come out for a beer.
>
> *(p. 155)*

Another person reported being only one of five people under 35 in their workplace. The second challenge is that "the work [students] had to perform in order to obtain their degrees often can be entirely different from the work that is necessary to get the jobs they desire" (p. 170). Frustration and second-guessing over the fields they studied – and the tuition expenses that went along with their education – thus afflict many students. Third, even if one is fortunate enough to obtain a job without having majored in a field that matches their workplace, one may experience the "impostor phenomenon" (Clance & Imes, 1978; Mak et al., 2019), a feeling of being fake and unworthy of one's accomplishments. One of Robbins and Wilner's interviewees described just this situation: "I always doubted myself and my abilities because I didn't know how I got the job. I still think it was a fluke" (p. 175). Now, this student who felt like an impostor reported attending the company's information session at her university only to receive a free hat, so perhaps it is not surprising that she did not feel a strong connection to the firm!

Silva (2013), whose writings about the working class we learned about in Chapter 2, also identified some social/organizational challenges experienced by the people she interviewed. A 25-year-old woman who held a fulfilling job in a restaurant – one with mentorship, advancement, and the feeling of being part of a well-functioning team – had it all fall apart when her manager died suddenly of cancer and the new leadership did not follow through with the previously successful business practices. Another lost her manufacturing job when the company shifted its plant to another country, and another missed out on a job he was on the verge of getting, due to a positive marijuana test. Things like this can happen to people of any economic status at any company, but one gets the impression from Silva's book that they create the most havoc for the most vulnerable workers.

Job-Hopping

By several measures, young adults tend to move around fairly frequently from job to job. A 31-year-old woman interviewed by Silva (2013) had worked in a toy factory (putting products in boxes) and in an electrical plant (inserting little springs into electrical switches), and as "a waitress, a truck driver, a field hand, a telemarketer," a hospital aide, and in logging (p. 112). These eight jobs may sound like a lot – and are – but are pretty much spot-on with the national average. Statistics from the

US Bureau of Labor Statistics (US BLS, 2014) showed young workers holding an "average of 6.2 jobs from age 18 through age 26," with a follow-up report six years later updating the figure to an "average of 8.2 jobs from age 18 through age 32" (US BLS, 2020).

Young adults seem to sense, when they are in one job, that there is a good chance they will soon be moving to another. In the 2015 Survey of Young Workers (Federal Reserve Board, 2016), only about 30% of workers expected to remain at their current employment for more than two years. Twenty-four percent said they didn't know how much longer they would stay, whereas the remaining 46% gave answers ranging from "less than two months" to "one to two years." Arnett (2015b) noted that, in a national (US) poll of 21–29-year-olds he commissioned, 46% of respondents agreed with the statement that "My job with my current employer is temporary." Grosemans et al. (2020), who reviewed the available literature on job explorations, concluded that individuals in the emerging-adulthood age range "do actually expect to hold different jobs" (p. 806). These authors observed some differences between nations, specifically that "some emerging adults (students in the United Kingdom) hold different jobs before obtaining a satisfying one, whereas others (students in Finland and Germany) directly get a satisfying job after education" (pp. 806–807).

Ben Casselman, a journalist who has written on statistical topics for many leading publications, has had enough of hearing about job-hopping millennials (Casselman, 2015). Whereas some of the statistics above refer to average numbers of the job held by a certain age, Casselman looks at young adults' job turnover differently. His statistic of choice is the percent of people (in this case, 22–29-year-olds) who change jobs in a given month. In any one month, not that many people change jobs, usually around 3–4%. Still, Casselman was able to discern some meaningful trends. In 1996, around 4% of US workers aged 22–29 (who were born between 1967 and 1974, i.e., pre-millennial) were changing jobs in a given month. Among millennials (born beginning in 1981 and reaching their twenties in the early 2000s), the rate of monthly job-moving dipped, first to around 3.5% and then to around 2.5–3.0%. Not a huge difference, but Casselman is technically correct that, at least up until 2015, "today's young people are actually less professionally itinerant than previous generations."

Although frequent job-switching may sound unappealing for a variety of reasons – another round of paperwork, less chance to get to know people, and so forth – Casselman (2015) points out one definite advantage. As he notes, "Changing jobs is a key way for workers to make more money. That's especially true for younger workers, who often need to move around to find the job that suits – and pays – them best." What's that word we keep coming back to? Exploration!

Some workers may not need to explore so much, however. They may see a given occupation as a "calling," something they have wanted to do for a long time and feel is their role or niche in life. The idea of a calling comes from religious contexts (Hahnenberg, 2020), but now is used to describe just about anything one is drawn to. Wilson (2018) administered, among other measures, the Calling and Vocation Questionnaire (Dik et al., 2012) and a work-engagement questionnaire to over 500 working Americans. Participants' average age was around 37 years, which is older than the emerging-adulthood range, but the results are still informative. The calling questionnaire represented three component themes: *feeling called* (a sample item being "I was drawn by something beyond myself to pursue my current line of work"), *purpose* (e.g., "My work helps me live out my life's purpose"), and *helping* ("My work contributes to the common good"). A sample item to measure work engagement was "At my work, I feel bursting with energy." Wilson found all three aspects of work as a calling to correlate with work engagement, such that the greater someone's feelings that they were called to their job, that it gave them a sense of purpose, and it allowed them to help others, they also felt greater engagement and energy on the job. Averages on the three calling subscales (calling, purpose, helping) ranged from 2.12 to 2.41, with 4 being the maximum score one could get (standard deviations were around 0.90, so roughly two-thirds of participants would have scores between 1 and 3). In short, not that many people would seem to consider their jobs a calling.

"Gig"/Freelance Economy

If there isn't a job you see as a calling and, even after working for several different companies, nothing seems to click, then perhaps working for yourself is the answer. Unlike some jobs, such as public-school teacher, where the students come to you, self-employment requires you to find your own clients and entice them to hire and retain you (remember the "enterprising" orientation in the RIASEC job-interest framework). Self-employment therefore is sometimes referred to as "gig" employment, as in a local rock-and-roll band that must find itself a gig for the upcoming weekend. The term "freelance" also applies, as in a freelance writer who independently works on articles and sells them to magazines.

According to a large, nationally representative online survey commissioned by Upwork and the Freelancers Union in 2015 (Upwork, not dated), more than one-third of US workers engage in freelance work. Forty-three percent of 18–34-year-olds reported freelancing. In each of the older age groups (35–44, 45–54, and 55 and older), between 29% and 31% freelanced. Further, 18–34-year-olds were more optimistic about freelancing and more likely to recommend it to others than were older individuals. These findings are what I would have expected, as the features young people say they want in a job (e.g., flexible hours and working conditions; ability to express one's personal identity) match what freelancing offers. Many young adults also have considerable technological savvy (for creating websites and apps), which can help them publicize and run their businesses.

One of the most noteworthy new phenomena of 2021 is the "Great Resignation," with millions of Americans leaving the labor force (Bruner, 2021). This trend may stem partly from continuing COVID-related uncertainty but also from general burnout, people spending less than usual during the pandemic and thus having some savings and the feeling that a large number of job openings will make it relatively easy to re-enter the job market. Young adults are a major part of the Great Resignation (Bruner, 2021). Bruner quotes economist Lawrence Katz to the effect that the Great Resignation "is less about young workers leaving the labor market entirely, but instead about 'trying out new things, and taking advantage of new opportunities and not sticking with the old bargain.'" Perhaps some of these "new things" will include self-employment and the gig economy.

Many types of solo practitioners have been around for ages: hairstylists (some of whom rent a chair in larger salons), gardeners, housepainters, tutors, music teachers, and others. Newer business models, however, allow individuals to do things they ordinarily do on their own but with guests. For example, one can drive their own car but take on passengers (Uber, Lyft) or simply open their home to lodgers (Airbnb). Even though these lines of work involve large companies, there is still a sizable self-employment component in some of them, as individuals can decide when they do and do not want to participate (Chen et al., 2019). Berkowitz et al. (2021), analyzing data from 2014 to 2017, concluded that, whereas the 2010 Affordable Care Act (ACA) may have helped the self-employed obtain health insurance to some extent, "a substantial portion of self-employed individuals remain uninsured. Further … transitioning to self-employment is strongly associated with losing insurance coverage" (Berkowitz et al., p. 254).

Personal Money Management

General

Once individuals start earning money – or *anticipate* receiving money – they then must manage it. One might expect college students and graduates to be good at money management as, after all, they got into college. As we discussed in Chapter 5, however, some maintenance work on twenty-somethings' brains (myelinization, pruning, continuing development of the prefrontal cortex) is still going on. Also, many aspects of finance are complex, such as interest rates, loans, and debt. Suffice it to say, finance can be complicated for anyone, and young adults are no exception. Did you know, for example, that "Defaulting on your student loan can leave a stain on your credit history for up to seven years after your loan is paid in full"? (Sumrak, 2017).

Walking over to the Student Union on my campus in the late 1990s and early 2000s, I used to see a familiar sight. A table would be set up, with signs offering students the opportunity to sign up for a credit card. In fact, if they did so, they would receive a "free" gift, such as a T-shirt or large jug of cola. According to financial educator Jennifer Wallis (2004),

> Many college students sign up for the cards without realizing that they may be starting a cycle that can take years to escape from. I have heard numerous times from college students that they signed up for the card to get the free stuff and just planned to cut up the card … Instead, they found themselves strapped for cash and discovered that they could use the credit card … When graduation came, the high paying job did not and along with student loan payments …, they found themselves overwhelmed.

I haven't seen that credit-card table much in recent years, thanks in part to the 2009 Credit Card Accountability Responsibility and Disclosure (or C-CARD) Act of 2009 (Cothern, 2021), which imposed greater regulation of credit-card companies' dealings with those younger than 21.

The above examples highlight the importance of a field known as personal financial planning (PFP). While available to adults of all ages, PFP has taken on particular relevance to those in emerging adulthood. Not only is there a growing body of research on young adults' financial literacy and behaviors (some of which we will review). Also, institutions including the University of North Texas, University of California, Los Angeles, University of Oklahoma, University of Oregon, and Texas Tech University offer financial advising, coaching, or wellness organizations on campus, which are open to students interested in workshops and other services to strengthen their money management.

One of the largest recent studies of US college students' financial behavior is the 2019 Money Matters on Campus survey (Zapp, 2019). The 30,000-plus participants consisted largely of undergraduates at four-year institutions, with small proportions of two-year undergrads and of graduate students. Ninety-one percent of participants reported having a checking account, but only 59% checked their account balances. Only around 40% engage in budgeting. Older students were more likely to practice good financial behaviors, generally, than were younger students, with 22-year-olds' rates of engagement typically around 5–10 percentage points higher than those of 18-year-olds. According to the report, "The percentage of students using credit cards in college has increased from 28% in 2012 to 46% today as has the percentage of students with more than one card from 25% to 45%" (Zapp, 2019). As of 2018, most students' (around 65%) amount of credit-card debt was under $1,000, and a little below 20% had debt in the range of $1,000 to $2,499. Roughly 7% had debt between $2,500 and $4,999, whereas 5% each had debt of $5,000–9,999 and $10,000 or more.

Another major study is the **A**rizona **P**athways to **L**ife (Success) for **U**niversity **S**tudents (A-PLUS) project (Serido & Shim, 2017). The project began with an initial survey of roughly 2,000 first-year college students in the spring of the 2007–2008 academic year. A second assessment occurred in the fall of the 2010–2011 academic year, when students were beginning their senior year. Two additional follow-ups took place, one in summer 2013 (third assessment) when students had been out of college for two years and the other in summer 2016 (fourth assessment), when students had been out for five years (assuming the students graduated in four years, which is not always the case). I have read various reports from the A-PLUS crew over the years and what follows are what I consider some of the most interesting findings. One measure of young adults' financial independence (one of the "Big Three" markers of adulthood in laypersons' minds, as discussed in Chapter 1) is whether parents can claim their children as dependents on the parents' income tax returns. A key criterion for parents to be able to claim someone as a dependent is that the potential dependent "Receive[s] more than half their support from [the tax-filer]" (Bieber, 2020). In the second assessment (students' senior year of college), the A-PLUS survey inquired into this issue and found that 22% of respondents could not be claimed as a dependent (i.e., were independent in the sense of receiving less than half of their support from parents), compared to 11% in the first year (first assessment). In the fourth assessment (five years after college), the researchers inquired into participants' strategies for dealing with financial difficulties. Among 14 possible options, the most highly cited were working additional hours (41%), foregoing medical or dental care (35%), asking parents for money (30%), and moving in with parents or other relatives (21%).

Research has linked young adults' financial behaviors with the extent to which they see their lives matching Arnett's (2015a) themes of emerging adulthood (Vosylis & Klimstra, in press). The greater participants' sense of self-focus (i.e., taking responsibility for oneself), the more they engaged in financial planning/goal-setting and controlled spending. Feeling in between adolescence and adulthood, on the other hand, was associated with less-diligent financial behavior (less planning, less monitoring of cash flow, less saving, and less controlled spending).

Housing

Among workers' most important expenses is their housing. In fact, going back to the beginning of this book, leaving home and living independently from one's parents is one of the traditional milestones of reaching adulthood (Henig & Henig, 2012). The 2015 Survey of Young Workers (Federal Reserve Board, 2016) included a few questions that probed respondents' living arrangements and how they paid for housing. Forty-five percent of these 18–30-year-old respondents' living situations represented full adult-like arrangements: 8% lived alone and 37% had started their own household and lived with their spouse/partner and/or dependent children. Thirty-nine percent lived with their parents (or spouse/partner's parents) and 13% lived with roommates (small percentages had other living arrangements). Participants also reported on how they paid the rent or mortgage for their housing (referring to themselves if they lived alone or themselves and a spouse/partner if they lived together). Forty-one percent of respondents (or respondent-partner pairs) paid fully for their housing, 17% contributed partially (with assistance from others such as parents), and 39% did not pay at all.

Finally, Census Bureau researcher Kurt Bauman (2017), without intending to, ties together the previous (education) and current chapters of this book. In Figure 7.3, which is based on his work, we see different combinations of work, school, and living situations from ages 16 to 34. Between ages 16 and 18, for the most part, people were living with their parents while attending high school (light gray). Starting around 19, four sizable areas of coloration emerge: attending college and living in a dormitory (dark green), attending college and living with parents (medium green), living with parents while working full-time (dark gold), and living with parents while working part-time or not working (dark gray). As we move into the early twenties, additional zones open up: never-married and working full-time (beige-cream color), never-married and not working full-time (light blue), and in college and living independently (light green). The expansion of the college/living-independently group makes sense, as large numbers of college students move into apartments after living in campus residence halls for their first year or two. Finally, two groups that really start growing around age 25 are ever-married and working full-time (yellow) and ever-married but not working full-time (blue). One can see hints of Osgood and colleagues' (2005) groups, which we covered in Chapter 1, in the color diagram. The independent-living, college-attending group (light green), for example, could be similar to Osgood et al.'s educated singles and educated partners. In addition, those living with parents and not working full-time (dark gray) could be like the slow starters. Think of Figure 7.3 as Osgood and colleagues in technicolor!

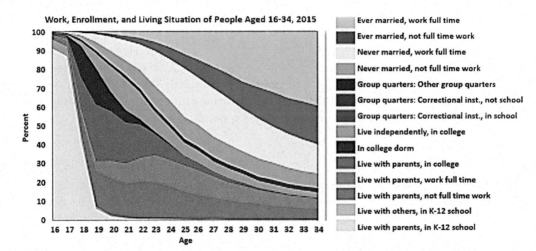

FIGURE 7.3 Percentages of individuals with different combinations of work, school, and living situations (as of 2015), by age (Bauman, 2017, US Census Bureau).

Source: Data from American Community Survey. International copyright, 2022, US Department of Commerce, US government.

Review

EIGHT jobs (roughly) being the average number held by Americans by age 32 (US BLS, 2020).

SEVEN years being the length of time defaulting on your student loan can mar your credit history (Sumrak, 2017).

SIX dimensions or domains of career interests: RIASEC (Hoff et al., 2018; Holland, 1959; Nauta, 2010).

FIVE years or more (by one interviewee's estimate) is the age difference a newly hired college graduate is likely to experience with their more senior coworkers (Robbins & Wilner, 2001).

FOUR criteria for what makes a good job: wages, benefits, hours, and satisfaction (Ross et al., 2018).

THREE social challenges for young workers identified by Robbins and Wilner (2001): most of your coworkers being a lot older than you are; skills you learned in college not mapping onto what is needed at your job; and the impostor phenomenon.

TWO ways to think of one's work: as a job or as a career (Willkomm, 2020).

ONE country (among those for whom research was reported in this chapter) in which a higher percentage of women than of men were self-employed: Mexico (OECD, 2021b).

Possible Class Activities

1. As discussed above, the CERI/MonsterTRAK survey (Chao & Gardner, 2007a, Table 1) lists 15 possible features of jobs that people can rank from most to

least important. You can find the list online (https://ceri.msu.edu/_assets/pdfs /young-pro-pdfs/JobChar4-16.pdf) and take the survey yourself.

2. The 2019 Money Matters on Campus survey (Zapp, 2019) is available online (https://everfi.com/white-papers/financial-education/money-matters-report -19/) and contains six financial-literacy questions (the quiz is introduced in the closing lines of text on p. 17, the actual questions appear on p. 18, and discussion follows on p. 19). See how you do!

Notes

1 There is even a term, "Zillennials," for people near the dividing line of Generation Z and Millennials (Bruner, 2021).

2 Epstein (2019) explains that, although Malamud's (2010) research design does not randomly assign students to either specialize or sample courses broadly, which a true experiment would require, the fact that England and Wales use one system whereas Scotland uses another can be considered a "natural experiment" (p. 129). This is defensible, in my view, as long as it is more or less random that students grow up in England or Wales, as opposed to Scotland.

3 For those of you who have taken statistics, the normal curve should ring a bell (sorry). Anyway, if we assume the data are normally distributed, roughly two-thirds (68%, exactly) of people will fall between plus or minus one standard deviation (SD) of the mean (Galarnyk, 2018). In the Survey of Young Workers, the mean (average) salary was \$38,175 and the SD was \$34,679. Hence, the mean minus the SD yields the lower boundary I mentioned in the text and the mean plus the SD yields the upper boundary.

8

Romantic Relationships

> In the space of a half century … we have seen the widest pendulum swing in
> family life in American history. We have gone from a lockstep pattern of getting
> married young, then having children, and for the most part staying married, to
> a bewildering set of alternatives.
>
> – Cherlin (2009, p. 8)

Many aspects of relationship, marriage, and family life have indeed changed dramatically since 1960 (which is roughly 50 years before the prominent family sociologist Andrew Cherlin wrote the above passage in 2009):

- As we saw in Chapter 1, the US, many European countries, Australia, and parts of Asia have seen their typical (median) age of first marriage rise to 30 years old (give or take a year or two), compared to the median US ages of 23 for men and 21 for women in 1970 (Buchholz, 2019; US Census Bureau, 2020).

- According to Carbone and Cahn (2014), "A half-century ago, female college graduates were less likely than their peers with less education to be married; today they are the top catches in the marriage market" (p. 14).

- Marriage equality for same-sex couples was not even a widely discussed issue among the US public until the mid-1980s, so that major public-opinion polls did not begin assessing attitudes on the issue until 1988 (Baunach, 2012). In 1988, support for allowing same-sex couples to marry was only 12.6%, but by 2010, it had skyrocketed to 47.4%. By 2019, after the US Supreme Court's decision in *Obergefell v. Hodges* (2015) striking down laws limiting marriage to heterosexual couples, support for marriage equality was consistently in the 60s (Polling Report, 2021). At present, 30 countries have now adopted policies of marriage equality for same-sex couples (Human Rights Campaign, not dated).

- The number of US divorces rose from 9.2 per 1,000 married persons in 1960 all the way up to 22.6 in 1980, then fell back down to 14.9 in 2019 (Wang, 2020).[1]

- On-off/cyclical relationships, in which the same partners break up and reunite, have probably existed for a long time. However, the amount of information we

DOI: 10.4324/9781003156567-11

have about them has grown tremendously (Dailey, Pfiester, et al., 2009; Dailey, Rossetto et al., 2009; Vennum et al., 2014).

■ Cohabitation (originally known as "living together") was barely discussed until the late 1960s. My now-retired Texas Tech colleague Judith Fischer (then known as Judith Lyness) published one of the first scholarly articles on the topic (Lyness et al., 1972). So new was the concept at the time that she and her colleagues needed to provide a very basic definition: "the situation where a man and woman who are not married to each other … occupy the same dwelling" (p. 305). Further, the researchers' participant sample included 91 married couples, 31 non-cohabiting dating couples, and only 18 couples who were living together (even in liberal Boulder, Colorado). As we will see, cohabitation is now extremely common.

To help keep different relationship stages and concepts in order, I have created the following diagram (Figure 8.1). It does not aim to capture every conceivable relationship type but only what appear to be the most common ones. Specifically, the diagram depicts a two-partner, exclusive relationship that fits many relationships in Western, industrialized countries and that likely leads to marriage. Nothing in the diagram rules out long-term unmarried unions, which are common in places such as Europe (Hiekel, 2014), however. Other types, such as polygamous and polyamorous relationships, are not addressed. Nor are arranged marriages, a well-known tradition in India (see Suri, 2020, for background). Note that steps in the diagram can be skipped (e.g., a single person can go straight to casual dating or go through the pre-dating steps; seriously dating/committed couples can go straight to marriage or go through cohabitation).

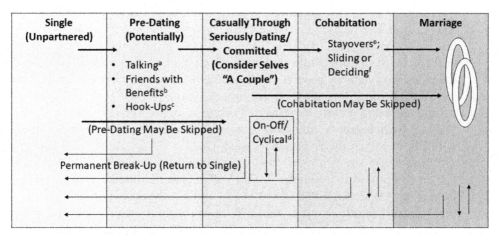

[a]Powell et al. (2021); [b]Claxton & van Dulmen (2013); [c]Bogle (2008); [d]Dailey et al. (2009) & Vennum et al. (2014); [e]Jamison & Proulx (2013); [f]Stanley et al. (2006).

FIGURE 8.1 Common stages of romantic relationships and associated concepts. Up-and-down arrows signify the potential for on-off or cyclical relationships, in which partners break up but then reunite. Although breakups are depicted as taking people back to being single, it is also possible that people could instead revert to an earlier stage (e.g., cohabiting to dating without cohabiting).
[a]Powell et al. (2021); [b]Claxton & van Dulmen (2013); [c]Bogle (2008); [d]Dailey, Pfiester, et al. (2009); Dailey, Rossetto et al. (2009); Vennum et al. (2014); [e]Jamison & Proulx (2013); [f]Stanley et al. (2006).

Dating and Relationship Development

Adolescence

By emerging adulthood, many individuals already have experience with dating and romantic behaviors. I briefly discuss adolescent dating for some context. Multiple studies of adolescent dating relationships, both national and local in scope, suggest that by 11th grade, between 44% and 68% of teens report being in a relationship (Furman & Hand, 2006). Different studies' survey items have defined relationships differently (in terms of liking someone and they like you back; time spent with someone one is "seeing" or "going out with;" and whether respondents consider themselves to be in a "special romantic relationship," with additional prompts about holding hands, hugging, and kissing; Furman & Hand, pp. 174). These different wordings are a possible reason for the variation in results between different studies (also, some studies asked about dating in the past year, whereas others referenced the past 18 months). Syed and Mitchell (2016) report some racial–ethnic differences in adolescent relationships, with Black teens being less likely than their White counterparts to report being in a relationship.

Emerging Adulthood

Pre-dating

As Figure 8.1 illustrates, individuals (particularly college students) may go through some "pre-dating" activities with a prospective partner before actually beginning to date them. Whether we should consider pre-dating a relationship stage is questionable, I admit. I've included it in the figure, however, because pre-dating activities *can* lead to dating in some instances. One such pre-dating activity is "talking" (Powell et al., 2021). Emerging adults widely see talking, in which potential partners discuss their desire to date each other or reasons pro and con, as something that can lead to a relationship, but is not itself the same as dating (Powell et al., 2021). Powell and colleagues found a clear majority of college students to be familiar with the term "talking," whereas in a young-adult sample obtained from an internet participant pool, about half of the respondents were.

Claxton and van Dulmen (2013) developed the umbrella term Casual Sexual Relationships and Experiences (CSRE) to encompass hook-ups, one-night stands, friends with benefits (FWB), booty calls, and f--- buddies (which I'm sure stands for "friendly buddies," wink, wink). With the exception of hook-ups, which can be ambiguous as to whether they involve sexual intercourse or only hugging and kissing, the other terms imply a high likelihood of intercourse. Claxton and van Dulmen proposed that CSRE behaviors can be differentiated on two dimensions: whether a given couple partakes only once (e.g., one-night stand) or on multiple occasions (e.g., booty calls and FWB), and whether the actors are strangers or acquaintances (e.g., one-night stand) or friends with each other (e.g., FWB). Bogle (2008), who focused specifically on hooking up on two college campuses, found that some students (predominantly women) hoped hook-ups would lead to longer-term relationships. However, "The least likely outcome of hooking up is that it leads to becoming a couple" (p. 42).

Dating

Emerging adults' dating relationships therefore are likely to develop through means other than pre-dating activities. Some question whether traditional dating – in which one person asks another if he or she would like to go out on a specified future date to engage in some activity (e.g., concert or movie) – still exists (Williams, 2013). What seems to pass for dating, at least in some people's minds, is a late-night text, asking if the invitee would like to join the requestor and their friends at a bar (Williams, 2013). When covering this topic, I regularly ask my classes if anyone has ever asked a person out on a date or been asked, and typically, the number of affirmative responses can be counted on one hand. My students' experiences fit with what Bogle (2008) found in her research. One of Bogle's student interviewees characterized dating as "like a culture from … my parents['] time" (p. 44). Instead of such old-fashioned dating, according to another student, "we would just hang out or go to a party or whatever" (p. 45). Going out with someone in a manner resembling a date did occur under one situation, however: *after* a couple had established itself as boyfriend(s)/girlfriend(s). Another rapidly growing technique for meeting potential dates and romantic partners, of course, is through mobile and online dating apps. A detailed review of electronic dating apps is beyond the scope of this chapter, but there are additional sources for readers interested in this topic (Finkel et al., 2012; Niehuis et al., 2020).

The dating process is in some ways similar for same-sex and different-sex couples but also different in some ways (Macapagal et al., 2015). Same-sex partners may meet through school or "talking," as do different-sex partners, and their dates often consist of simply "hanging out" (Macapagal et al., 2015). Also, relationship quality, on average, is similar between same-sex and different-sex partners (Reczek, 2020). However, identifying potential partners is typically more difficult for LGBT individuals. As Macapagal and colleagues note,

> heterosexual young adults by default gain information about heterosexual relationships, which are the predominant model of intimate relationships in society and in the media. In addition, heterosexual young adults' social networks likely consist primarily of openly heterosexual peers, and as such they experience little need to ascertain the sexual identity of a potential partner.
>
> *(p. 310)*

Young adults seeking same-sex partners, on the other hand, rely more on contexts in which LGBT individuals are likely to be visible or "out" (e.g., social networks with known LGBT individuals and social-networking websites; Macapagal et al., 2015).

Whatever the methods young adults use when they do manage to pair off, here are some statistics on dating relationships. According to national data reported in Regnerus and Uecker (2011), never married, 18–23-year-olds fall into the following categories (data available for heterosexual individuals only):

- Not in a relationship (men 40%, women 27%).
- Dating and having sex (which includes cohabiting; men 52%, women 66%).
- Dating but not having sex (men 5%, women 4%).

- Just having sex, in the manner of Claxton and van Dulmen's (2013) Casual Sexual Relationships and Experiences (men 3%, women 2%).

Regnerus and Uecker explain that fewer men than women reporting being in a relationship is a "very common survey artifact" (p. 16) or anomaly. Syed and Mitchell (2016) note some racial–ethnic differences in emerging-adult relationship statuses. African American emerging adults had a higher rate of being in steady relationships than did Whites. Short-term relationships were more common among Whites, however, so that their overall number of relationships was higher than African Americans' and Latinos'. Differences, such as they existed, were not large, though. As Syed and Mitchell explained, "The overall average number of relationships in the prior 6 years was about three, and the difference between whites and blacks was about 2/3 of a relationship and whites and Latinos about 1/3 of a relationship" (p. 91). There was no difference between Whites' and Asian Americans' numbers of relationships.

Historically, researchers have examined sequences by which potential romantic partners progress from acquaintanceship to casually dating, regularly dating, seriously dating, and so forth. During this progression, relationships increase in self-disclosure, commitment, and maintenance behaviors such as complimenting and making sacrifices for one's partner (Ogolsky & Monk, 2019). Scholars of early relationship development – of which my wife Sylvia Niehuis is a leading one – also investigate dating couples' timing of *relationship milestones* such as partners' first sexual intercourse with each other and first feeling in love with and wanting to marry the partner. Passionate, whirlwind romances are a literary archetype and sometimes happen in real life. The question is, do they tend to lead to better or worse relationships. Niehuis et al. (2016) addressed this very question in a sample of heterosexual newlyweds who were tracked for two years after their weddings. Each newlywed participant (working independently from their spouse) first provided information on a timeline representing the entirety of their premarital relationship, from first date to wedding day. Specifically, they noted (retrospectively) the month in which they first felt feelings of love for the partner, first decided that they wanted to marry the partner, and first had sex with the partner (if occurring before the wedding day). The quicker these events occurred after the first date, the more "passionate" the couple's courtship was considered to be. Also, at the newlywed assessment and one- and two-year follow-ups (i.e., after couples had been married for one and two years), participants reported on affectionate maintenance behaviors in their relationship (e.g., compliments, sharing emotions, physical affection). Results showed that couples with the most passionate courtships – those who had sex, felt in love, and wanted to marry their partner shortly after their first date – may have burned out their passion. In other words, those with quickly moving, passionate courtships exhibited "the sharpest yearly decline in affectionate expression during the first two years of marriage" (p. 1092). Couples who took the longest time to attain the relationship milestones (possibly a sign of a floundering relationship) also experienced a notable decline in affectionate behaviors. Only couples who reached the milestones in a moderate length of time – neither too quickly nor too slowly – maintained their affectionate behaviors steadily over time.[2] Another possible interpretation is that partners whose relationships were heavily passionate early on did not spend as much time learning about each other's personalities, values, and beliefs – which is necessary to build a strong foundation for the relationship – as did the moderate-passion couples (Niehuis et al., 2016). There does not appear to be research on the implications of same-sex couples' timing of relationship milestones. However, some research suggests that female couples tend to wait longer to have sex than do male couples (Macapagal et al., 2015).

Many LGBT couples experience additional challenges in their relationships. For example, when two same-sex partners differ in their levels of outness, it can create tension when in public (e.g., one partner preferring to show affection, whereas the other wanting them to appear as platonic friends; Macapagal et al., 2015). Recalling our discussion of intersectionality in Chapter 2, the combination of minority statuses both in sexuality and race-ethnicity can lead to difficult relationship dynamics (Reczek, 2020). These can include experiencing both homophobia and racism and receiving less social support from family (Reczek, 2020). Transgender individuals and their cisgender[3] partners also experience many challenges, including discrimination and stigma related to public displays such as holding hands and introducing one's partner to others (Reczek, 2020).

Cohabitation

Well within my lifetime (up until I was around six years old), cohabitation was almost unheard of in the US, at least going by official statistics. According to Gurrentz (2018), "in 1968, living with an unmarried partner was rare. Only 0.1 percent of 18- to 24-year-olds and 0.2 percent of 25- to 34-year-olds lived with an unmarried partner, according to the Current Population Survey." The frequency of cohabitation then began to grow, attracting the attention of media outlets such as *Newsweek*, *Esquire*, *TIME* and *Life* magazines, and of academic researchers (Lyness et al., 1972; Macklin, 1972). Driving a good deal of this attention (as best as I can tell, as I was too young at the time to know what was going on) was a "seemingly innocuous" 1968 article in the *New York Times* on cohabitation (Barnard College, not dated). An undergraduate student named Linda LeClair at New York City's Barnard College (the all-women's counterpart to Columbia University, which was all-men at the time), using the pseudonym "Susan," revealed that she was living with her boyfriend, unleashing a disciplinary process that ended in her expulsion. My first experience seeing couples of roughly my age, whom I knew, start moving in together was during graduate school (1984–1989). Despite occurring only 16 years after the "LeClair Affair," neither these cohabitations nor any others raised any shock or outrage that I could discern.

More recent statistics show how commonplace cohabitation has now become in the US. Susan Brown (2005) noted that, around the start of the new millennium, "More than half of young adults in their 20s and 30s ha[d] experienced cohabitation" (p. 33). About a decade ago, Scott Stanley and colleagues launched a national (US) survey of individuals 18–34 in dating relationships (Stanley et al., 2011). At study onset, 32% of respondents were currently cohabiting and of those not currently living with a partner, 25% had done so in the past; together, these percentages roughly replicate Brown's earlier figures. Finally, according to Fox (2014), "two-thirds of couples married in 2012 shared a home together for more than two years before they ever waltzed down an aisle." Interestingly, for how strongly many observers link cohabitation to college campuses (perhaps stemming from the LeClair Affair), a completely different demographic has shown the highest prevalence of cohabitation. As Brown (2005) noted, "Historically, unmarried cohabitation was most common among the lower [economic] classes, for whom marriage held few social, legal, or economic benefits" (p. 33).

Unmarried couples may wish to cohabit for a variety of reasons, including saving money on housing, having increased opportunities for sex, and preparing and testing compatibility for marriage (Brown, 2005; Lyness et al., 1972; Stanley et al., 2011). Macapagal et al. (2015) note that parents' disapproval of same-sex relationships may lead gay and lesbian couples to cohabit, perhaps earlier than they otherwise would have. Few issues in the study of close relationships have seen conventional wisdom jump around as much as has the question of whether cohabitation is good preparation for marriage. As best as I can tell, experts' thinking on cohabitation has gone through at least the following four phases (note that not all experts would agree with each proposition):

1. Before much (if any) scientific research on the topic existed, some writers in the 1960s, 1970s, and 1980s assumed that cohabitation would be beneficial for later marriage (among those cohabiters who wed). Their reasoning was that living together would allow partners to learn about each other, gauge their compatibility, and see the kinds of issues that could arise in domestic life (Niehuis et al., 2013; Pleck, 2012).[4]

2. Early studies tended to show greater divorce in married couples who had cohabited beforehand than in those who did not cohabit. Cohabitation was seen as harmful (perhaps because it led couples to "slide" into marriage rather than actively and intentionally "decide" to wed; Stanley et al., 2006). Based on multiple studies beginning in the 1970s, "On average, researchers concluded that couples who lived together before they tied the knot saw a 33 percent higher rate of divorce than those who waited to live together until after they were married" (Fox, 2014). This phenomenon became known as the "cohabitation effect" (Stanley et al., 2006).

3. Later research suggested that, if couples began cohabiting after committing themselves to marriage and thus saw cohabitation as a lead-in to wedlock, cohabitation was not harmful. As summarized by Chalabi (2014), one major study showed that couples who had not lived together before marriage and those who cohabited while engaged had similarly high rates of marital intactness over 20 years of marriage (more so in men than in women). However, couples who lived together for a considerable time without being engaged, and who then married, had lower rates of intactness than those who never cohabited. More specifically, the cohabitation-without-engagement group was around five percentage points less likely to be intact than the no-cohabitation group after 10 years of marriage in men and around 10 percentage points less likely to be intact after 10 years in women.

4. Finally, a young scholar named Arielle Kuperberg (2014a) published a study in the rigorously reviewed *Journal of Marriage and Family*, drawing upon three

versions (1995, 2002, and 2006–2010) of a leading family-studies dataset, the National Survey of Family Growth, challenging what we thought we knew about cohabitation and divorce. Kuperberg essentially showed the typical correlation between cohabitation and divorce likelihood in some initial analyses, then demonstrated how statistically controlling for age at co-residence (the age when beginning to cohabit for those who cohabited, otherwise the age at marriage) diminished the harmful effect of cohabiting.[5] Most of the earlier research had what some now consider a major flaw, namely "comparing couples by their age at marriage rather than by their age when they moved in together" (Kuperberg, 2014b). Kuperberg (2014b) concluded from her research that "cohabitation doesn't cause divorce and probably never did."

Note that, even with Kuperberg's (2014a) findings, we are not quite at the point of going back to the original thinking that cohabitation is affirmatively better than not cohabiting (item 1 above). Saying that cohabitation doesn't increase the divorce rate (compared to non-cohabiters) is basically saying it's a tie. It's not the same thing as saying cohabitation actually lowers the divorce rate compared to marrying directly without premarital cohabitation.

A study by Rhoades et al. (2012), using the same national survey of dating couples mentioned earlier (Stanley et al., 2011), also suggests that things are not so bad for cohabiters. Many of the participants transitioned from non-cohabitation to cohabitation (with the same partner) within roughly the first two years of the study, so they could be compared on several measures (e.g., commitment, self-rated marriage likelihood, relationship satisfaction, and communication quality) during their dating vs. cohabiting days. On many of these measures, participants' relationship functioning increased when they were dating during the year before cohabiting, but then either leveled off or declined slightly during the first year of cohabitation. For example, participants' relationship satisfaction increased on average from 4.0 (on a 0–6 scale) one year before cohabitation to 4.2 at cohabitation onset but then declined to around 4.1 after a year of living together. Hence, no major decline in satisfaction occurred after cohabitation onset.

Stayovers

A phenomenon that may or may not simply be a miniature version of cohabitation, leading up to full-fledged cohabitation, is that of "stayovers" (Jamison & Proulx, 2013). Jamison and Proulx studied stayovers as an established routine for couples, requiring that one partner stay overnight at the other partner's home at least three nights per week (i.e., beyond just weekends) while the two partners maintained separate residences the rest of the time. Hence, occasional stayovers were not examined. Whereas some prior research findings depicted stayovers as seamlessly linked to eventual full-time cohabitation, others emphasized differences between the two (e.g., stayovers provided greater opportunity than cohabitation for partners to spend time apart; even some people philosophically opposed to cohabitation nevertheless participated in stayovers; Jamison & Proulx, 2013). A larger study by Jamison and Proulx confirmed this mixed picture of stayovers. Supporting the underlying similarity of stayovers and cohabitation, among participants with the most favorable attitudes toward cohabitation, 80% had engaged in stayovers. Also, prior experience in full-time cohabitation was correlated with higher odds of engaging in stayovers. On the other hand, 47% of those with unfavorable attitudes toward cohabitation engaged in stayovers, suggesting they saw cohabitation and stayovers through separate lenses. Jamison and Proulx concluded from their study that "New and innovative research is building a case that coresidence is a fluid concept with variations and norms that have yet to be fully explored" (p. 168).

Marriage

Getting married – eventually – remains an important priority and value for American young adults. However, in line with the statistics showing a delayed onset of marriage compared to prior generations, only 26% of unmarried 20–24-year-olds agreed that they wanted to be married *now* (Scott et al., 2009). In contrast, 83% of unmarried young adults considered it "very important" or "important" to get married "someday" (Scott et al., 2009). Support for the importance of eventual marriage has been around a long time: in fact, between 1977 and 2001, from 85% to 88% of male high school seniors and 91–94% of their female counterparts said it was "quite or extremely" important to "have a good marriage and family life" (Institute for Social Research, 2002a). Though supportive of marriage, young adults are not absolutist: half of 20–29-year-olds in another poll (Barlette, 2008) answered that they "don't believe that they need to be married to validate the commitment of a long-term relationship." Despite the relative recency of marriage equality in the US, there has been research on LGBT individuals' attitudes toward marriage. According to Reczek (2020), it shows "that marriage is important to same-sex couple stability; the ability to legally marry, coupled with general social tolerance towards marriage, is associated with higher desire for long-term relationships and stronger monogamy beliefs among [sexual and gender minority] populations" (p. 309).

Despite most young adults' apparent aspirations for marriage at some future time, research has appeared within the last decade suggesting that many lower-income Americans have "all but given up on marriage as a way of life, even if they still idealize the white picket fence" (Carbone & Cahn, 2014, p. 14). Silva (2013) argues that a combination of chronic stress, previous disappointments in their family, educational, work, and love lives, and lack of income have made relationships and marriage a low priority for many working-class individuals. Brown (2005) noted that "Financial security and stable employment, home ownership, and money for a wedding are not always attainable and represent an insurmountable barrier to marriage for many Americans" (p. 34). Or, as one of Silva's heterosexual male interviewees put it in more down-to-earth terms, "no woman wants to sit on the couch all the time and watch TV and eat at Burger King" (p. 4).

As the preceding paragraphs illustrate, attitudes toward marriage are more multifaceted than simply wanting or not wanting to marry. Willoughby and Hall (2015) have taken the assessment of attitudes toward getting married in an interesting direction, in my view. By asking respondents (unmarried college students in their study) about aspects of their marriage-related thinking (e.g., age at which they expect to marry; age they consider ideal to do so; desire to have an expensive and elaborate wedding), Willoughby and Hall's method can assign respondents to one of three groups. These are the "enthusiasts" toward getting married, the "hesitant," and the "delayers." The enthusiasts' ideal marriage age (24.2 years) was younger than the hesitants' (25.6) and the delayers' (30.1). Note, however, that even the enthusiasts think it best to marry at a later age than Americans used to marry (i.e., 23 for men and 21 for women in 1970). I have created a classroom activity based on Willoughby and Hall's measure, described at the end of this chapter, so readers can see where they fall regarding their marriage inclination. In Willoughly and Hall's sample (taken from a "large public university in the Midwest"; p. 126), enthusiasts comprised 32%, the hesitants 58%, and the delayers 10%. These percentages may well differ at other universities and in non-university settings. How might enthusiasts, hesitants, and delayers have developed their respective outlooks? Willoughby and Hall's results suggested that parents' divorce might be a factor inclining individuals toward hesitancy or a desire to delay marriage, whereas greater religiosity might point people toward greater enthusiasm for marriage.

Now that we know most unmarried college students seem to be in no immediate hurry to marry (being either hesitants or delayers), the next question is, why the desire for delay? Regnerus and Uecker (2011) compiled a set of reasons for delay from interviews they conducted and sources in the literature. These include the following (pp. 182–194):

- "Can't afford it," need to be "financially set," and the importance of education and career.
- Need time to become one's "own person," go through changes in personality and outlook.
- Early twenties "too soon" to have children.
- Want to travel, explore the world.
- "Parental resistance" to early marriage, as they want their children to finish their education and become financially independent.
- The need to search for a partner who is the "right fit," with whom person has "sexual chemistry."
- Losing confidence in the "institution" of marriage (e.g., due to high divorce rate).

Of these, the one I find most interesting is the parental resistance to their children marrying young, even though in many cases the parents themselves married young. A lot of times, we think that how we did something must be the right way. Hence, it is interesting to see some parents evolving in their thinking on the best time to marry.

Finally, I want to draw readers' attention to some neat, animated graphs from Flowing Data (Yau, 2007–2021) on US marriage trends. These illustrate how, after delaying marriage for some number of years, more and more people start getting married as they get older. In men (based on 2016 statistics), the percent married rises sharply (and in a straight linear fashion) from almost none around age 20 to about 60% at age 40. At that point the proportion of married men stays level until age 50. At 40, about 15% of men are separated or divorced, and around 25% remain never married. In other words, by 40, three-quarters of men have married, although some of these unions have ended. In women, the percent married rises from near 0% at age 20 to about 60% even more quickly – by the mid-late thirties – than in men. A solid 20% of women are separated or divorced between around 40 and 65. The proportion of women who are never married shrinks from around 20% around age 40 to below 10% by 65. Because most marriages are heterosexual and men tend to die earlier than women, the proportion of women who are widowed begins to expand beyond just a few percent around 50. This is getting a bit beyond emerging adulthood, but for general interest, *nearly all* women who are alive past age 90 are widowed.

Divorce

Divorce trends among different age groups in different eras have shown some interesting patterns (Kennedy & Ruggles, 2014). Whereas married women 30 and older exhibited higher divorce rates from 2008 to 2010 than did similar-age women in 1970, 1980, and 1990 (i.e., divorce becoming more common in the new millennium among older women), a very different trend has emerged in younger married women. Among 20–24-year-olds in the 2008–2010 data, there were around 35 divorces per 1,000 married women, in contrast to the roughly 45 divorces per 1,000 20–24-year-old married women in 1980 and 1990. Similarly, among 25–29-year-olds in 2008-2010, the divorce rate was also around 35 per 1,000, whereas it was 40 per 1,000 in this same age group in 1980 and 1990. Kennedy and Ruggles (2014) raise the question of why divorce has become less common among young adults in the 2000s and answer it as follows:

> The decline in divorce rates among women under age 25 probably reflects increasing selectivity of marriage. Fewer young people are getting married: over 40 % of the population in 2008 had not married by their 30th birthday, marking a fourfold increase since 1980 … As pressures to marry recede, people can be more selective about their partners; thus, it makes sense that marriages may become more stable.
>
> *(p. 596)*

What's that word I've been citing over and over? Exploration! Here we see how increasing selectivity in choosing a mate – that is, meeting many different possible romantic partners and exploring who might be best for you – can promote marital stability in the long run.[6] Marrying young is associated with increased divorce, so with young adults waiting longer to marry, they are avoiding a high-risk situation for divorce.[7]

Regnerus and Uecker (2011) make the good point, however, that we do not merely want our marriages to last but also to be highly satisfying. As discussed in the next section, people sometimes stay in unsatisfying relationships because they face daunting barriers to leaving or *constraints* (Stanley & Markman, 1992), such as a lack of money to live independently. Regnerus and Uecker cite a meta-analysis (aggregation of multiple studies) by Glenn et al. (2010), which suggests marrying between ages 22 and 25 maximizes the odds of both staying together and being satisfied in one's marriage. In some analyses, those who married between ages 26 and 29 also experienced relatively high-quality marriages, although not as high as those who married between 22 and 25. Glenn et al. urged caution in interpreting their results, however, noting that "at least some of the persons who married relatively late would not have had better marriages if they had married earlier" (p. 798). Glenn and colleagues also had some specific advice for young adults, namely that "a 25 year old person who meets an excellent marriage prospect would be ill-advised to pass up that opportunity only because he/she feels not yet at the ideal age for marriage" (p. 799).

I also don't want to leave the impression that marital age is the primary or only predictor of marital success. Warmth and quality of the early marital relationship, when many spouses are within the emerging-adulthood age range of 18–30, is also tremendously important. Huston et al. (2001), having tracked couples for the first 13 years of their marriages (or as long as their marriage was intact), drew the following key conclusions. First, "couples destined for marital happiness more than 13 years later … had a stronger marital bond as newlyweds than did couples who later found themselves less happily married." Second, "The married-happy couples also had a stronger romantic bond as newlyweds than did the divorced-early [2–7 years after marriage] couples" (quotes from p. 244).

Because marriage in same-sex couples is relatively new, a lot of older research compared the dissolution rates in married heterosexual, cohabiting heterosexual, and cohabiting gay/lesbian couples. Findings from these studies are mixed, with some showing similar breakup rates in same-sex and different-sex couples and others showing dissolution to be more common in same-sex relationships (Reczek, 2020).

On-Off/Cyclical Relationships (with the Same Partner)

As you may recall from the discussion of "spaghetti graphs" in Chapter 1 (Figure 1.2), one of the central tenets of this book is that life in general, and emerging adulthood in particular, is not linear. There are ups and downs, and steps forward and backward. In the domain of close relationships, many couples break up but get back together within a short amount of time, often with multiple iterations. Accordingly, these types of relationships are known as on-off or cyclical relationships. Given the length of time between their stints as a couple (2002–2004 and 2021–onward), movie stars Ben Affleck and Jennifer Lopez, also known as "Bennifer," probably would not count, however.

Much early research on on-off/cyclical relationships came from the lab of René Dailey (Dailey, Pfiester et al., 2009; Dailey, Rossetto et al., 2009). In one study, 18.5% (43/232) of current dating couples in a randomly selected metropolitan sample (ages 19–35) were on-off/cyclical (Dailey, Rossetto et al., 2009). Two college-student samples helped refine our knowledge of these types of relationships further (Dailey, Pfiester et al., 2009). Sample 1 participants were asked if a *current or prior* relationship had been on-off. According to Dailey, Pfiester et al.,

> Of … 445 participants, 61.6% (*n* = 274) had experienced an on-off relationship … Of these 274, 66 (24.1%) reported they had broken up and renewed only once, 81 (29.6%) reported renewing twice with the same partner, 59 (22.2%) reported three, and 64 (23.6%) reported four or more.
>
> *(p. 32; numbers do not add to 100% due to missing data)*

In Sample 2, "A little less than half (… 39.4%) reported that their relationship (whether current or past) had an on-off nature" (Dailey, Pfiester et al., p. 38). Note that the higher prevalence (61.6% and 39.4%) of on-off/cyclical relationships in Dailey, Pfiester et al.'s (2009) college-student samples than in Dailey, Rossetto et al.'s (2009) metropolitan sample (18.5%) likely stemmed from the former including past relationships and the latter not.

Vennum et al. (2014) examined the prevalence of on-off/cyclical relationships among cohabiting and married couples in a national (US) survey. The researchers focused on a survey item that asked, "Did you and your current partner ever separate and get back together?" (yes or no; pp. 415–416) with reference not only to their current state (i.e., cohabiting or married), but also prior states (cohabiting or dating for married couples; dating for cohabiting couples). For married couples, the researchers deemed only trial separations and reunions as cyclical; they did not count divorce and remarriage to the same person as cyclical. As a final criterion, Vennum and colleagues labeled as cyclical "couples in which at least one partner indicated they had broken up and gotten back together at least once" (p. 416). Spouses/partners overwhelmingly agreed on whether they had broken up and reunited at the different stages, with discrepancies in their reports occurring in fewer than 5% of cases.

Vennum and colleagues' (2014) results showed on-off/cycling behavior to be more common among cohabiting than among married couples. Among currently cohabiting couples, 22% had broken up and reunited while cohabiting and 25% had done the same while dating. The researchers divided married couples into those who did and did not cohabit prior to marriage. Among married couples who had cohabited, 4% went through a trial separation and reunion while married, 6% cycled during the time they cohabited, and 12% cycled while they were dating their future spouse. Finally, among couples who went straight from dating (without cohabitation) to marriage, 3% went through a trial separation and reunion and 8% cycled while they were dating. Other interesting findings emerged. First, cycling begets cycling. In other words, couples who broke up and reunited at an earlier stage were more likely to do so again at a later stage. Second, contrary to the researchers' hypothesis that on-off cycling would be associated with the absence of a commitment to marriage, cohabiters who had previously cycled were just as likely to have made a commitment to marriage before moving in as were cohabiters who had never cycled (findings in married couples were inconsistent between husbands and wives). Finally, "cohabiting and married participants with a history of cycling reported greater uncertainty in the future of the relationship and lower relationship satisfaction than noncyclical couples" (p. 421).

If on-off/cyclical relationships are less satisfying than non-cyclical ones, you may be wondering, then why do so many couples engage in them. Vennum and colleagues (2014) borrowed the concept of "constraint commitment" from Stanley and Markman (1992), which refers to staying together not because of overwhelming love and dedication to one's partner, but due to perceived barriers to leaving the relationship. And indeed, Vennum et al. found that potential barriers to leaving the relationship such as the presence of children, need for childcare assistance (which cohabitation can provide), and relatively low financial resources were more common in cyclical than non-cyclical couples. Cyclical relationships can also be a sign of severe relationship distress, with Vennum and colleagues observing that "It is concerning that those partners who experience the most conflict are those that are choosing to renew their relationship instead of permanently ending it" (p. 412). Greater societal awareness of the potential problems with on-off/cyclical relationships is warranted, as are therapeutic interventions for premarital couples, as Vennum et al. advocate. For further information on this topic, Dailey (2020) has published a book on on-off/cyclical relationships.

Re-partnering (with Someone Else) after Breakup

That the US has a high rate of marriage and divorce is well-known. What Andrew Cherlin's (2009) book *The Marriage-Go-Round* drew attention to was Americans' strong propensity for *re*-partnering. Whether it is economic strain, loneliness, or embarrassment after a breakup or divorce, or something else, many people are eager to find a new partner quickly. Some do not merely want to find a new partner but move in together and even marry quickly. Cherlin points to a statistic that captures the dynamics of repeated re-partnering: the percentage of a country's residents who have experienced three or more live-in relationships (cohabitation or marriage) by age 35 (cohabitating with and then marrying the same person would count as only one relationship, so an individual must have lived with or married at least three different people). Drawing upon research by Jeffrey Timberlake (not to be confused with Justin Timberlake), Cherlin summarizes different countries' percentages of women who had lived with three or more partners by age 35:

> almost no one in Italy or Spain, less than 2 percent in France or Canada, and 3 percent in Germany … 4.5 percent in Sweden and 4 percent in New Zealand. But in the United States, 10 percent of women had three or more husbands or live-in partners by age thirty-age.
>
> *(p. 19)*[8]

Why might this be the case? Cherlin argues that the US exhibits a "unique" combination (p. 4) of supporting marriage (e.g., with marriage-preparation courses and government healthy-marriage programs), but also promoting self-expression, which could encourage people to leave unfulfilling unions.

Sexual Identities and Emerging Adulthood

Research and teaching on diversity in sexual identities appear to be greater on university campuses than they were a decade or more ago. Even with these improvements, however, queer-spectrum and trans-spectrum students continue to report higher rates of psychological distress (e.g., loneliness, depression) than heterosexual and cis-gender students, respectively (Rankin et al., 2019). In keeping with the theme of emerging adulthood being a time of exploration, let's look at research examining individuals' exploration of their own sexual identities. In an older but still informative and thought-providing study, Lisa Diamond (2003) conducted repeated interviews over a five-year period with young women (18–25 years old at study onset, mostly White and well-educated) from college and community samples regarding their sexual identities, experiences, and attractions. Anecdotally, women of this age were thought to re-examine and possibly re-label their sexual identities, with terminology such as "LUGs" (lesbian until graduation) being bandied about.[9] Diamond's study sought to obtain quantifiable data on retention and change of sexual identities. Based on Diamond (2003) and a book she later published on the topic (Diamond, 2008), I created the following graphic (Figure 8.2). As can be seen, roughly half of Diamond's 80 sexual-minority or queer (non-heterosexual) participants retained their sexual identities over the five years of the study (22 continuing to refer to themselves as "lesbian," 12 continuing to refer to themselves as "bisexual," and 7 continuing to decline to label their sexual identity). Figure 8.2 depicts consistency or retention of sexual identities with horizontal lines, each line representing one woman. Hence, wider bunches of lines denote greater numbers of people. There were also shifts in identities (diagonal lines from the earlier to the later identity). Some initially lesbian women switched to bisexual or unlabeled, whereas some initially bisexual women switched to lesbian, unlabeled, or heterosexual. Some initially unlabeled women switched to lesbian, bisexual, or heterosexual. In short, there was both considerable stability and considerable change, although not all possible forms of change (e.g., lesbian to heterosexual) occurred.

Finally, Morgan (2012) summarized the available research at the time on sexual identity through the lens of emerging adulthood. Several key points made by Morgan are as follows:

■ "Developing a meaningful sense of one's sexual orientation and identity is an important undertaking during emerging adulthood" (p. 52).

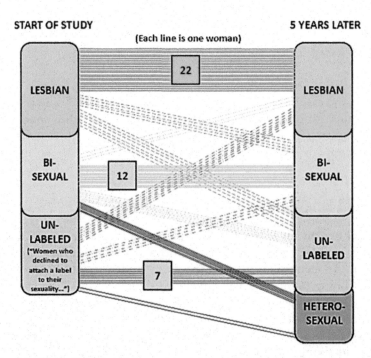

FIGURE 8.2 Stability and change in women's sexual identity over a five-year period. Each line represents one woman.

Source: Based on Diamond (2003, Table 2) and Diamond (2008).

- "sexual orientation and identity development during emerging adulthood, especially for those whose sexuality might diverge from normative models, may be both rife with opportunities for exploration and simultaneously constrained" (p. 53).
- "Non-exclusivity" (e.g., gay- or lesbian-identified individuals indicating other-sex attraction, or vice-versa; p. 57) is not uncommon.
- At least five pathways of EA sexual development exist:

> there is a cohort of sexual minority youth who transition into emerging adulthood having [1] already developed a highly integrated sexual-minority identity. There [are also] emerging adults who are [2] just starting to explore same-sex interests and may continue to do so into young adulthood. There [are also] emerging adults who [3] subscribe to two or more different sexual orientation labels and another cohort [4] who will maintain the same sexual orientation label throughout emerging adulthood and beyond. Some emerging adults [5] will resist labeling their sexual orientation altogether.
>
> *(p. 61)*

Some of Morgan's (2012) points are things we saw in Diamond's (2003) study, such as some of her female participants refusing to label their sexual identities. Morgan's points about exploration fit with the larger context of emerging adulthood, but her claim about some adolescents and young adults feeling constrained in their sexual expression is well-taken. Even though overt discrimination toward and mistreatment of sexual-minority individuals is less than it once was, it has not disappeared.

Review

We have:

SEVEN reasons young adults give for delaying marriage (Regnerus & Uecker, 2011).

SIX major changes in romantic-relationship and marriage patterns over the past 50–60 years. These include delayed marriage in many countries (Buchholz, 2019; US Census Bureau, 2020); college-educated women going from a low to a high rate of marriage (Carbone & Cahn, 2014); marriage equality for same-sex couples; the US divorce rate rising and then falling (Wang, 2020); patterns such as on-off/cyclical relationships gaining tremendous attention (Dailey, Pfiester, et al., 2009; Dailey, Rossetto et al., 2009; Vennum et al., 2014); and the enormous rise in cohabitation (Stanley et al., 2011).

FIVE pathways of emerging-adulthood sexual and sexual-identity development (Morgan, 2012).

FOUR stages of experts' thinking on whether cohabitation, on the whole, is beneficial or harmful for couples: it was (1) initially assumed beneficial, then (2) found harmful, then (3) found not to be harmful if couples entered cohabitation already committed to marry, and (4) most recently, in retrospect, considered to have possibly never been harmful at all (it only looked harmful due to a statistical artifact).

THREE subgroups of young adults based on their outlooks toward getting married (Willoughby & Hall, 2015): enthusiasts, hesitants, and delayers.

TWO seemingly opposing social forces – support for marriage (requiring two people to blend into a shared identity), but promotion of self-expression – that may explain why Americans pair up, split up, and find new partners so quickly and repeatedly (Cherlin, 2009).

ONE, which is where the US ranks (among those countries that have been studied) in the percentage of women who have had three or more live-in relationships (cohabitation or marriage) by age 35.

Possible Class Activities

1. I created a classroom activity based on Willoughby and Hall's (2015) research, which I published in Reifman (2020; available online at: https://view.publitas .com/iarr/rrn-december2020/page/1). Find out if you are an enthusiast, a hesitant, or a delayer regarding when you would like to get married! Or, if you are/were already married, what do you think would have been the ideal time for you?

2. The chapter lists several reasons young adults have for delaying marriage (based on Regnerus and Uecker, 2011). Either as an individual survey or as a class discussion, students can share their thoughts on which of these reasons may or may not apply to them.

Notes

1 Scholars have long disagreed about how to calculate and interpret US divorce statistics. Kennedy and Ruggles (2014) contend that divorce increased between 1990 and 2008, although mainly among people older than 35. In younger couples, divorced has stabilized or declined.

2 This finding suggests that passionate courtships are a "goldilocks" phenomenon, so named after the porridge in the children's story *Goldilocks and the Three Bears* (Southey, 1837) needing to be "not too hot," "not too cold," but "just right." The same appears to hold for how quickly couples have sex, fall in love, and decide they want to marry.

3 "Cisgender, or cis, means that the gender you identify with matches the sex assigned to you at birth. Transgender is when your gender identity differs from the sex on your birth certificate" (Watson, 2020).

4 As Pleck's (2012) history of cohabitation describes, the idea of a trial, test, or probationary marriage (for childless couples) to see how well a couple functioned goes back to the 1920s.

5 Statistical control can be a challenging concept, not only for undergraduates but even graduate students and experienced researchers. Suppose that children who attended private schools performed better on standardized tests than did those who attended public schools. A skeptic might then come along and question whether the families of the private-school students were wealthier than those of the public-school students and therefore the parents of private-school students could more readily afford test-prep services for their children. In

other words, maybe it was the private-school parents' *money* that led to their children's high test scores, not the actual private education. One would then want to control statistically for family income. In principle, this would mean looking at subgroups of families with similar income (e.g., comparing a set of private- and public-school parents all with income between $50,000–59,999; comparing another set all with income between $60,000 and 69,999; and so forth). By keeping income relatively constant within a comparison, one therefore removes the influence of income and allows a sharper comparison of private- and public-school students' standardized test scores, beyond any effects of income.

6 Glenn et al. (2010) allude to a very similar idea, the *length of search thesis*, which posits that "the longer a person searches for a mate and 'circulates' on the marriage market (at least to a certain point), the greater is the probability of a good marital match when he/she marries" (p. 789). This idea goes back a long way, to Levinger (1965) and others.

7 Sources offer somewhat different characterizations of what marriage ages, specifically, carry the greatest risk for youthful divorce. Regnerus and Uecker (2011) contend that "Most sociological evaluations of early marriage note that the link between age-at-marriage and divorce is strongest among those who marry as teenagers … Marriages that begin at age 20, 21, or 22 are not nearly so likely to end in divorce as most Americans presume" (p. 180). Fox (2014), in discussing Kuperberg's research, states that the latter "found that individuals who committed to cohabitation or marriage at the age of 18 saw a 60 percent rate of divorce. Whereas individuals who waited until 23 to commit saw a divorce rate that hovered more around 30 percent."

8 Within family sciences, a lot of statistics are reported only for women. I am not sure why, my best guess being that many vital-statistics data (e.g., marriages, births) come from fertility studies, which concentrate on women. For example, the National Survey of Family Growth "was designed to be nationally representative of ever-married women 15–44 years of age in the civilian, non-institutionalized population of the United States." Men were added to the project only after nearly 30 years (US Centers for Disease Control, 2020a). https://www.cdc .gov/nchs/nsfg/about_nsfg.htm

9 Although Baumeister (2000) discussed the possibility that "male sexuality is more determined by genetic factors" than is women's (p. 356), Diamond (2003) suggested studying men's stability and change in sexual identities (as she did for women) as a topic for future research.

CHAPTER

Becoming a Parent

> *We had never discussed having children. It was a different era. You didn't think,*
> *'Do I want to do this?' or 'Is it time' or 'Are we mature enough?' None of those*
> *questions ever arose. We were typical of most Fifties couples: we got married;*
> *we had babies.*
>   — *Former Texas Governor Ann Richards (quoted in Reid, 2012, p. 19)*

Becoming a parent is the final remaining task for us to discuss from Henig and Henig's (2012) list of five traditional milestones used to define adulthood (Chapter 1). For most people, parenthood is a profoundly transformative life event, solidifying the transition from the self-focus of emerging adulthood (Arnett, 2015a) to the other-focus of caring for a child (and perhaps also a spouse or partner). This chapter on becoming a parent, as will become apparent, is organized into four major sections: statistical background on parenthood, young adults' plans for starting a family, how becoming a parent changes a person, and the transition to parenthood in lower-income populations.

Statistical Background

Percentage of Adults Who Are Parents

A very high proportion of Americans become parents. As of 2016, 86% of 40–44-year-old women had given birth at some point in their lives (Livingston, 2018). This proportion includes 90% of ever-married and 55% of never-married women. The percentage of individuals in (roughly) the emerging-adulthood age range who are parents is smaller. According to the Clark University Poll (2015), 33% of 21–29-year-olds had children (19% with one child, 14% with two or more). Another data source with similar items is the National Longitudinal Survey of Youth (NLSY) 1997 version, whose participants were born between 1980 and 1984 (US Bureau of Labor Statistics, 2021). When the study commenced in 1997, participants thus ranged from 13 to 17 years old. NLSY staff interviewed participants annually

DOI: 10.4324/9781003156567-12

from 1997 to 2011, after which interviews were conducted every two years (2013, 2015, 2017, etc.). I wanted to plot the percentage of NLSY respondents who had had one or more biological children by each five-year increment (1997, 2002 [when participants were 18–22], 2007 [23–27], etc.), but there was no 2012 interview; hence, I used 2013 [29–33] and then 2017 [33–37; see Figure 9.1). The percentage of NLSY participants with biological children rose steadily, from virtually no one at ages 13–17 to 18.5% at ages 18–22 and 42.0% at ages 23–27. This latter figure is in the same ballpark as Arnett's Clark University Poll (2015), which reported 33% of respondents in their twenties having children. By ages 29–33, 63.1% of NLSY respondents had had children, and by 33–37, 71.4% had.

According to the Williams Institute at UCLA Law school (perhaps the leading research organization on LGBT individuals and families), "Between 2014 and 2016, 16.2% of all same-sex couples, 8.1% of same-sex male couples and more than one in five same-sex female couples were raising children, with higher rates of childrearing among married same-sex couples" (Goldberg & Conron, 2018). Same-sex couples who become parents do so through a variety of pathways (Reczek, 2020). The most common way LGBT adults have children is via previous heterosexual relationships, which may reflect the greater stigma surrounding sexual-minority relationships in the past (Reczek, 2020). Other ways include adoption, reproductive technology, and surrogacy (primarily with gay fathers). The monetary expense of some of these techniques and legal restrictions in some states and countries may make them unattainable for some people (Reczek, 2020).

Note that the Williams Institute statistics on same-sex parenting came out right around the same time as the 2015 US Supreme Court decision declaring marriage equality the law of the land. As time goes by and more gay/lesbian couples marry,

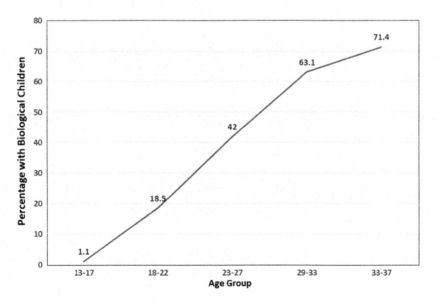

FIGURE 9.1 Percentage of respondents to the National Longitudinal Survey of Youth 1997, who had had one or more biological children at (roughly) five-year increments. Participants were 13–17 years old in 1997, 18–22 in 2002, and 23–27 in 2007. There was no 2012 interview, so 2013 (when participants were 29–33) was used. Finally, participants were 33–37 in 2017.

therefore, it seems likely that more families headed by same-sex couples will include children.

Timing of Having First Child

As with the typical age of first *marriage* in the US, the typical (average) age at first *childbirth* for women increased from 2000 to 2014 (Mathews & Hamilton, 2016). Overall, average age at first birth rose from 24.9 to 26.3, a difference of nearly a year and a half. As shown in Figure 9.2, regardless of racial–ethnic group, American women were having their first child at an older age in 2014 than in 2000.

As I have noted before, many family and fertility statistics cover only women's experiences. I did, however, manage to track down some information on typical ages of fatherhood from the *Columbus Dispatch* (Ohio) newspaper (Gordon, 2012). The *Dispatch* article informs us that

> Although statistics on the number of first-time fathers older than 40 are elusive, research by the National Center for Family and Marriage Research shows the average age at which men have their first child ha[d] risen from 25.3 in 1987 to 27.4 in 2010.

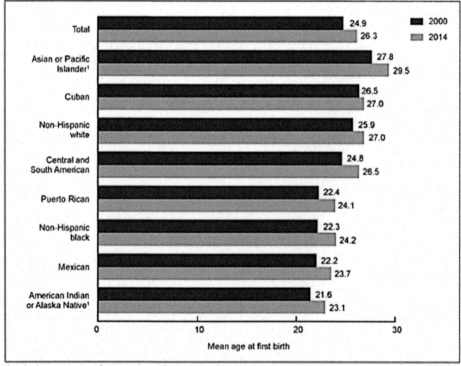

[1] Includes persons of Hispanic and non-Hispanic origin.
SOURCE: CDC/NCHS, National Vital Statistics System.

FIGURE 9.2 Mean age at first birth, by race and Hispanic origin of mother: United States, 2000 and 2014 (Mathews & Hamilton, 2016). According to document: "All materials appearing in this report is in the public domain and may be reproduced or copied without permission."

Even though some men may have wanted to have children earlier than they did, according to the article, "In many ways, older fathers say, their age makes them better equipped to be dads. They often are in better shape financially to support a child, and they have a maturity and perspective they lacked as younger men."

In Australia, where a recent media article reported a mean age of first-time parenthood of 29.3 years (Jennings-Edquist, 2020), quotes from the article revealed different women's outlooks on having children at different ages. One mother, who had two children in her early twenties, said that

> I'm young enough that I can play with them and enjoy them and hopefully be around when they have children of their own … I think being younger my body doesn't struggle as much with sleep deprivation, and also carrying the babies I just feel better.

In contrast, a woman who had her first child at age 36 saw this age as a good fit for her, as it gave her "the chance to study and develop a career before raising children."

Fertility at Different Ages

One consideration in women's and their partners' timing of pregnancy and childbirth, of course, is the odds of successful conception at different ages. According to the American College of Obstetricians and Gynecologists (ACOG, 2021),

> A woman's peak reproductive years are between the late teens and late 20s. By age 30, fertility (the ability to get pregnant) starts to decline. This decline becomes more rapid once you reach your mid-30s. By 45, fertility has declined so much that getting pregnant naturally is unlikely for most women.

Whereas difficulties becoming pregnant are less common in women's twenties than later in life, they can still occur, however (Weiss, 2021).

Pregnancy and Parenting during Emerging Adulthood

Lefkowitz and Gillen (2005) offered a rare look at pregnancy and parenting issues in emerging adulthood. Compared to teen pregnancy, according to these authors, "Less attention has been devoted to pregnancy during emerging adulthood. National data on college students suggest that 15% of college students have experienced their own or a partner's pregnancy." However, women in the EA age range are likely to be in better shape than their younger counterparts, with Lefkowitz and Gillen positing that "becoming pregnant during emerging adulthood in comparison to adolescence may be somewhat less risky for mothers and their children because the mothers may be in more committed relationships from which they can garner physical, emotional, and financial support" (quotes from pp. 243 to 244). This latter point would likely apply to EA women regardless of whether they attended college. Lefkowitz and Gillen offer a final caution, however, namely that even though many women attend college during or after pregnancy, having a child may disrupt college education (in the short term, at least), which could have the ripple effect of reducing young parents' exposure to career options.

Planned and Unplanned Pregnancies

Another dimension along which we can view parenthood is the extent to which pregnancies are planned (Mosher et al., 2012). According to Mosher and colleagues, numerous studies have "shown that births that were unintended by the mother are at elevated risk of adverse social, economic, and health outcomes for the mother and the child" (p. 2). Hence, it is important to study whether pregnancies are intended or not. Further, from the perspective of emerging adulthood, it is also worthwhile to inquire into possible links between women and their partners' ages and the likelihood of planned vs. unplanned pregnancies (the survey measures used in this research, being older, tend to focus only on male partners). In this research area, social scientists ask participants questions such as "Right before you became pregnant …, did you yourself want to have a [or if they already had one, *another*] baby at any time in the future?" and "So would you say that you became pregnant too soon, at about the right time, or later than you wanted?" (Mosher et al., 2012, p. 4). From responses to these and other items, Mosher and colleagues created three categories of pregnancy: intended (at the right time), unwanted (no pregnancy was intended), and mistimed (earlier than desired; this category is sometimes subdivided into mistimed by less than two years and mistimed by two years or more).

Figure 9.3 shows the percentage of births from intended pregnancies by age and marital status. During what we might call "early EA" (20–24 years old), 50% of births were intended, roughly double the rate for those 15–19. For the age group 25–44, the percent intended rose to 75%. The span from 25 to 44 years old is a long one, however, so we cannot immediately tell if there is a narrower band (e.g., 25–29, 30–34, 35–39) in which intended births rose dramatically.

Mosher and colleagues' (2012) report also contains the percentages of mistimed births by age group. Mistiming by 2+ years, meaning that the mother "wanted the birth to occur at least 2 years later than it did" (p. 7), was common in teenagers

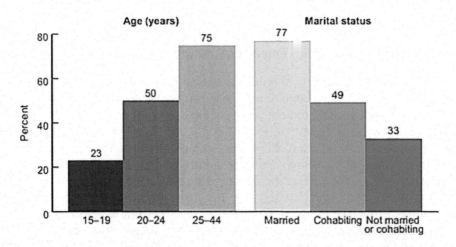

FIGURE 9.3 Percentage of births that were intended at conception, by mother's age and marital status at birth: United States, 2006–2010 (Mosher et al., 2012; Figure 2 in original).

Source: Data from Centers for Disease Control and Prevention/National Center for Health Statistics and National Survey of Family Growth. According to document: "All materials appearing in this report is in the public domain and may be reproduced or copied without permission."

(51% of their births), relatively rare (22%) in the 20–24 age group, and very rare (4.8%) in the 25–44 group. Also as shown in Figure 9.3, married women (77% of their births) had a higher rate of intended births than did cohabiting women (49%) or those whose relationships did not involve living together (33%).

Socioeconomic trends in (un)intended pregnancies are also apparent. In 2011, according to the Guttmacher Institute (2019), women below the federal poverty level had roughly 110 unintended pregnancies per 1,000 women. Those moderately above the poverty line had roughly 60 per 1,000, and those well above the poverty line had around 20 per 1,000. Likely reflecting African American and Hispanic families' lower income than that of Whites (Wilson, 2020), unintended births were higher in these minority groups than in White women during the years 2006–2010 (Mosher et al., 2012; data based on ever-married women).

Unplanned or unwanted pregnancies can occur for different reasons. Some readers may imagine scenarios in which couples engaged in sexual intercourse without contraception or using faulty contraception, despite not wanting to get pregnant. Indeed, women who had experienced births from unintended pregnancies cited reasons such as not expecting to have sex when they did, not thinking they could get pregnant, being worried about birth control side-effects, and male partners either not wanting to use birth control themselves or not wanting the woman to use it (Mosher et al., 2012). Individuals' core philosophies about the meaning of parenting and children are also linked to attitudes toward family planning (Luker, 1984). Based on in-depth interviews with pro-life (anti-abortion) and pro-choice (abortion rights) activists, Luker concluded that planning the timing of one's pregnancies was a higher priority to the pro-choice than to the pro-life advocates. "This is not to say that pro-life people do not approve of planning," Luker acknowledged (p. 171). However, rejecting terms such as "unplanned" or "unwanted" pregnancies in favor of the term "surprise pregnancy," pro-life women are "well equipped to believe that an unanticipated pregnancy usually becomes a beloved child" (p. 198). This idea of not necessarily planning to have a baby but being open to it (a "surprise pregnancy") indeed appears to characterize a segment of the American population. In the survey on planned and unplanned pregnancies discussed above, 23% of women selected, as a reason for their unintended births, that they "Didn't really mind if [they] got pregnant." Finally, historical era is important. Governor Richards, in the quote to open this chapter, alluded to becoming an adult in a "different era," the pre-Pill 1950s. In that era, family planning apparently was not very common. Almost certainly, Governor Richards became more of a family-planning advocate over time, as her oldest child, Cecile, became president of the organization Planned Parenthood (Cottle, 2018)!

Young Adults' Plans Starting a Family

As we have seen, unplanned pregnancies (either unwanted or mistimed) are fairly common, for a variety of reasons. However, many couples do plan, more or less systematically, for when they would like to start and expand their families. The Cornell Couples and Careers Study (Altucher & Williams, 2003; Moen & Sweet, 2002), though an older study, nicely illustrates some of the key issues in family planning. Altucher and Williams analyzed qualitative interviews with 94 individuals, mostly from married couples, but with a small number from cohabiting couples or single. The sample had an average age of 38 (although some on the younger end were between 25 and 30), with 75% of participants being White, 74% having a bachelor's degree or higher, and roughly one-third each having no children, one child, or two children. The study consisted of three groups of couples and individuals with reference to their family situations. One group was still in the family-formation process (either waiting to have their first child or to have additional children), not having completed their families during EA; a second group had already had the number of children they intended to; and a third group was likely to remain childless (e.g., past childbearing age). Factors individuals might consider in deciding when to have children included parents' ages, the biological clock, the adults' vitality ("presumably youthful energy needed to cope with young children," p. 55), and the parent–child age gap. Altucher and Williams further divided those who were still in family-formation mode into three subgroups, based on their time-urgency or lack thereof.

- One subgroup, despite the sample on average being in their late thirties, still saw having their first (or additional) children as something off in the future. As Altucher and Williams (2003) noted,

  > Many [in this subgroup] are still single and talk about planning to get married and then at some point having children, usually two. Having children is not a major preoccupation for them. Many younger married women and men see childbearing as something distant and abstract.
  >
  > *(p. 55)*

- A second subgroup, in contrast, was feeling pressure to have children immediately. In addition to biological clock/fertility issues, as one woman said, "I want to get started because I don't want to be 50 when the kid is still in high school or something (laughs)" (p. 56).
- A third subgroup was still "trying to find the 'right' time" (p. 56) to have a baby that would be least disruptive to their careers or education. As Altucher and Williams (2003) characterize this group, its

  > calendar is not set by age but by educational or career paths. People trying to find the right time to have children speak of a "buffer year" in which a baby would be less problematic or of how to have a child without compromising their resumes. The challenge of coordinating work and family careers is most pronounced for them because they have not yet reached a solution for the problem of fitting it all in.
  >
  > *(p. 56)*

Whether people can actually find the "right" time to begin a family is an open question, in my view. They may be able to find a time that is *satisfactory* to them, but that doesn't mean there was one ideal time. Looking at biological variables, one can examine correlations between women's ages when trying to conceive and various markers of maternal and child health: successful fertility (highest in women's late teens and in the twenties), rate of birth defects (lowest when mothers are 26), and infant mortality (lowest when mothers are 32) (Henig, 2012). The British publication *Medical News Today* contends that "There is no right age to have a baby that works for everyone," noting that "Economic issues, lengthy educational careers, and personal preference now mean that for many people, the time when they are the most fertile may no longer be the best or most practical time for them to have a baby" (Villines, 2020). All one can do is evaluate, within the context of their lives, the biological, psychological/emotional, and financial considerations in deciding if/when to begin (and possibly expand) their family (Villines, 2020).

Unfortunately, even carefully formulated plans don't always come to fruition. A National Public Radio (NPR) segment (Wilson, 2008) vividly illustrates the uncertainty involved in trying to start a family. One of the interviewed women had not conceived by age 38, despite two years of fertility treatments. As she told Wilson, "When I look around and see these people getting pregnant at a drop of a hat, by accident … it makes me very angry." Wilson added that this interviewee had vaguely expected that "as long as I try to start to get pregnant by the time I'm 38, 39, 40, I'll be fine." I like the NPR segment and hope that you will listen to it. If it has a limitation, however, it is that it focuses exclusively on relatively well-off couples (e.g., dual-income or a large enough single income for the couple to live on; ready availability of childcare through the baby's grandmothers). In a later section, we will examine the transition to parenthood in lower-income contexts.

How Becoming a Parent Changes a Person

The transition to parenthood involves "adjustment to new experiences, changes in relationship expectations and mental health, as well as potential for self-expansion, relationship enhancement, and conflict" (Mickelson & Biehle, 2017, p. 271). At a practical level, new parents can expect sleep disruption, possible postpartum depression (more so in mothers than in fathers), and other sources of stress (Mickelson & Biehle, 2017). My focus, however, is on how parenthood changes one's larger concept of oneself as a person (e.g., less immature, better at caring for others). Qualitative studies of the transition to fatherhood by Palkovitz et al. (2001) and of motherhood with toddler-age children by Prikhidko and Swank (2018) illustrate many key points.[1]

Palkovitz and colleagues (2001) recruited 40 fathers from a community in the eastern US via newspaper ads. Nearly 80% of these fathers were White and 20% were African American, with a small Hispanic representation. Participants ranged in age from 20 to 45 at the time of the interviews, with the average age when they became fathers being 26 years old. Specific employment information was absent, other than the article citing "diversity in … occupational achievement and status" (p. 52). Interviews lasted for at least one hour, probing how the men perceived fatherhood as affecting their lives in several areas (e.g., marriage/relationship, friendships, work, values, religious beliefs). The researchers really pressed the men to introspect, asking "how can you be sure that it's fatherhood that has changed you? How do you know that it's not just maturity or aging or your job or your marriage or your education?" (p. 54).

As we have seen in some examples throughout the book, qualitative researchers often try to extract *themes* – or commonly recurring ideas – from participants' responses to the questions. If many respondents independently convey the same idea (e.g., that fatherhood has made them cut down on possibly risky behavior), then we can infer that what is being discussed is a fairly common experience of fatherhood. On the other hand, if only one father mentions something (e.g., that fatherhood has made them follow current events more closely than they had before), then we would not consider this experience to be a common or normative part of becoming a father (which is not to say that the one father's experience is necessarily uninteresting, just uncommon). Palkovitz et al. (2001) discovered five themes, each with reasonably frequent occurrence, from their analyses of interview transcripts:

- *Settling down* (mentioned by 45% of fathers). As Palkovitz et al. (2001) noted, "Some men communicated the theme in terms of eliminating 'wildness' from their lives, while others focused more on needed direction, maturity, and focus" (p. 56).

- *Less self-centered/more giving* (35%). The researchers characterized this group of men in the following manner: "fathers had come to see that they were selfish and self-centered prior to having children. Interestingly enough, marriage did not seem to bring this revelation" (p. 57).

- *Major responsibilities* (32%). As Palkovitz et al. acknowledge, this theme is similar to the previous one (less self-centered). The researchers quote one father that "I have to look out for [his children] and not just me … If it wasn't for my children I would probably blow a lot of money" (p. 58). Another father noted that "You have responsibility for another life and that changes your direction of what you want to do, what you can do, or what you don't want to do" (p. 58).[2]

- *Generativity* (29%). Many readers will know that, in Erik Erikson's (1968) lifespan theory, generativity – or sharing one's wisdom with, and guiding, younger generations – is the central task of middle adulthood (Hagerty, 2016). However, considering that becoming a parent revolves so heavily around interacting with member(s) of the new generation, I don't find it surprising that generativity would show up in these new fathers' discourse. Underlying fathers' sense of generativity, according to Palkovitz and colleagues, was "their desire to see their children do better than they had personally." Some fathers also mentioned wanting to leave a legacy after they were gone.

- *A "jolt"* (29%). Some of the men saw fatherhood as a major transformation or "shock to the system" (p. 61), compared to their pre-fatherhood lifestyle. One father, who thought he would be in prison if fatherhood had not turned his life around, noted that he did not want his daughter to see him "through eight inches of glass" (p. 61).

Palkovitz et al. (2001) also asked one quantitative question: "In terms of rough percentages, if we take a look at who you are today, as a person, as a man, what percentage of you is who you are because of being a dad?" (p. 54). In other words, did some of these men believe that being a father was 50% of who they were or 30% or 90% or what? Take a moment to think about this and guess what the average was for the men in Palkovitz et al.'s study. The average was 56%, with a range from 20% to 100%. I've proposed a possible class activity based on this item (see end of chapter).

What about motherhood's effects on women? Prikhidko and Swank (2018) interviewed 13 self-identified middle-class mothers of toddlers aged two to five. For

10 mothers, the toddler was their first child, whereas for three mothers it was their second child. The mothers were 26–38 years old, predominantly White (nine, with two each African American and Hispanic), and predominantly married (10, with three divorced). Mothers did not appear to be asked directly whether they worked in the labor market, but some respondents' references to work indicate that some did. Individual interviews, lasting 40–60 minutes, included questions such as "How would you describe ideal motherhood?", "[W]hat are your beliefs about motherhood?", and "[H]ave you ever felt guilt in your role as a mother (please explain)?" Note that these kinds of questions are likely to get participants to speak at length on their beliefs – which is good for qualitative research – as opposed to yes/no questions. You know what's coming next, right? Themes! Four themes emerged, but the percentages of mothers who alluded to each one were not reported.

- *Uncertainty*. Mothers remarked upon the lack of clear instructions or directions for their (and in many cases, their partner's) childrearing task. As one of the interviewed mothers said, "Sometimes you don't know if you made the right decision or not, and if what you are doing will somehow impact them down the road" (p. 280). Using family and friends who respondents thought were good parents as role models and discussing parenting issues with them were ways the participants coped with this uncertainty.
- *Juggling*. The ability to balance or juggle work, career, and motherhood was seen as characteristic of the ideal mother. Participants alluded to different kinds of balancing, actually, such as in time spent with different family members and in showing warmth and support vs. discipline and structure as parents.
- *Social context*. This theme refers to worries over being judged on the quality of their parenting by others in society, including one's friends.
- *Struggles*. Lastly, some mothers alluded to striving to live up to their "ideal" standards of motherhood and feeling guilt when they fell short in their minds. One mother discussed her feelings toward spending time with her daughter: "I do not want to [miss] seeing her first something. I do not want to put so much importance on being a working woman and a professional [that] it takes away from time I should spend with her" (p. 281).

Whereas the fatherhood themes uncovered by Palkovitz et al. (2001) mostly represented positive or growth-oriented developments (e.g., feeling more settled down, more responsible, and less self-centered), the motherhood themes revealed by Prikhidko and Swank (2018) centered on stress and anxiety (uncertainty, juggling, worrying about being judged, and struggling to adhere to ideal standards and avoid guilt). It is possible that men (on average) judge themselves more generously and mentally beat themselves up less than do women. There are many reasons why this conclusion would be premature, however. The two studies' sample sizes were very small and not representative of the US population of men and women, the studies were conducted perhaps 15–20 years apart,[3] and the respective research teams' lines of questioning appear to have been different (the motherhood, but not the fatherhood, study asking specifically about ideals and guilt, which may have put mothers in a more pessimistic mindset). There could be other differences, as well, that are just not as obvious as the ones listed already.

Focus on Lower-Income Parents

As we have seen, academic researchers (Altucher & Williams, 2003) and the media (Wilson, 2008) have sometimes focused on parents in relatively advantaged circumstances. Increasingly, however, academic researchers have examined the lives of lower-income parents. Many parents in the younger half of emerging adulthood (18–24, as opposed to 25–30) are likely to be from lower- or middle-income backgrounds. Figure 9.4 features a graph I created from data reported in Edin and Tach (2011). These data show that 73% of US women whose family income was under $20,000 had become parents by age 24 in the years 2006–2008. In the family income range of $20,000–50,000, a smaller though still large percentage (60%) of women had become parents by 24. Above $50,000, 39% of women had. This trend or gradient of lower parenthood rates with higher family income also holds in men, but not as dramatically as in women.

As we discussed in Chapter 4, Silva (2013) argued from her extensive interviews with working-class individuals that parenthood and their children (among those who had them) were the major source of these young adults' identities. Though lower/working-class individuals may derive satisfaction from being a parent and draw inspiration from it to improve their standard of living, life clearly is not easy for these parents.

First, per Edin and Tach (2011), "Almost 60% of first births to young adult men, and almost 65% of first births to young adult women occurred outside of a marital union" (p. 189). These authors also noted, however, that "In contrast to popular images, most unmarried men are not eager to flee their parental responsibilities as soon as the child is conceived" (p. 193). For nearly half of children of unmarried young adults, their parents are cohabiting; for a third of these children, the parents remain romantically involved, but not cohabiting (Edin & Tach, 2011). That leaves 20% of children born to unmarried parents who are no longer together (Edin &

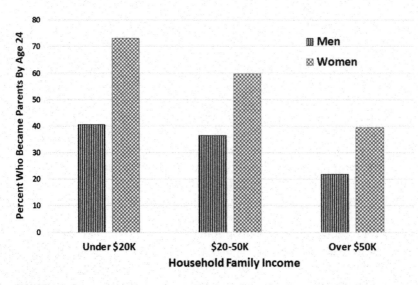

FIGURE 9.4 Percent who became parents by age 24, according to gender and income.
Source: Based on data presented in Edin and Tach (2011) from the National Survey of Family Growth in 2006–2008.

Tach, 2011). Beyond the old "culture war" debates over childbearing in and out of marriage (Chapman, 2014), during which single mothers were unfairly criticized in my view, having two committed parents to care for children presumably makes life easier than if one parent must do it all. Overall, 74% of unmarried fathers financially supported the mother during pregnancy.

Second, according to Edin and Tach, "Young parents are also more likely to have used drugs or spent time in jail, although these experiences are much more common for unmarried parents than they are for married parents" (p. 192). Third, the relationships of young parents represent a "glass half-empty/glass half-full" scenario in terms of stability. Of young-adult mothers who were married to the baby's father at the time of birth, 57% were still married to them five years later (the glass being a little more than half-full). Of young-adult mothers who were cohabiting with the baby's father at the time of birth, 54% were still together five years later (cohabiting or married). When the mother and father were in a romantic relationship at the time of the child's birth (but not married or cohabiting), they had a 27% chance of still being together five years later, and if there was no relationship at the time of birth, 9% of parent couples were together five years later (Edin & Tach, 2011). Of the mothers no longer together with the baby's father after five years, many found new partners (remember the "marriage-go-round," Cherlin, 2009, from the previous chapter) and had additional children with their new partners. According to Edin and Tach,

> Twenty-one percent of divorced young mothers and 26% of formerly cohabiting mothers had a new child by a new partner within 5 years of the focal child's birth. Over 35% of mothers who were in romantic nonresident relationships with the father prior to splitting up had new children by new partners, and fully 40% of mothers who were not involved with the baby's father at the birth had new children by new partners.
>
> *(p. 198)*

Such multi-partner fertility (Guzzo & Dorius, 2016) can create new problems of its own. Edin and Tach note that "Prior partners, who often continue to engage with the mother via child visitation, are a significant source of tension in new couple relationships, as the prior partner's visits to see the child fuel jealousy from the current partner," among other difficulties. On a more positive note, "Unmarried mothers who repartner typically do so with men who have considerably more human capital [education and skills] and fewer behavioral problems than their prior partners … but we know next to nothing about the quality of the subsequent partnerships" (quotes from p. 199). Edin and Tach conclude that "young adults who transition to parenthood typically do so in challenging circumstances, and their children often end up in family constellations that are highly unstable and enormously complex" (p. 202). This is not to say that some young-adult parents and their children cannot thrive. However, the glass seems at best half-full.

The Child & Family Research Partnership (CFRP), directed by Cynthia Osborne at the University of Texas-Austin, has conducted extensive research on promoting father involvement (which they see as beneficial in the vast majority of cases). Dr. Osborne and her team have also barnstormed the state of Texas in recent years, leading workshops on the topic (I caught the one they gave in Lubbock in July of 2019). According to one of CFRP's written reports (Osborne et al., 2017),

> Many men are becoming fathers in particularly disadvantageous situations. Young, unmarried, and lacking in education, these men face a multitude of barriers to being the fathers they want to be, from poor employment prospects and high incarceration rates, to juggling multiple parenting roles among the children they live with and the ones with whom they do not.
>
> *(p. 6)*

(Recall that "juggling" was also a theme uncovered in Prikhidko and Swank's [2018] study of motherhood.)

Osborne and colleagues have identified several factors associated with positive father involvement with their children. I would like to focus on four key ones but interested readers can consult the original sources (CFRP, 2018; Osborne et al., 2017) for the full set. To remember these four factors, I created the acronym CRED, as in the shorthand for "credibility." First, fathers must be *confident* (C) in their parenting abilities. As Osborne et al. note, "Compared to mothers, fathers often lack confidence in their parenting skills or abilities and are less knowledgeable about child development" (p. 97). Many programs for fathers seek to instill greater parenting confidence in participants (Osborne et al., 2017). Second is the *relationship* (R) between the father and mother of a child. Per Osborne and colleagues,

> a substantial body of research supports the notion that when parents get along, both the quantity and quality of father involvement are higher. Fathers who are romantically involved with their child's mother are consistently more likely to be involved with the child across a wide range of demographic, economic, and residential domains. In fact, some scholars identify the quality of parents' romantic relationship as the strongest predictor of paternal involvement.
>
> *(p. 19)*

Third are *economic* (E) factors, as "Several studies … connect a father's education, income, and employment to supportive parenting and frequency of father–child contact" (Osborne et al., p. 19). Finally, fathers must avoid *destructive* (D) conduct. Osborne and colleagues note, of course, that "Fathers with a history of incarceration, abusive behavior, or drug and alcohol problems pose a high risk to positive interaction and are less likely to maintain contact with their children over time" (p. 19).

Sick and colleagues (2019) have also conducted in-depth research on young parents (whom they define as those having their first child between 16 and 24), including those with low income (defined as less than double the US federal poverty level, which under today's standards, is around $44,000 for a family of three; see Chapter 2 of this textbook). Sick et al. found that 27% of low-income young parents were high school dropouts and only 5% had obtained a college degree. Some people, if they are so inclined, can return to school after missing out during the usual years (e.g., 18–22 for college) if their family and economic circumstances permit. Low-income young parents are rarely able to do so, however. Roughly 5% (based on my retinal inspection of Sick and colleagues' graphs) of low-income young adults were able to attend school (without also working) from ages 23 to 30. An additional 10% of this group were able to attend school while also holding a job. Among all young parents in school from ages 23 to 30 (not just low-income ones), about 40–45% (depending on the specific age) were in vocational/job-skills training, 30–35% were attending two-year community colleges, 25–30% were attending four-year colleges and universities at the undergraduate level, and perhaps 2–8% were attending graduate school (i.e., master's, doctoral, professional) (Sick et al., 2019).

Childcare is another important issue for young parents in terms of being able to seek educational and occupational opportunities, while not exhausting a large share of their family budget. According to a recent survey,

> 81 percent of Millennials and Gen Zers identified access to affordable high-quality child care as an important issue, and nearly 3 in 4 (72 percent) of respondents identified the lack of high-quality child care programs and their cost as a barrier to achieving their professional goals.
>
> *(Bohanan & Cohen, 2020)*

One article notes that "In roughly 20 states [of the US], average annual child care costs are more expensive than housing" (Marte, 2015). Another way in which the difficulty of obtaining childcare can (indirectly) create hardships for parents is via their work hours. According to Marte (2015), "Millennials with children are also twice as likely to work an after-midnight shift in order to free up time they can spend with their children during the day."

In conclusion, being a parent is difficult for anyone. Lower-income parents appear to have some additional challenges, although as we have discussed, many of them derive a positive identity from parenthood. In Chapter 12, we will discuss government and business policies that might be able to ease the transition to adulthood for those facing various disadvantages. Childcare will be one we discuss.

Review

We have:

FIVE themes representing the ways in which fatherhood changes one as a person: settles them down, makes them less self-centered and more giving, increases their sense of responsibility, evokes generativity, and delivers a "jolt" to men's existing lifestyle (Palkovitz et al., 2001).

FOUR themes representing the ways in which motherhood raises important issues in women's lives: uncertainty, juggling, social context, and struggles (Prikhidko & Swank, 2018); and FOUR key factors (forming the acronym CRED) that promote father involvement in disadvantageous situations: confidence, relationship with the mother, economic, and (refraining from) destructive conduct (Osborne et al., 2017).

THREE subgroups of couples looking to start or expand a family: those envisioning childbirth off in the future, those feeling pressure and trying now, and those still trying to find the right time (Altucher & Williams, 2003).

TWO types of unplanned pregnancies: unwanted (not planned at all) and mistimed (getting pregnant earlier than planned) (Mosher et al., 2012).

ONE, representing parents' first child, which they typically had around age 26 for US women and 27 for US men (as of the 2010s). These ages are a year and a half to two years later than women's and men's typical ages at first birth in 2000 and 1987, respectively.

Possible Class Activities

1. The audio of Wilson's (2008) NPR interview on the transition to parenthood (referenced in the chapter) remains available at: https://www.npr.org/templates /story/story.php?storyId=90227229. At slightly under nine minutes, playing the audio out loud fits nicely within a class period, and typically generates good discussion.

2. If you have a friend in their twenties who has recently become a parent, text them with Palkovitz et al.'s (2001) question about what percent of who they are stems from being a parent. I got this idea from a student who, during a class in which we were discussing parenthood, raised her hand to announce that she had just texted her parents to find out what percent of their overall identities stemmed from being parents.

Notes

1 Mickelson and Biehle (2017) recommend that the transition to parenthood be studied from three perspectives (if the child is being raised by two parents): that of each parent individually and that of the parents jointly ("hers, his, and theirs," with heterosexual parents; p. 271). These authors acknowledge, however, that "little is known about the joint adjustment to the transition" (p. 272).

2 Recall from Chapter 1 the study in which college students were able to list activities that might be socially acceptable to undertake as an undergraduate, but not "later on when you settle down as an adult" (Ravert, 2009, p. 381). The above quote from one of the fathers in Palkovitz et al.'s (2001) study suggests, therefore, that many people retain an appreciation of age-appropriate (and inappropriate) behaviors well beyond their college years (or beyond their late teens and early twenties, if they did not attend college).

3 It can take a few years from when a study is completed until it is published. Hence, publication year is not a precise indication of when a study was conducted.

Healthy Transitions to Involved Citizenship

Mental Health and Substance Use

Many of you have probably heard the saying that health is "not merely the absence of disease," a phrase that originated with the World Health Organization (WHO) in 1946 (WHO, 2022). Rather, health is said to consist of positive psychological characteristics (happiness, life satisfaction, contentment, a sense of meaning and purpose, etc.), physical vigor, community involvement, and other qualities. Terms such as wellness, well-being, flourishing, and thriving have been used to characterize this broad conception of health (Su et al., 2014). Su and colleagues developed the Comprehensive Inventory of Thriving, a 54-item questionnaire that inquires into 18 areas of life (three items for each area). Just a few of these 18 areas include *life satisfaction* (e.g., "My life is going well"), *skills* (e.g., "I get to do what I am good at every day"), *community* (e.g., "I pitch in to help when my local community needs something done"), *belonging* ("I feel a sense of belonging in my community"), and *meaning and purpose* (e.g., "I have found a satisfactory meaning in life").

Part IV of the book, which includes our final three chapters, covers young adults' health (broadly speaking) and involvement in one's community and the larger society. Chapter 10 explores mental health and substance use in young adults, differentiating behaviors that (in moderation) can be pleasant and healthy (e.g., moderate alcohol consumption; CDC, 2020b), that are moderately unpleasant but highly common (e.g., occasionally feeling sad or anxious), and those that are clinically significant, debilitating, and possibly threatening to health or life (e.g., major depressive disorder, alcohol or other drug-use disorders). Chapter 11 examines civic engagement, specifically the extent to which young adults volunteer in their communities, serve in the military, become politically involved, and participate in organized religion. Engagement in these activities can provide the different facets of thriving listed above, such as life satisfaction, belonging, and meaning. Finally, Chapter 12 delves further into the political/public-policy arena, examining government programs to ease the transition into adulthood. These include subsidies for young adults to find their own housing (Sweden) and various initiatives to assist vulnerable populations (e.g., children in US foster care).

DOI: 10.4324/9781003156567-14

> All of these factors – intense self-doubt, problems with learning a new work or social protocol, being overwhelmed by everything happening at once, losing the college anchor, dashed expectations – can contribute to the sense of helplessness that many twentysomethings feel in the years after graduation.
>
> – Quarterlife Crisis *authors Robbins and Wilner (2001, pp. 112–113)*

Robbins and Wilner's (2001) notion of a quarterlife crisis (QLC), modeled after the idea of a midlife crisis (Levinson, 1978),[1] raises some interesting issues to begin this chapter on mental health. First, how do we define mental and psychological health and distress, so we can assess how many people are doing well or not? Second, even though there unquestionably are *some* individuals aged 18–30 who experience psychological difficulties, does the epidemiological (statistical) evidence support the idea of a *widespread* quarterlife-crisis period? Third, the idea of the twenties as a quarterlife crisis is not unreasonable. As you'll recall from Chapter 1, one of the five features of Arnett's (2015a) theory of emerging adulthood is that it is a time of stress and instability. Experiencing a lot of change, if not actual turmoil, certainly could create a crisis for some.

Clinical vs. Sub-clinical Criteria for Psychological Distress

Most, if not all, people feel sad or anxious at some point. We cannot control everything that happens to us, so it is natural that things that we did not want to happen will happen and that we will worry about important upcoming events, of whose outcomes we cannot be certain. How, then, do we distinguish between everyday sadness, anxiety, and other kinds of distress, on the one hand, and clinically significant mental disorders, on the other? Mental-health professionals (psychiatrists, psychologists, marital/family therapists, social workers, and other counselors)[2] use the *Diagnostic and Statistical Manual (DSM) of Mental Disorders*, now in its fifth edition, known by its abbreviated title, *DSM-5*[3] (American Psychiatric Association, 2013). *DSM-5* presents diagnostic criteria for 157 disorders (Murphy & Hallahan, 2016). To my mind, there are two crucial features of *DSM-5* diagnoses. To be diagnosed with some type of disorder, an individual must (1) exhibit *multiple symptoms* of that disorder, for (2) *sustained periods* of time. This way, a very brief or limited spell of psychological distress would likely not qualify for a *DSM-5*, clinically significant diagnosis. Table 10.1 presents examples of diagnostic criteria for some well-known disorders.

There are several things to notice from this table. First, even though symptoms must last for some appreciable duration to warrant any kind of diagnosis, there is variation in these durations. Generalized anxiety disorder (GAD), for example, has a time window of six months. Rutter and Brown (2015) note that *DSM-5* characterizes GAD as a "chronic" condition; thus, a long timeframe makes sense. Why major depression has a two-week window is not clear from the sources I could find. However, given that depression can lead to suicidal behavior, it seems like a good idea for its diagnosis to focus on severe symptoms over a relatively short period of time.[4] Second, some disorders have core symptoms that must exist before a condition can be diagnosed, whereas others do not. For example, among the five or more symptoms necessary for a GAD diagnosis, two must be excessive anxiety/worry and

TABLE 10.1 Brief Summary of *DSM-5* Diagnostic Criteria

Disorder (Sources for Further Discussion)	Number of Symptoms Needed	Example Symptoms	Duration of Symptoms Needed
Major Depression (Bennett, 2017)	Five or more*	Depressed mood, loss of interest, weight loss, too little or too much sleep, feelings of worthlessness, fatigue, suicidal thoughts	Two weeks (most of the day, nearly every day)
Generalized Anxiety (Laboratory for the Study of Anxiety Disorders, 2021)	Five or more**	Excessive anxiety, difficulty controlling it, difficulty concentrating, irritability, muscle tension, sleep disturbance	Six months (more days than not, during this time)
Anorexia Nervosa (Harrington et al., 2015)	Three	Restricted eating leading to low body weight, intense fear of weight gain or fatness even though at low weight, body-image disturbance	Three months***
Alcohol Use Disorder (National Institute on Alcohol Abuse and Alcoholism, 2016)	Two or more	Unable to cut down even when wanting to; drinking interfered with family, work roles, etc.; in dangerous situations (e.g., driving) during or after drinking; tolerance (having to drink more than previously to get same psychophysiological effect); withdrawal symptoms	Past year

*At least one of the symptoms must be depressed mood or loss of interest or pleasure in a previously enjoyed activity.

**Two core symptoms (excessive anxiety and worry; difficulty controlling it) plus at least three more symptoms.

***Three-month window mentioned in determining restricting vs. binge-purging subtype.

difficulty controlling it; the remaining three or more symptoms can be any on the list. For alcohol use disorder, on the other hand, any two symptoms from the list of 11 possible ones can suffice. Third, across the four disorders described in Table 10.1, the symptoms cover an impressive range of the human experience, such as thought processes, emotions, challenges (e.g., difficulty cutting down on substance use), and processes that combine psychological and physiological elements (e.g., sleep, weight, muscle tension).

Therapists commonly conduct detailed interviews and/or have individuals complete questionnaires to arrive at a clinical diagnosis. Allen and Becker (2019) describe how

> Interview style changed dramatically over the years but always involved a process whereby a clinician elicits a combination of social, medical, education, familial, psychological, developmental, and other information from the client and sometimes informants who know the client well (e.g., parent, spouse).
>
> (p. 307)

Some clinical interviews can take 2.5 hours or longer to conduct (Kelly, 2020).

In contrast to the in-depth assessments needed to diagnose *DSM-5* clinical disorders, researchers sometimes use just a few questions to measure psychological distress and well-being. For example, Vanhalst et al. (2012) used a six-item measure of depressive symptoms (such as "During the last year, I felt unhappy, sad and depressed"; p. 780), whereas Hodgkinson et al. (2010) employed a five-item depression measure (e.g., "Do you feel bad, down, sad or depressed a lot?"). Use of brief measures is most common when a researcher seeks to survey hundreds or thousands of respondents, as in-depth clinical interviews with that many participants would not be feasible for most studies. Because these studies do not involve actual clinical diagnostic interviews, therefore, any reported psychological distress (e.g., sadness, anxiety) is considered sub-clinical ("sub," in this instance, meaning "below," as in submarine or subterranean). Although surveys with abbreviated mental-health measures cannot generate clinical diagnoses, they can still give a sense of whether samples of people are doing well and what other variables might be correlated with mental health.

Peak Ages for Mental Health Disorders

According to a report from the National Institute of Mental Health (NIMH, 2021) comparing different adult age groups, 15.2% of 18–25-year-olds in the US meet *DSM-5* criteria for an episode of major depressive disorder, compared to only 8.9% in the 26–49 age category, and 4.7% in those 50 and older (based on a 2019 national survey). The 26–49 category, of course, groups together a wide range of ages, so we do not know what the depression rates would be for narrower bands (e.g., 26–30, 31–35). It is possible that people 26–30 have comparably high rates to those 18–25, but we don't know. Having said this, the fact that adult rates of major depression are highest between 18 and 25 would appear to support Robbins and Wilner's contention of that many young adults experience a quarterlife crisis. However, the national survey referenced here did not include one important age group: adolescents. The teen years are, of course, known – by reputation, if not actual fact – as a time of emotional turmoil. Fortunately, we have research comparing depression in adolescents and young adults.

A large national (US) study, with over 18,000 respondents, permits such a comparison, as it followed participants who initially were 13–18 years old for seven years, until they were 20–25 (Adkins et al., 2009). It would have been extremely difficult for the researchers to have obtained full diagnostic clinical interviews from this many respondents, hence they had to use a survey measure. The survey measure was a very good one, however, namely 9 items from the 20-item Center for Epidemiologic Studies Depression Scale (CES-D; Radloff, 1977). The researchers combined the nine items into an overall depression score, which is commonly done. Figure 10.1 presents the results by gender and race–ethnicity, with the shown curves representing mathematically simplified shapes that fit the general trends of the data.

Whichever gender or racial–ethnic group you look at, depression peaks at around 17 years of age, during adolescence. From ages 20 to 25, depression is trending downward. These findings therefore call into question whether the twenties represent a quarterlife crisis.

What about disorders other than depression? The Simmons Longitudinal Study, a 30-year project headquartered at Simmons College in Boston, compared regional participants' rates of several *DSM* conditions when they were 21, 26, and 30 years old (Tanner et al., 2007). The researchers interviewed participants and applied the

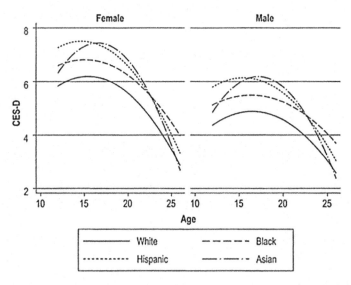

FIGURE 10.1 Depression (CES-D) levels of female and male participants of four racial–ethnic groups. *Source*: From Adkins et al. (2009, Figure 2 in original work). Reprinted with permission.

DSM criteria that were in place at the time (i.e., *DSM-3* at 21, *DSM-4* at 26 and 30). The percent of participants meeting clinical criteria for phobias was much higher at age 21 (17%) than at 26 and 30 (each under 5%). Post-traumatic stress disorder (PTSD) was rare throughout (around 2–3%). The Simmons project examined prevalence of major depressive disorder, as well, with results showing minimal increases from age 21 (5%) to 30 (roughly 8%).

For some international perspective, Gustavson et al. (2018) report the prevalence of mental-health disorders (using *DSM-4*) in Norway. Among those 19–29 years old, 6.2% of Norwegians (7.2% of women and 4.4% of men) met the criteria for a past-year diagnosis of major depressive disorder. This is comparable to the findings of the Simmons (Boston) study. Although the age ranges are somewhat different – 19–29 in the Norwegian study and 18–25 in the American study reviewed above (NIMH, 2021) – the US appears to have a higher rate of young-adult depression than does Norway. Also as in the Simmons (Boston) study, the Norwegian one revealed a high level of phobias (17% in the past year) in the 19–29 group (this percentage refers to *specific* phobias, which create "impairment in circumscribed situations" [p. 2] such as flying on an airplane or standing in a confined space).

Focus on College Students' Mental Health

As noted in Chapter 1, emerging adulthood represents individuals in the 18–30 age range who feel they are going through a time of identity exploration, self-focus, transitioning from adolescence to full-fledged adulthood, and so forth (Arnett, 2015a). There is no requirement that someone attend college to be considered an emerging adult! Still, because so much of emerging-adulthood research has been conducted with college students (in the US, at least), the field has accumulated a large body of findings on those attending university. Accordingly, let's look at what we know about college students' mental health. We should note first that many college students are advantaged socioeconomically and campuses provide a number of support services for students (e.g., academic advisors, counseling centers). Still, as I wrote a decade ago (Reifman, 2011b):

> Think about what many college students go through. Leaving the family home, feeling intense pressure to obtain high grades in connection with career aspirations, taking final exams, trying to establish a romantic/social life, dealing with (often very high) costs of college and possibly working at a job during the school year. What kind of jobs (if any) students can get after college also remains tenuous given the multi-year recession [I was referring to the 2008–2009 Great Recession, but in the 2020s, you can substitute COVID-related economic concerns]. On top of all that, students in many parts of the U.S. must deal with snow and subfreezing temperatures that, in the words of a colleague who once taught in Buffalo [New York], leave students "really dragging by December" … Considering the above, how can college students **not** be highly stressed out?

Thanks to the American College Health Association (ACHA, 2021)/National College Health Assessment (NCHA), there exist mental health (and other kinds of well-being) data on over one million students over a period of many years. Oswalt et al. (2020) report on changes in the prevalence of several psychiatric/psychological conditions between 2009 and 2015 in a total sample of 454,029 students! As we have suggested, full clinical interviews are not feasible with this many respondents (or even a small percentage of these respondents). ACHA/NCHA investigators therefore came up with a very clever way to obtain clinically relevant data from a large sample. They asked participants "Within the last 12 months, have you been diagnosed or treated by a professional for any of the following" conditions, including anorexia, anxiety, bulimia, depression, and schizophrenia, among others (Oswalt et al., p. 43). Figure 10.2 shows the percentages of students who reported that they had been diagnosed with each condition, in each year from 2009 to 2015. As this figure conveys, not only were anxiety and depression clearly the most common disorders all through this period, but they also grew substantially from 2013 to 2015. Panic attack, a *DSM-5* category within the domain of anxiety disorders (Ankrom, 2020), was the third most common condition among college students, followed by attention-deficit hyperactivity disorder (ADHD). Most other conditions were reported by 1% or 2% of students. In addition to providing the annual prevalence of each condition, Oswalt and colleagues reported that, consistently over the 2009–2015 period, roughly 15–20% of respondents had received mental-health services from their current institution.

Mental Health in Underrepresented Minorities

Unlike college students, who can be reached for research purposes through their campuses, other young adults in the US are more difficult to reach. These include the homeless, minorities, rural residents, and LGBT+ individuals. West-Bey and

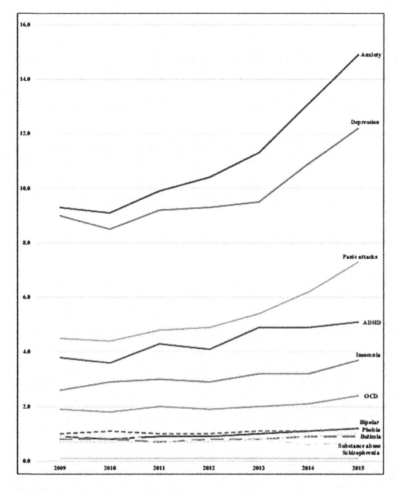

FIGURE 10.2 US college students' diagnoses on clinical conditions, 2009–2015.
Source: From Oswalt et al. (2020, Figure 1 in original work). Reprinted with permission of Taylor & Francis
        Ltd, (www.tandfonline.com).

Mendoza (2019) interviewed 26 low-income youth (16–25), who comprised five
focus (discussion) groups. According to this report,

> Learning about small and hard-to-reach populations presents a challenge for
> researchers and policymakers. Sometimes called "asterisk groups" because their
> data is replaced with an ★, these groups' numbers are often too small in nation-
> ally representative samples to be considered reliable or, in the case of hard-to-
> reach communities, they belong to groups that are likely to be undercounted
> by conventional sampling methods.
>
> *(p. 5)*

The authors summarized some of their key findings as follows: "Youth in small
and hard-to-reach communities experienced similar mental health threats to those
of urban and rural African American youth. These include trauma in the form of
financial strain, exposure to violence, and racism and discrimination" (p. 3). A sample
quote from one respondent is as follows:

One thing is that I get to witness a community that's depressingly in decline, because we're from an area that's known for coal and nothing else. ... And since the coal-mining industry is dying out, um, I get to be a part of a group that is trying to improve the living standards, while we're losing our one source of income.

(p. 8)

Another person, in a different context, discussed sexual minorities:

One thing that people in areas like this struggle with a lot, are just, there is a lot of queer people that are like, their struggle is and then as a person are just thrown to the side, because they want to ignore the fact that those people exist.

(p. 11)

Final Notes on Mental Health

Personal experience with, and exposure to others', substance-related problems can also contribute to mental-health problems. Alternatively, mental-health problems may lead to heavy substance use. It is not uncommon for someone to be diagnosed with two or more mental disorders at the same time, a phenomenon known as *comorbidity* (National Institute on Drug Abuse, 2018). One study showed, for example, that 11% of young adults (18–24 years old) met criteria for both alcohol use disorder and major depressive disorder (Brière et al., 2014). We examine substance use and associated disorders next.

Substance Use and Associated Disorders

Substance use, in itself, does not necessarily constitute a clinically significant disorder – one must look at *DSM-5* criteria for that. However, even occasional use (or overuse) of a substance can be harmful to the individual and others. As usual, let's begin with some basic statistics. In the US, these come from the annual National Survey on Drug Use and Health (NSDUH), conducted by the Substance Abuse and Mental Health Services Administration (SAMHSA, 2021). Young adults drink heavily and use marijuana frequently, at least according to their public image. Is this image correct?

Researchers measure alcohol use in several different ways. These include the number of drinks one has consumed;[5] number of times someone has consumed a sizable number of drinks in one sitting (usually defined as five for men, four for women, due to differences in body size); and the number of times a person reports having gotten drunk. Researchers also specify a timeframe during which the reported drinking occurred (e.g., past week, past two weeks, past month, past year). Given young adults' reputation for heavy drinking, let's look at frequency of 5/4-drink episodes (which the NSDUH labels "binge" drinking). NSDUH results from 2020 show that 31.4% of 18–25-year-olds engaged in at least one binge (5/4 drink) episode in the past month (this percentage is similar to ones reported from a different dataset in Chapter 2).

A multinational team collected similar data in nine countries (Chaiyasong et al., 2018). These researchers examined whether individuals consumed more than six drinks in a single occasion, at least once per week (which they labeled "higher-risk drinking") and compared age groups ranging from 16–19 to 55–65. Higher-risk drinking reflects greater intensity of drinking than the binge-drinking measure used in the NSDUH, as it involves consumption of a greater number of drinks (at least 7 vs. 4/5) and in a shorter timeframe (one week vs. one month). Results varied by country, gender, and age. Among men in four countries (England, Scotland, Australia, and New Zealand), the 20–24 age group engaged in higher-risk drinking to a much greater extent than did any other age group. This pattern was particularly evident in Scotland. There, over 60% of early-twenties men exhibited higher-risk drinking, with men 25–34 and 35–44 the next closest at slightly above 40%. In England, Australia, and New Zealand, roughly 45–52% of 20–24-year-old men engaged in higher-risk drinking, with most other age groups in these countries falling within 30–40%. Among men in the other countries (South Africa, Mongolia, Thailand, Vietnam, and the Caribbean island nation of St. Kitts and Nevis), higher-risk drinking occurred at similar rates in the 20–24, 25–34, 35–44, and 45–54 age groups. In no age group within any nation did women's higher-risk drinking reach 30%. Also, among women, this type of drinking occurred at similar rates in the 25–34 and 20–24 groups. Adding some social context to the drinking behavior of European young adults, Anderson and Baumberg (2006) observed that, with little exception, young adults preferred to drink in bars and restaurants rather than at home with meals. Also, most European studies have shown that "the frequency of drinking to intoxication is highest in young people compared with older groups" (Anderson & Baumberg, 2006, p. 115).[6] There are also some international data on the prevalence of alcohol use disorder. NSDUH (SAMHSA, 2021) estimated that 15.6% of US 18–25-year-olds met criteria for this condition. In Norway, in the 19–29 age group, 6.0% did (Gustavson et al., 2018). The two percentages are not directly comparable due to differences in the age ranges, but they suggest the US probably has a higher prevalence of alcohol use disorder in young adults.

What about marijuana (also referred to as cannabis), a drug that states increasingly have been legalizing in recent years? NSDUH reports only past-year (rather than past-month) use for some drugs, including marijuana (SAMHSA, 2021). Results showed that 34.5% of respondents in the 18–25 group had used marijuana at least once in the past year. From the available data, therefore, a broad segment of the US 18–25 population lives up to its reputation for marijuana use and heavy drinking. The European Monitoring Centre for Drugs and Drug Addiction (2017) reports past-year marijuana-use statistics for "across the pond" from the US, although only for the 15–34 age range, which is not very specific. As of 2013–2015 (depending on each country's data availability), the European nations with the most prevalent past-year marijuana use among young adults (broadly speaking) were: France (22%), Spain and Denmark (both around 17.5%), and Finland, Ireland, and Germany (all just short of 15%).

Other well-known drugs are not that widely used in the US among young adults or other age groups (SAMHSA, 2021). Rates of past-year use among 18–25-year-olds for various substances are as follows: hallucinogens (including Ecstasy), 7.3%; cocaine (including crack), 4.3%; prescription pain-relievers (used inappropriately),

4.1%; and methamphetamine, 0.5%. Cigarette smoking has declined heavily in the past 20 years; only 13.9% of 18–25-year-olds smoked in the past month, whereas in 2002, 40.8% had. Some of the decline may reflect a shift from cigarette smoking to nicotine vaping; 11.7% of 18–25-year-olds had engaged in the latter behavior in the past month during 2020.

Influences on Young-Adult Drinking and Other Substance Use

Social contexts – where you live, who you spend time with, where you hang out, and so forth – are important, as we've seen (remember the reference to neighbor-hoods at the beginning of Chapter 2). In addition to the country in which you live, other contexts that affect young adults' drinking include college attendance (vs. going straight into the workforce or obtaining career and technical education) and whether one is married. We address these contexts next.

College Influences on Students' Drinking

US universities are awash in alcohol, some argue. Sperber (2000) argues that, as much as college administrators speak out against underage drinking, their schools send mixed messages via "large displays in campus bookstores and gift shops of beer mugs, shot glasses, and other party paraphernalia – all with the school's logo on them" (p. 152). Perhaps the closest blending of campus and alcohol culture has occurred at the University of Wisconsin-Madison (a school at which I have taught during summer terms in a visiting capacity). At Badger sporting events, the school band plays the advertising jingle for Budweiser beer. But at the song's crescendo, the crowd sings "When you say *Wisconsin*, you've said it all" (exemplified at https://www.youtube.com/watch?v=n7WseDlzcyY).

Wechsler and colleagues (Wechsler, Lee, Kuo et al., 2002) conducted a series of four large surveys of US college-student binge drinking (using the 5/4 drinks per episode criterion). Each survey had roughly 14,000–15,000 student respondents (except for one that had approximately 11,000). Findings were remarkably consist-ent over an eight-year span, as the percentages of US college students reporting at least one binge episode in the past two weeks were 43.9%, 43.2%, 44.5%, and 44.4% in 1993, 1997, 1999, and 2001, respectively. Underlying these overall percentages, men's binge-drinking rate was around 49% and women's around 39% in each of these surveys. Here are some questions you may have about Wechsler and colleagues' college-drinking research.

It has been over 20 years since the final survey in the sequence (2001). Are college-student binge-drinking rates still around 44% today? I am not aware of any recent large-scale surveys of US college students' binge drinking like those conducted by Wechsler, Lee, Kuo et al. (2002). However, a relatively recent (2014–2016) survey of roughly 3,400 students from seven colleges and universities in the US state of Georgia found binge-drinking rates over repeated assessments of the students of between 41% and 46% (Haardörfer et al., 2021). The Georgia study used the 5/4-drink criterion for binge drinking, but referred to anytime in the previous four months, as opposed to the two-week window used by Wechsler and colleagues, which allows greater opportunity for binge episodes to have occurred. Hence, the binge-drinking rates in the Georgia study may by inflated somewhat, relative to Wechsler et al.'s national surveys. Still, if one is willing to assume that Georgia is similar to the US as a whole, then college-student binge drinking appears to be occurring at a similar rate today to what it was 20–30 years ago.

How accurate are people's self-reports of a sensitive behavior such as heavy drinking, as used not only by Wechsler, Lee, Kuo et al. (2002) but also by nearly all other alcohol researchers? Wechsler, Lee, Hall et al. (2002) used a clever method to confirm the validity of students' reports. The researchers were able to see which colleges had the highest and lowest rates of binge drinking reported by their students. They then surveyed non-student adult residents living near these campuses, asking

> if they have seen or witnessed negative consequences of others' drinking (litter, noise or disturbance, vandalism, people who are drunk, fighting or assault to others, vomit or urination, and automobile accidents) one or more times in their neighborhood in the past year.
>
> *(p. 428)*

The local residents were also asked if they attributed the problems they observed to students at the nearby colleges. Note that the crucial data came from two *independent* sources: schools' status as high- or low-binging was determined from students' self-reported drinking, whereas the neighborhood disturbances were reported by non-student residents. Results showed that a higher percentage of adults who lived near campuses with high rates of binge drinking (16%) reported student littering in their neighborhood than did adults living near low-binge campuses (5%). The same result emerged for noise or disturbances: this was reported by 14% of those living near high-binge schools vs. 8% of those adjacent to low-binge schools.

OK, so large percentages of people report having four or five or more drinks in one sitting. Considering that someone might have had five drinks over several hours during the binge episode or might have only had one such binge episode over a span of several weeks or months, are there long-term effects of heavy drinking during college? Of course, even a single instance can lead to horrible tragedy, such as drunk driving. Over the longer term, however, a team from the University of Missouri showed that first-year undergraduates who engaged in binge (five-or-more-drink) episodes four or more nights per week – which, to be sure, is a considerable amount of drinking – had a nearly 50% chance of meeting the criteria for an alcohol use disorder 10 years after starting college (O'Neill et al., 2001).

Wechsler and colleagues' national college-drinking studies (Wechsler, Lee, Hall et al., 2002; Wechsler, Lee, Kuo et al., 2002) unquestionably yielded a great deal of information. However, because they included only college students, they were unable to compare college students to their same-age non-college counterparts. Studies began to emerge in the early 2000s showing that going to college appeared to raise students' drinking beyond what it would have been had they chosen a different direction after high school. I had access to a dataset that I thought was excellent for addressing potential college-attendance effects on heavy drinking, so with some colleagues, I plowed ahead (Reifman et al., 2010).[7] The dataset included a random, representative sample of families in the Buffalo area who had an adolescent child between 13 and 16 at study outset, with roughly 300 of these early adolescents ultimately attending college and roughly 200 not. In addition, the study consisted of six annual interviews, so participants were 18–21 by the end of the study. Figure 10.3 shows the results from comparing college- and non-college-bound youth at ages 13 through 21 on their heavy drinking (a composite of amount of alcohol, times drunk, and frequency of binge drinking, i.e., five or more drinks in a single occasion). Consistent with earlier research (Schulenberg et al., 2001), we found that, at ages 15, 16, and 17, college-bound students drank somewhat less than did their non-college-bound counterparts (Reifman et al., 2010). In other words, during high school, studying for college protects against heavy drinking. However, at ages 18 and 19 (when college-bound students were in college and the non-college-bound were in the workforce or pursuing other activities), the college students had surged above their non-college counterparts in heavy drinking. Hence, consistent with the idea of colleges supporting drinking cultures, university life appeared to drive up student drinking.

Marital Influences on Young Adults' Drinking

Research strongly suggests that getting married reduces the heavy drinking of those who drank heavily while single (Bachman et al., 1997; Miller–Tutzauer et al., 1991). Observers frame this research as illustrating the power of marriage and other adult responsibilities to make people "mature out" of heavy drinking and other substance use. Bachman and colleagues examined national (US) data that followed individuals at two-year intervals through their twenties to assess possible correlation between the transition to marriage and binge (5-plus-drink) episodes. Though some of the details of this research are complex, the major points are straightforward. First, single people in their twenties drink more heavily than their married counterparts. Around 55% of single men and 35% of single women reported at least one binge episode in the past two weeks, compared to 35% of married men and 15% of married women. Second, and most interesting in my view, people in the transition from singlehood to marriage moderate their drinking from what is characteristic of a single person to what is characteristic of a married person. For example, in women who went from single (S) at one point to engaged (E) two years later to married

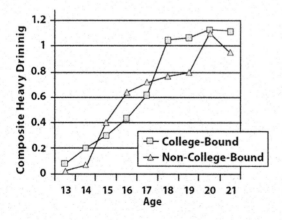

FIGURE 10.3 Trajectories of heavy drinking in college- and non-college-bound youth from Buffalo, New York. From Reifman et al. (2010, Figure 2 in original work). Reprinted with permission of the *Journal of the First-Year Experience & Students in Transition.*

(M) two years after that (an S-E-M sequence), their prevalence of binge drinking dropped from 35% (just like single women as a whole) to roughly 25% during their engagement (halfway between single women's binge-drinking prevalence of 35% and married women's 15%) to a little over 15% when married (similar to married women as a whole). Men followed a similar pattern. Also, if married people got divorced, their binge-drinking prevalence would rise back up to the prevalence characteristic of single people (perhaps because they started going to bars and parties again as part of dating to find a new spouse). Another finding from this research, which may surprise some, is that transitions to parenthood did not reduce drinking as much as did transitions to marriage (Bachman et al., 1997). One possibility is that people reduce their drinking (or as some students term it, curtail their party lifestyle) so heavily upon marriage that there isn't much room to reduce it further when having a child.

Gambling

Gambling does not involve ingestion of substances the way drinking alcohol, smoking marijuana, and other forms of drug use do. However, gambling shares many of the same markers of addiction and clinical disorder as substance use. According to one state health office in the US (Massachusetts Office of Problem Gambling Services, 2021), the *DSM-5*'s gambling disorder lists nine symptoms, of which someone is required to show at least four in the past 12 months to warrant a diagnosis. Some of these symptoms closely resemble those for substance use disorders, namely "Needs to gamble with increasing amounts of money in order to achieve the desired excitement" (similar to tolerance of a substance), "Has made repeated unsuccessful efforts to control, cut back, or stop gambling," and "Has jeopardized or lost a significant relationship, job, or educational or career opportunity because of gambling." Making an occasional small bet on a sporting event or buying an occasional lottery ticket do not represent clinically serious gambling. However, advertising for government-run lotteries and ubiquitous sporting events (including football games on US college campuses) may create contexts that increase the likelihood of young-adult gambling.

Extensive studies of gambling have emerged from the UK and US. Hollén et al. (2020) reported the results of a large study of young-adult gambling in the UK. By age 24 (the oldest age at which participants were studied), men were classified as non-gamblers (28.5%), occasional/less-than-weekly gamblers (54.3%), and regular/at-least-weekly gamblers (17.2%). Women's percentages were not that different (36.5% non-gamblers, 55.7% occasional, and 7.9% regular). Men's most common forms of gambling at age 24 were online betting (47.4%), national lottery (30.3%), football (soccer) pools, and scratch cards (each 17.5%). Women's two most common forms of gambling were, far and away, playing the national lottery (44.1%) and scratch cards (40.0%). Welte et al. (2015) conducted US gambling surveys in 1999–2000 and 2011–2013, with mostly similar results emerging in the two projects. Within the 18–30 age group, 7.7% of respondents engaged in *frequent* gambling within the past year (at least twice a week), whereas 5.4% met criteria for what the researchers deemed *problem* gambling (three or more *DSM-4* criteria). Young adults' frequent gambling was less common than in the 31–45, 46–60, and 61-plus age groups (whose prevalence ranged from 9.2% to 12.3%). However, young adults' problem gambling rate resembled that of the 31–45 group (5.1%) and was higher than in the two oldest groups.

Physical Health

Hardly a word has been said about young adults' physical health in this chapter. Whereas 18–25-year-olds enjoy a low rate of major illnesses such as cancer, heart disease, diabetes, and stroke, this does not mean they have no health concerns (Bonnie et al., 2014). According to Bonnie and colleagues, during the early and mid-twenties, "they are less likely to eat breakfast, exercise, and get regular physical and dental checkups, and more likely to eat fast food, contract sexually transmitted diseases, smoke cigarettes, use marijuana and hard drugs, and binge drink" (p. 63). Focusing heavily on mental health and substance use, which this chapter has done, seems most appropriate to me. However, good physical health in your twenties should not be taken for granted and ignored.

Review

We have:

FIVE alcohol drinks within a single occasion or sitting as the most common definition of binge drinking, although some studies differentiate between five for men and four for women or use more than six drinks.

FOUR countries (England, Scotland, Australia, and New Zealand) in which men in the 20–24 age group exhibited higher-risk drinking much more than did any other age group.

THREE ways to assess potential psychological problems: full clinical interviews with *DSM-5* criteria, questionnaires (which take less time, but can be administered to large numbers of respondents), and asking people if they have been diagnosed by a professional as having a clinical disorder.

TWO weeks as the time window during which the necessary symptoms must have occurred, to warrant a diagnosis of major depressive disorder.

ONE clinical condition that shares many of the characteristics of substance use disorders but does not involve ingesting any substances: gambling disorder.

Possible Class Activities

1. My friend from graduate-school days Chris Crandall developed the Undergraduate Stress Questionnaire (USQ) three decades ago (Crandall et al., 1992), which he updated in 2019. It lists 83 stressful events, some school-related (e.g., final-exam week) and others broadly applicable to young adults (e.g., learning of a romantic partner cheating on you). Students in class can complete

the USQ and count how many events they have experienced. Class discussion can focus on how events on the USQ may lead to the kinds of mental-health issues covered in the chapter. The instructor should make clear that no student is required to share either the number or content of events they have experienced but can do so voluntarily. The USQ is available at: https://www.researchgate .net/publication/335456070_Revised_USQ_a_newer_Undergraduate_Stress _Questionnaire

Notes

1 The frequency of midlife crises appears to be overstated. If you ask middle-aged individuals if they have experienced distressing circumstances (e.g., divorce, job loss), many will respond affirmatively. However, if you ask whether they have entertained the kinds of thoughts specifically characteristic of a midlife crisis – that life is passing them by, that their dreams will never be fulfilled, and that drastic action is needed to reclaim their youth (e.g., buying a motorcycle) – then only about 10% of adults experience a midlife crisis (Hagerty, 2016).

2 Perhaps the two best-known types of mental-health practitioners are psychiatrists and clinical psychologists. Psychiatry is a branch of medicine, so psychiatrists hold an MD degree, which allows them to prescribe medications for clinically significant disorders. Clinical psychologists hold either a Doctor of Philosophy (PhD) from university psychology departments with an American Psychological Association-accredited clinical training program, which prepares one for research and teaching, as well as psychotherapy practice, or a Doctor of Psychology (PsyD), which comes from a practice-oriented training institution (Michalski & Fowler, 2016).

3 For whatever reason, the *DSM-5* uses the numeral "5," whereas the previous edition was known as *DSM-IV* (Roman numeral for 4). To keep things simple, I will use numerals for all versions of the DSM that I discuss.

4 According to the book *DSM: A History of Psychiatry's Bible* (Horwitz, 2021), the manual's diagnoses of depression (including major depressive disorder, MDD) have been conceptually weak over some of its editions. Noted Horwitz, "the DSM-III diagnostic criteria for depression were a mess. MDD combined into a single entity two depressions, one of which was widespread but often not severe and the other incapacitating but uncommon" (p. 71). Horwitz also cites a source from roughly 60 years ago that argued "A depression is judged to be pathological if there is insufficient specific cause for it in the patient's immediate past, if it lasts too long, or if its symptoms are too severe" (p. 69). Hence, the two-week window may stem in part from someone's judgment that anything over two weeks is "too long."

5 A convenient aspect of alcohol research is that what experts call a *standard drink* "contains roughly 14 grams of pure alcohol," regardless of whether someone is drinking beer, wine, or distilled spirits/hard liquor (National Institute on Alcohol Abuse and Alcoholism [NIAAA], not dated). Hence, researchers can simply ask about the number of drinks (in general) one has consumed. According to the same NIAAA document, the alcohol content of these different beverages matches because the one with the least alcohol (beer, 5% alcohol) is consumed in a large serving (e.g., a 12-ounce can), whereas the beverage highest in alcohol (hard liquor, 40% alcohol) typically comes in a small serving (a 1.5-ounce shot glass). Wine falls in between (12% alcohol, typically served in a 5-ounce glass).

6 There is also research showing that US college students increase their drinking when they participate in study-abroad programs in Europe and elsewhere (Pedersen et al., 2010).

7 These data were initially gathered by the now-retired Grace Barnes of the Research Institute on Addictions in Buffalo. I worked with Dr. Barnes and a lot of great researchers during my years in the city best known for snow blizzards. Summer and fall in Buffalo are great, though.

11

Engagement with Broader Society

Ask not what your country can do for you. Ask what you can do for your country.
– President John F. Kennedy, Inaugural Address (January 20, 1961)

A key part of how individuals transition to adulthood and explore their possible future directions is through engagement with their broader communities and societies. Recall from Chapter 4 that participating in some type of "identity project" (which often occurred in conjunction with a community organization) helped disadvantaged youth stay on a productive path of education and work, as opposed to ending up in "the street" (DeLuca et al., 2016). Hence, not only does community involvement help the individual participant, but it provides some tangible benefit to the broader society. In this chapter, we examine four different types of involvement: volunteerism, military service, politics, and religious involvement. There can be overlap between these four activities, such as if someone, acting out of a religious commitment, volunteers with underprivileged children. However, it is easier to discuss the activities as four separate domains. It must also be acknowledged that individuals' investments of time and even personal risk (e.g., being sent to fight a war through the military) can vary widely. In the political realm, simply casting a ballot usually does not take much time[1] but still represents a contribution to those democratic systems around the world. In each of the four arenas, however, considerable development in young adults' attitudes, values, and skills can occur. We now review the four arenas.

Volunteerism

Just a little over three months before stating the immortal words quoted at the beginning of this chapter, candidate John F. Kennedy stood at the front of the Michigan Union on the University of Michigan campus during a campaign stop in the 1960 election. According to Tobin (2010), "Legend has it that he first proposed the idea of the Peace Corps here. The truth is a little more complex, but far more interesting." The Peace Corps, for those not familiar with it, is a US government program that

DOI: 10.4324/9781003156567-15

sends volunteer Americans ages 18 and older to different countries around the globe to contribute some type of service (host countries were described as ones "emerging from colonialism in Africa, Asia and South America"; Tobin, 2010). Volunteers receive extensive training (including technical/skills, language, cultural, and health/safety) and then spend a set amount of time in their host country (27 months for a conventional volunteer position; 3–12 months if participating in response to a call for specific technical expertise). Peace Corps recruiters regularly visit college campuses (at least before COVID-19). Some of the background story of JFK's Michigan speech is as follows (Tobin, 2010). The Kennedy campaign had already raised the idea of the Peace Corps in a press release, but to little notice, so the proposal was not technically original to the Michigan rally. However, the confluence of events – Kennedy looking for a way to demonstrate initiatives for world peace and a UM professor having developed some of the ideas and consulted with Kennedy – appeared to bring the Peace Corps proposal back to the forefront of Kennedy's mind minutes before he was to address the Michigan crowd. As Tobin noted, Kennedy phrased his proposal indirectly, in the form of questions, such as "How many of you who are going to be doctors are willing to spend your days in Ghana?"

To this day, the Michigan Union marks the occasion of Kennedy's Peace Corps speech with a plaque by the building's entrance and a medallion on the ground where JFK stood. Figure 11.1 presents some pictures I took on a visit back to the University of Michigan, where I attended graduate school from 1984 to 1989.

As human development scholars, our aim is to evaluate the potential impact of experiences on individuals' attitudes, psychological development, behaviors, and other possible outcomes. Large-scale evaluations of the Peace Corps have been

FIGURE 11.1 Commemoration of then-candidate John F. Kennedy's 1960 speech at the University of Michigan, in which he proposed the idea for the Peace Corps. The upper picture in the center shows the main entrance to the Michigan Union, with the commemorative plaque to the left of the doors. A close-up of the plaque appears to the left. On the far right is a photo of the full tower of the Michigan Union. The two circles (lower-middle) include a photograph of the actual medallion on the ground marking where Kennedy stood and a schematic (given how faintly the medallion's letters appear).

Source: Photographs by the author.

conducted, but do not appear to probe deeply into psychological development. According to Tarnoff (2016):

> While most volunteers do rate their overall experience highly, volunteer anecdotal accounts suggest some degree of poor programming and staff support still occur. The 2015 volunteer survey found that 17% of volunteers did not think they had enough to do at their work site, and 23% were dissatisfied with support received from Peace Corps staff in site selection and preparation. … One sign of volunteer dissatisfaction – the cohort resignation rate – has improved in recent years, with 15.6% of those who entered service in [Fiscal Year, FY] 2011 resigning prior to completing their term, representing a steady annual decrease from the FY2005 cohort level of 27.6%.

Smaller-scale evaluations typically allow the researchers to go into greater depth, although their results may apply to fewer people. A study of US college students who devoted their Spring Break to volunteering in an impoverished community of orphan children in Nicaragua (Cox & McAdams, 2012) nicely illustrates what researchers can learn. These researchers were interested in how students' feelings about their volunteer experience might correlate with their interest in remaining involved with the Nicaraguan community they visited (e.g., by staying in touch or donating to relief organizations). To assess students' feelings about their experiences, the researchers had them write a series of essays about different parts of the trip. Cox and McAdams then conducted content analyses of the essays, looking for expressions of (wait for it) … themes. The researchers were interested in three themes. One was *helplessness* (a student stating in an illustrative quote that "Everything was magnified and intensified at the Dump [where people scavenge for recyclable items that can be sold]. I sort of had an emotional breakdown – I felt very overwhelmed," p. 34). A second was *sympathy* (e.g., "I felt that [one boy] had never had a proper childhood where he didn't have to always look out for his siblings. It made me so sad, because I realized how lucky I was and how I always took it for granted as a child," p. 32). Finally, the third was *personal transformation* (e.g., "I realized that these kids, and people in general, just need love, that that may come in different forms, such as feeding a little boy, but that love can have such a profound impact on a person," p. 31). Of the three themes, the only one that correlated with continued involvement with the Nicaraguan community three months after the trip was that of transformation. In other words, the more strongly the college students expressed ideas of self-transformation in their essays, the more involved they stayed.

Not all young adults, of course, are as committed to volunteerism as the students who devoted their Spring Break to helping disadvantaged children. How common is volunteering among young adults, anyway? Many researchers in this area (e.g., Salamon et al., 2018) divide volunteerism into *organization-based* (e.g., helping build houses through Habitat for Humanity or delivering food to elderly persons in need through Meals on Wheels) and *direct* (e.g., helping someone move). International comparisons show young adults (broadly defined as 15–25 years old) to volunteer at high levels, generally (Salamon et al., 2018). Regarding direct volunteerism, nearly half of young adults participated in Denmark, whereas roughly 25% did in Hungary, Poland, Italy, and Portugal. Young-adult participation was lower, slightly over 10%, in South Africa. In most of these countries, direct volunteerism was around 10–20%

higher in older age groups. Organization-based volunteerism is generally lower than the direct form. Organizational volunteerism showed different trends in different nations. It was highest in Australia (32% in 15–25-year-olds), Austria (32% in 15–19 and 30% in 20–29-year-olds), and Japan (20% in the 15–25 group). In Poland and Canada, 15–25-year-olds participated at a roughly 15% rate, which was higher than in older groups. Portugal's participation was 8% in young adults, with the rate also declining in older groups. Organizational volunteering was slightly below 8% in the US and Italy in both 15–25 and 26–35 age groups, with the rate rising a couple of percentage points in middle age (Salamon et al., 2018). Data for Mexico were available in a different form altogether, being divided into institutional, church, alone, or with informal groups. Volunteering through an institution, alone, and informally were all around 40% in 15–24-year-olds; church-related volunteerism characterized 15% in this age group. Institutional volunteering rates in Mexico rose up through the 35–44 age group, alone and informal declined slightly by 25–34, and church-related rose gradually up to ages 55–64 (Salamon et al., 2018).

Researchers have also studied the factors that appear to promote volunteerism and civic engagement. Wray-Lake et al. (2020) found greater involvement from ages 18 to 30 (assessed via the item: "How often do you participate in community affairs or volunteer work?") in a US sample among African American participants than in those from other racial–ethnic groups, with slight declines in all groups with increasing age. Women exhibited slightly higher engagement/volunteerism than men at age 18, with the difference disappearing at age 24, and then women's greater participation reasserting itself at 30.

The book *Bowling Alone* (Putnam, 2000), a classic study of community engagement in the US, shows an interesting trend regarding youth involvement. Across numerous domains of community engagement – membership in professional service organizations, military-veteran associations, and yes, the American Bowling Congress; entertaining friends in one's home; regular card games – participation declined from 1950 (give or take a decade) to 2000. A major reason for this decline was that young adults at the turn of the millennium did not participate heavily in these kinds of activities, thus lowering the nationwide average, as members of heavily participating older generations passed on.[2] Putnam pointed out, however, that

> Against this bleak picture of social isolation and civic disengagement among recent generations must be set one important countervailing fact: Without any doubt the last ten years [1990–2000] have seen a substantial *increase* in volunteering and community service by young people.
>
> *(p. 265)*

Putnam acknowledges that the increase may stem from high school graduation requirements to engage in community service (or students' attempt to burnish their credentials on college applications). American youths' lower volunteerism than their counterparts in other countries (Salamon et al., 2018) supports the idea that a broad wave of civic involvement has not swept the US since 2000 (the immediate aftermath of the 9/11 attacks in 2001 being a possible exception).

Another explanation for the seemingly low civic engagement of American youth is that they actually are socially engaged, but in direct rather than organization-based volunteering. Watters (2004) coined the term "urban tribes" for tight-knit groups of friends (typically 4–12 of them) in their twenties and thirties, who are either single or dating. These tribes meet regularly, such as having weekly dinners at a restaurant and do various fun things. As Watters describes,

> [his] group of friends … came together to tackle group projects such as painting a living room, critiquing someone's rough cut of a documentary, or caring for someone who had fallen ill. We moved each other's furniture, talked each other through breakups, and attended each other's parents' funerals. Those who had money loaned it to those who didn't. Everything we owned, from books to tools to furniture to cars, was shared, or loaned or given away on an ongoing basis.
>
> *(p. 37)*

As one can see, volunteerism can take many forms. As the study by Cox and McAdams (2012) illustrates, it may be the meanings one takes away from volunteer experiences more so than the actions themselves that profoundly affect our lives. Ask not …

Military Service

Military service, though less common of an experience in the US than it used to be, can be a powerful experience in shaping young adults' lives. As Trace Evans (2015) writes in his first-person account, entitled "This Is What the First 36 Hours of Marine Boot Camp Is Like," each young recruit "is broken down to that of a whimpering boy, then rebuilt into what the Marine Corps wants in its warriors." Sleep deprivation, constantly being yelled at, having to clean up messes created specifically for your training, it's all there. Not to mention the concluding test, conducted over 54 hours in which soldiers "hike over 45 miles while taking on several obstacles that require strong problem-solving and teamwork," before going up a steep, 700-foot-tall hill (Kirkpatrick, 2019). With heavy backpacks. A television news story about an organization that puts on outdoor activities for veterans (Batman, 2020) quoted one as saying, "It's a brotherhood that's unbreakable and it's not going to change." Hart and Lancaster (2019) found indeed that, in a sample of US military members and veterans, respondents scored highly on multiple measures of bonding with the military (e.g., identity "fusion" or seeing one's identity as inseparable from the military; willingness to help veterans). The reason military experience is less common than before (in the US, at least) is, in part, the 1973 switch to an all-volunteer force instead of a military draft (Rostker, 2006). Whereas nearly 9% of the US population served in the military during World War II and roughly 2% did during the Korean and Vietnam Wars, only about half of 1% has done so in recent decades (Pew Research Center, 2011). For our purposes, we want to look specifically at 18–25-year-olds (roughly). Over the past 20 years, around 3% of this age group has served, 3.5–5% of men and 0.5–1% of women (Jekielek & Brown, 2005; National Center for Education Statistics, 2011; Statista, 2021b).[3] Kelty et al. (2010) observed that:

> Although military service might be playing a larger role in the transition to adulthood for women and for racial and ethnic minorities than it did in the

past, and might do so in the future for homosexuals, it is less inclusive across the socioeconomic spectrum than it was during periods of wartime conscription.

(p. 190)

Military service differs greatly around the world. The NationMaster (2003–2021) website lists every country's type of service (required or voluntary), age eligibility, and minimum commitment length. Findings on the psychological correlates of current or previous military service in veterans from countries other than the US will be discussed as different topics come up in the following paragraphs.

Perhaps the best-known effect of military combat exposure (and exposure to traumatic events such as violent victimization outside of the military) is post-traumatic stress disorder (PTSD). This disorder consists of recurrent intrusive thoughts and flashbacks, avoidance of perceived threatening situations, and arousal/emotional symptoms (Gates et al., 2012). Multiple studies of PTSD prevalence have been conducted in the aftermath of each of four wars: Vietnam (which took place mainly in the 1960s and 1970s), the first Gulf War (1991), Afghanistan (2001–2021), and Iraq (2003–2011) (Gates et al., 2012). More than half of these studies have shown 10% or more of the studied veterans to meet criteria for PTSD at the time of the studies, a trend that was especially strong for Afghanistan/Iraq veterans (Gates et al., 2012). Gates and colleagues highlighted one particularly strong study of US veterans of the Afghanistan and Iraq wars (e.g., with a representative sample of veterans) that yielded a 14% rate of diagnosis (Tanielian & Jaycox, 2008). Gates et al. also examined PTSD in veterans outside the US. These studies, featuring UK veterans of Afghanistan and Iraq, produced lower PTSD rates, as did most studies of Australian, British, and Canadian soldiers from earlier wars.

Substance use is, of course, another concern. In response to heavy substance use during the Vietnam War,

> From 1972 onward, the Department of Defense has issued a series of policy directives aimed at prevention and treatment of all substance abuse among military personnel ... The zero tolerance policy for drugs was indeed effective in lowering rates of illicit drug use from 36.7% in 1980 to 6.9% in 2002, but heavy alcohol use has remained fairly constant between 1980 and 2002 [20–25%]. These statistics indicate that the military's policies and education programs regarding alcohol problems, while positive in intent, have not been all that successful in curbing heavy and binge drinking.
>
> *(Moore et al., 2007)*

Moore and colleagues also informed readers that

> It is important to note that the evidence suggests that the vast majority of drinking by members of the military occurs during off-duty time. However, as a perpetually on-call occupation, the division between work and leisure for the military is not as clear-cut as it is for other professions.

Ames and Cunradi (2004) compiled statistics on binge (5-plus drink) episodes in men and women within the different US military services, compared to civilians (Figure 11.2). In men, members of each military service engaged in greater binge

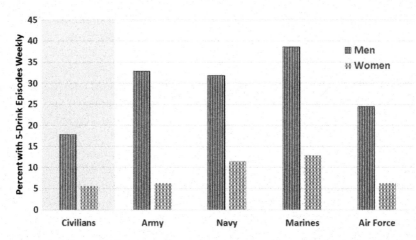

FIGURE 11.2 Percentage of 18–25-year-olds exhibiting weekly binge (5-plus drink) episodes in the past 30 days, according to military branch (or civilians status) and gender.
Source: Based on data presented in Ames and Cunradi (2004) from the 2001 National Household Survey on Drug Abuse and 2002 Department of Defense Survey of Health Related Behaviors Among Military Personnel.

drinking than did civilians. Among women, only those in the Navy and Marines exceeded civilians' level. Also, despite the expression "drunken sailor," Navy men were a few percentage points lower than the Marines and essentially tied with the Army. Navy women were just a little below the Marines, but higher than the other groups.

Researchers have also studied the romantic relationships in members of the military. Whereas some soldiers may be totally single/unpartnered, others may be married/partnered with fellow service members and yet others may be married/partnered with someone outside the military. According to Regnerus and Uecker (2011), young adults in the military are more likely to be married than same-age civilians (although some of the data are a bit old, e.g., late 1990s, early 2000s). Summarizing research by Jay Teachman, for example, Regnerus and Uecker note,

> At age 25 … 66 percent of white male soldiers had been married, compared with 51 percent of their civilian counterparts. Among African American men, the contrast is even more striking: by age 25, 57 percent of them had married, compared with only 25 percent of their civilian counterparts.
>
> *(p. 196)*

Finally, Regnerus and Uecker also cite research from Jennifer Lundquist. Her findings regarding male soldiers vs. civilians are similar to Teachman's. Further,

> The same pattern she documents for men holds true among women as well. Women in the military marry earlier and have more children than their civilian counterparts. The vast majority of married military women (86 percent) were wed to fellow soldiers.
>
> *(p. 196)*

Whether it is the early ages of marriages or the stress of being in the military (especially with soldiers being deployed away from their partners, spouses, and/or families, and facing possible life-threatening situations) or something else, military marriages have some notable difficulties. Specifically, divorce, marital conflict, and domestic violence have reached high levels in the military (Van Epp et al., 2008). To address and try to prevent these developments, a team of relationship educators and researchers (Van Epp et al., 2008) created and evaluated a program for single Army soldiers. Pre-post results of the evaluation study showed participants to increase their sense of importance of getting to know their partner. decrease some unrealistic beliefs (that "choosing a partner should be easy," p. 343), and increase their sense of knowledge and confidence about applying principles from the program to their own relationships, after experiencing the program.

Military experience may also intersect with some people's parenting. As seen in previous chapters, Silva (2013) interviewed a large number of working-class young adults on how they coped with economic and other challenges in their lives. One woman, a single mother who had joined the National Guard and was facing a possible third deployment to Iraq, told Silva she was torn between accepting the deployment or seeking a discharge to avoid it. Going back to Iraq would allow her to earn extra money (including combat pay, which is higher than the usual pay) to "do more for my son." On the other hand, she noted, "I missed the first two years of my son's life and now I might have to leave again. It's just rough. You can't win." Reflecting on this mother's dilemma, Silva observes that "the only path to economic stability and a better life for her son requires her to put her life in danger and to leave him" (quotes from p. 77).

Finally, the skills and values learned through military service can lead to other forms of community engagement. According to Núñez and Flanagan (2016), "military training socializes one into norms of service and solidarity and teaches members to overcome intergroup hostilities" (p. 488). In addition, the military instills organizational skills (e.g., planning) that are helpful for community work. Specific examples of military veterans' involvement in other forms of community activities are discussed in the closing section of this chapter.

To conclude this section, it is worth considering the ways in which military service may or may not fit with the typical experiences of emerging adulthood. Military training is obviously highly structured, especially in Marine boot camp (e.g., wake-up time, the extent of communication soldiers can have with their families). According to Kelty et al. (2010), this structure benefits soldiers in many ways, such as building personal responsibility and independence (i.e., forcing them to solve problems by themselves) and promoting personal growth. However, opportunities for EA-type free exploration (e.g., having late-night discussions with your buddies about the meaning of life) would seem to be limited. When I have discussed this issue with my classes, however, some students have pointed out that the military can expand soldiers' horizon in some ways. New recruits will almost certainly meet fellow recruits from different parts of the country, different race–ethnicities, and different social, cultural, and religious backgrounds. Further, in the case of overseas deployments, soldiers will be exposed to other cultures.

Political Involvement

Youth political involvement is a seeming paradox. On the one hand, teens and young adults have played major roles in many significant protest movements in the

US and elsewhere. On the other hand, however, in the US and most other countries, in election after election, a smaller percentage of the eligible 18–25-year-olds shows up to vote than the percentage of older citizens. This section provides additional detail on these trends and examines possible reasons for them.

Four major US protest movements of the past 60 years are the Civil Rights and anti-Vietnam War protests of the 1960s and Black Lives Matter (BLM) and Occupy Wall Street protests of the 2010s and 2020s. In all, college students and other young people played large roles. Among the catalyzing events of the Civil Rights Movement (along with Rosa Parks, a Black woman, refusing to give up her seat at the front of a Montgomery, Alabama, bus in 1955) was a series of daily sit-ins by four Black students in 1960 at North Carolina A&T University in the Whites-only section of a lunch counter in downtown Greensboro (Anderson, 2015; Conner, 2021; Wilson, 2020). During the nearly six months the protests went on, increasing numbers of students, not just from A&T but from high schools and other colleges as well, joined in. Antiwar protests, starting later in the decade, were heavily based on college campuses. An interactive map of Vietnam-era antiwar protests compiled by the University of Washington shows the many that took place in college towns (Miller, 2015–present). The Black Lives Matter movement (inspired by certain deaths of Black people at the hands of police or private citizens) is likewise disproportionately populated by young adults. In a 2020 survey conducted after the death of George Floyd in Minneapolis, 18–29-year-olds comprised 41% of those who reported that "they attended a protest focused on race or racial equality in the last month," whereas this age group makes up only 19% of all US adults (Barroso & Minkin, 2020). Finally, 64% of participants in the Occupy Wall Street movement against economic inequality were under 35 years old (*The Week*, 2015).[4]

Internationally, protests prominently featuring young adults have occurred in many countries, sometimes even resulting in the fall of the current government (Honwana, 2013; Maganga, 2020). According to Maganga,

> many young people in different countries in Africa have demonstrated against dictatorships, the extension of presidential term limits, the lack of transparency during elections and unpopular socio-economic policies. In many of these protests, youth movements have managed to gain considerable success in removing political leaders and effecting policy change, but they have failed to bring systematic political, social and economic change because of a lack of influence in post-protest politics and government.

Honwana specified that these protests have occurred in Sudan, Angola, Burkina Faso, Malawi, and Nigeria, along with other nations. Honwana contends that "The recent wave of youth protests can best be understood in the context of this generation's struggles for economic, social, and political emancipation" so they can validate themselves as adults (p. 2429). What Honwana cites as protestors' "enthusiasm and energy" may also be possible contributors to their activity (p. 2441).

As noted, however, the political activity young adults exhibit in protests rarely seems to translate into electoral participation. Election analysts typically divide voters (and potential voters) into broad age groups such as 18–29, 30–44, 45–59, and 60 and older or something similar (United States Elections Project [USEP], not dated). The US has held 18 national elections from 1986 to 2020.[5] And in each and every one of these 18 elections (nine presidential and nine midterm), 18–29-year-olds have shown up at the lowest rate. In 2020, for example, nearly 80% of eligible voters aged 60 and over voted, whereas only slightly over 50% of those in the 18–29 age group did (45–59-year-olds had the second-highest voting rate, slightly over 70%, and 30–44-year-olds had the third-highest, roughly 65%). Now, some years are better than others, relatively speaking, from the perspective of youth voting. In 2008, when the young (and to many observers, charismatic) Barack Obama was on the presidential ballot, the gap between the oldest (and most consistent) voters and the youngest voters was only 20% (roughly 70% vs. 50%), compared to the 30% difference in 2020.[6]

Smith and colleagues (2011) documented young adults' (18–23) low involvement with the political system through in-depth interviews, rather than simply voting behavior. Based on these interviews, Smith et al. deemed only 4% of these young adults to be "genuinely political." These were individuals who "expressed substantive knowledge of political matters, genuine interest in participating in politics, and specific descriptions of meaningful ways that they are civically or politically engaged" (p. 208). Participants in this category were also able to discuss particular issues with sophistication. Another 27% were labeled "marginally political." These participants "expressed some interest in politics, but it was far from clear how or even if they were actually civically or politically active" (p. 206). Even being generous and counting the marginally political as involved, therefore, only 31% of these young adults qualified. The other 69% fell into various categories of disengagement: disempowered (those with some political knowledge, but who felt incapable of impacting policy), 10%; distrustful (similarly, having political knowledge but citing a lack of trust in the political system as their reason for remaining on the sidelines), 19%; uninformed (those who claimed to not know enough about politics to be involved), 13%; and apathetic ("completely uninterested in politics," p. 197), 27%.

Scholars have also examined demographic differences in young adults' political involvement. As part of the same study in which Wray-Lake et al. (2020) examined community/volunteer activity (summarized above), they also investigated three types of political involvement (interest in government and current events; electoral participation [e.g., voting, working in a campaign]; and "political voice" [e.g., writing to a representative, demonstrating]). Political interest rose in Black, Hispanic, and White respondents from ages 18 to 30; it rose from 18 to 24 in Asian American participants, but then declined from 24 to 30. Electoral participation rose in all four racial–ethnic groups from 18 to 30, with the highest absolute levels being highest in African Americans. Political voice also rose from 18 to 30, with no absolute differences between racial–ethnic groups. Men reported greater absolute levels of political interest than did women by a fairly sizable margin; men also reported greater electoral participation and political voice than did women, but by much smaller differences. Syed and Mitchell (2016) suggest that "Gaining an understanding of how the sociopolitical context may affect their future leads minority youth to participate in efforts to reduce the impact of [structural and economic] barriers, both for others and for themselves" (p. 92). As some of the racial–ethnic differences found by Wray-Lake et al. suggest, therefore, minorities' efforts to fight structural barriers may, in part, take the form of political activity.

Many different theories of young adults' low voting and low involvement, some tested more than others through statistical analysis of survey data and some theories overlapping with each other, have been proposed (Table 11.1). Some of these theories are from journalists who cover politics, whereas others come from academic political scientists.

These theories generally locate the cause of young adults' voting or not voting in three domains: the individual young adult; socializing agents (e.g., parents, schools); or the political context (e.g., how inspiring the candidates are). Individual factors include young adults' degree of political identity formation (which Gentry [2018] models after Marcia's [1966, 1980] system of foreclosure, moratorium, achieved, and diffused), identification with a party (as opposed to being independent), sense of voting being a citizen's duty, sense of having a stake in the political/governmental system, ability to stay on top of one's voter registration, and sense of (dis)empowerment. Wattenberg (2015) and other researchers have documented that older age groups have a stronger sense that voting is a duty than do 18–29-year-olds. The idea of inspirational, hope-inducing candidates pertains not only to President Obama (as noted above), but also President Kennedy. Gentry (2018) found support for her "Three I's" theory through decades of US election-related polling. Young adults (18–24) who had more fully developed political identities, reported that they found one or both candidates in an election to inspire hope, and were not political independents showed higher turnout rates than those with less-developed political

TABLE 11.1 Theories of Why Young Adults Do Not Vote as to the Same Extent as Older Adults

Theory	Author
"Three I's": Voting most likely when a young adult has a strong political *identity*, an *inspirational* candidate is on the ballot who makes one feel hope, and one is not a political *independent* (which may reflect a lack of knowledge of the candidates and issues).	Gentry (2018)
Lack of socialization about the political system by parents and schools to build young students' interest and teens and young adults paying little attention to media coverage of politics.	Wattenberg (2015)
Recent generations do not perceive voting as being a citizen's duty to the same extent that older generations do.	Bennett et al. (2009); Blais (2000); Cramer & Bartels (2020); Dalton (2008)
"young people today do not feel they have much of a stake in society. Having children and owning property gives you a direct interest in how schools and hospitals are run, and whether parks and libraries are maintained."	DK (2014)
Schools do not prepare students to understand the political system.	Morris (2017)
"Younger people typically have busy more complicated lives and are more likely to find themselves in a situation where they are living in temporary accommodation and not registered to vote."	*Irish News* (2017)
"Any time a cause that people believe in becomes popular, the blowback from the cynics of society tear it at the seams. As a result, young people feel impotent. We feel like there's no hope that we could ever organize in a way that would change anything." (Similar to Smith et al.'s [2011] sense of disempowerment.)	Montenegro (2014)

identities, who did not find the candidates to inspire hope, and were independents. Other theories, to my knowledge, do not have as much research support.

A potentially important dynamic that might either enhance or hinder young adults' political involvement – and thus is not yet a definitive theory – is the role of communications technology (e.g., smartphones, social media) in young adults' political activity. Kahne and Middaugh (2012) noted that "Some observers argue that young people's use of social media will help spur activism, as in the Arab Spring; others worry that social media distract youth from the world around them. What we found is somewhere in between" (p. 54). Whereas participation on sites such as Facebook does not appear to spur political activity directly, a select group of young people who participate in non-political online interest groups (e.g., sports, hobbies) may have this activity spill over into political activity (Kahne & Middaugh, 2012).[7]

Religious Involvement

The final form of young-adult engagement with the broader society we will discuss is religious involvement. McNamara Barry and Abo-Zena (2014) collected a series of works from different authors for the volume *Emerging Adults' Religiousness and Spirituality*. McNamara Barry and Abo-Zena introduce the book with this quote:

> Although most children in the United States are raised in a faith tradition, their outward religious expression declines significantly by the time they are in their twenties, even though many claim religion and spirituality to be important.
>
> *(p. 3)*

The quote illustrates some of the core issues in the study of religiosity. One is the distinction between outward behaviors (e.g., attending religious services) and inner beliefs. Another is the continuity (or lack thereof) between the religious faith in which one was raised and the beliefs they hold as they become adults. Arnett (2015) concurs with McNamara Barry and Abo-Zena (2014), writing that "emerging adults' religious beliefs have only a limited connection to their religious training in childhood and adolescence, a reflection of their resolve to think for themselves and decide on their own beliefs" (pp. 212–213). In addition, according to Arnett, EA exposes individuals to new influences, such as college, which may prompt reconsideration of one's beliefs. Wuthnow (2007) agrees that those who go to college are less likely to hold certain beliefs (e.g., that the Bible should be interpreted literally) than are those who did not matriculate. Wuthnow also notes, however, that college education is linked to extensive community involvement (in general), so for that reason, college graduates' attendance at religious services remains strong. Hence, studying religiosity in emerging adulthood may not be as straightforward as one may have thought.

As usual, I have some statistics to start us off. First, the US rates as one of the more religious nations in the world. Data on 18–24-year-olds in 41 countries from the World Values Survey (Lippman & McIntosh, 2010) were used to divide these nations into three categories (Table 11.2). The US appeared in the category with the second-highest religious intensity, with an extremely high percentage (93%) of its young adults reporting belief in God, but only around 50% each saying religion and

TABLE 11.2 Country Categories of Religiosity According to the World Values Survey

Category	Definition	Countries in the Category
High spirituality and religiosity	"75 percent or more of young adults believe in God and find both God and religion to be important in their lives"	Indonesia, Pakistan, Egypt, Iran, Nigeria, Philippines, Turkey, Bangladesh
High belief in God, moderate importance of God and religion in life	75 percent or more report belief in God, but below 75 percent say God or religion is important	Poland, Italy, Brazil, Argentina, Mexico, the US, Canada
Moderate belief in God, low importance of God and religion in life	"40–73 percent of young adults reported a belief in God, but neither God nor religion was important to more than about 10 percent"	Taiwan, Russia, Spain, Great Britain, France, Germany, Sweden

Based on results reported in Lippman and McIntosh (2010, pp. 2–3).

God were "very" important in their lives. Other nations in this second-highest category included the countries to the immediate north (Canada) and south (Mexico) of the US, along with Poland, Italy, Brazil, and Argentina. Lippman and McIntosh noted that many countries in the highest-intensity category "have a history of an influential dominant religion (e.g., Islam) and a developing economy" (p. 2). Many of the countries in the lowest-intensity religious category were in Europe.

Within the US, there is evidence, however, that 18–29-year-olds are less attached to organized religion than are older individuals. According to the Public Religion Research Institute's (PRRI) 2020 American Values Atlas (PRRI, 2021), 36% of the 18–29 age group reported being religiously unaffiliated, compared to 25% for ages 30–49, 18% for ages 50–64, and 14% for 65 and older (for the percentages of Americans affiliating with different religious denominations, see PRRI [2021]). Lack of affiliation may not equate completely with absence of religious–spiritual beliefs, as someone could believe in a Supreme Being but not find any organized religion with which they are compatible. However, affiliation and belief probably are highly correlated. Other US surveys have asked directly about belief in God. One in 2012 by the Pew Research Center "showed that 31 percent of respondents under the age of 30 have doubts about the existence of God, compared to 9 percent of those polled who were 65 or older" (Jauregui, 2012).[8]

Chan et al. (2015) conducted a longitudinal study in Los Angeles, in which predominantly White, Hispanic, and Asian American participants were surveyed in 12th grade and two and four years after high school graduation. The study's purpose, in part, was to examine potential changes in participants' religious affiliations, religious identity (measured by items such as "I have a strong sense of belonging to my own religion," p. 1559), and attendance at religious services. In all racial–ethnic groups, smaller percentages reported having a religious affiliation four years after high school than during 12th grade. Hispanic students had the highest rate of affiliation in 12th grade, nearly 75%, but four years later, it had declined to 50%. Religious attendance declined in all racial–ethnic groups, but only slightly. Strength of religious identity showed a gender difference; female participants declined only slightly in their religious identity over the four years of the study, whereas male participants declined more sharply.

Two additional studies examined demographic characteristics associated with higher or lower frequency of attendance at religious services. Petts (2009) looked at trajectories of religious service attendance from ages 10 to 25 among a subgroup of participants with high early attendance, with special emphasis beginning at age 20, when many participants had moved out of their parents' home (Figure 11.3). As can be seen, those who had married by age 20 increased their religious attendance (on average) compared to other groups, whereas those who were cohabiting decreased their attendance. To me, the form of the graph warrants the alliterative name, the "Petts Pitchfork."

Wuthnow (2007) investigated how four factors – gender, age (from 20 to 45), getting married, and becoming a parent – were related to religious service attendance (going weekly or almost weekly). Certain trends were clearly evident. Married people attended more frequently than did their unmarried counterparts, women attended more than men, attendance rose with age, and those who had children went more than did their childless counterparts. Looking at combinations of characteristics, the highest attendance – around 40–45% participating weekly or almost weekly – belonged to women in their thirties or forties who were married and had children.

Thus far, we have not considered characteristics of the churches, synagogues, mosques, temples, or other houses of worship in attracting members and guests. Houses of worship vary greatly in physical characteristics, leadership style, and philosophy. Some are "megachurches," such as Lakewood Church, which occupies a former professional basketball arena in Houston, Texas, and Saddleback Church in Orange County, California. Megachurches are typically defined as houses of worship with at least 2,000 weekly attendees, although some attract between 10,000 and 44,000. Also, although any religion can have large attendance, the term megachurch tends to be applied only to Protestant Christian churches (Fieldstadt, 2018). For people who prefer something not so large, of course, there are numerous neighborhood houses of worship, which appear every several blocks in some US cities. According to one study, 90% of houses of worship have 350 or fewer attendees, with the average congregation size being 75 (these and many other statistics are available in the National Congregations Study, 2019).

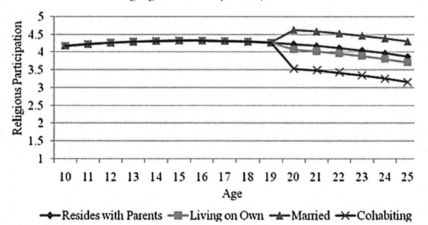

FIGURE 11.3 Trajectories between ages 10 and 25 in frequency of attending religious services, by relationship and residential statuses starting at age 20.
Source: From Petts (2009, Figure 2 in original). Reprinted with permission.

Some people may want something even smaller than traditional neighborhood houses of worship, however. In fact, some very small congregations have been popping up in recent years that cater to emerging adults' sense of exploration, experimentation, and wanting to decide on things for themselves. By coincidence, these congregations fittingly are called "emerging churches" (Bishop, 2009). Some do not even have their own space, instead renting out a meeting room in a larger church for a few hours each week. Bishop captures the environment at one emerging church in Minneapolis, Minnesota. Participants decorate the room with "small 'prayer stations' in the corners, with cushions, candles, and mosaics of Jesus," and a band plays "rockish praise songs" that resemble the sound of the Eagles and Grateful Dead. At an emerging church in Louisville, Kentucky, refreshments include "Ding Dongs, Hostess Cup Cakes, Twinkies, and fireplug-size jugs of Big K cola." Theologically speaking, emerging churches are "full of questions and doubt; the attitude is purposely non-judgmental." Bishop adds, though, "That's not to say the emerging church is squishy on faith or the Bible," with some of the ministers at emerging churches trained at traditional theological seminaries (quotes from Bishop, 2009, pp. 276–281). These features may allow some young adults to find their niche in terms of religion and spirituality. Emerging churches mainly appear in big cities and so probably do not reach many people in smaller towns like the one I'm in. Based on my unscientific polling (asking students in my class), only one student reported ever going to one.

Conclusion on Community Engagement

As I noted earlier, the four types of community engagement discussed in this chapter overlap with each other in various ways. In their overview of community involvement in emerging adulthood, Núñez and Flanagan (2016) note, for example, that

> the likelihood of voting is 23% higher for veterans compared to nonveterans (with the possible exception of veterans from the Vietnam War). Those veterans of the wars in Iraq and Afghanistan who spent most of their time on planning and reconstruction showed increased likelihood of volunteering and serving other military families back home compared to veterans who took part in combat.
>
> *(p. 489)*

Núñez and Flanagan (2016) also discuss community engagement from the perspective of immigrants and lower-income American youth. According to these authors, "Immigrant youths … engage in unique forms of civic participation, including serving as cultural brokers and translators for older and younger members of their communities and organizing to change policies that affect their ethnic group" (p. 482). An example of the latter might include working to improve undocumented immigrants' access to higher education (Núñez & Flanagan, 2016). Regarding socioeconomic class, Núñez and Flanagan (2016) note that the kinds of experiences during childhood and adolescence that socialize individuals into later community engagement (e.g., student government) "are unevenly distributed based on the social class and racial groups to which youth belong" (p. 486). More specifically, impoverished communities typically lack the civic organizations to inspire and promote youth involvement. Despite these potential hindrances to participation, however, Núñez and Flanagan (2016) report that roughly 30% of participants in US service programs overseen by AmeriCorps (e.g., environmental and health programs) are from disadvantaged backgrounds.

One final point about community engagement is that it may be good for our psychological health (Núñez & Flanagan, 2016). Although cautioning that it is difficult to distinguish whether community activity improves our health or people in good health are drawn toward volunteering, Núñez and Flanagan (2016) document that involvement and health do tend to go together in some fashion. As they write, "volunteering in adolescence and young adulthood enhances life satisfaction, confidence, self-esteem, sense of control over one's life, hope, optimism, and happiness and decreases depression, anxiety, distress, and antisocial behavior" (p. 485).

Review

We have:

SEVEN theories of why young adults do not vote and follow politics to the same extent as do older adults (Table 11.1).

FOUR aspects of religious attachment: belief in God, importance of religion to the self, religious identity, and attendance at religious services. Importance and identity overlap somewhat, as people with a strong religious identity would also likely state that religion was important to them.

THREE percent of US 18–24-year-olds who have served in the military at any given time in the past 20 years.

TWO types of volunteering: through an organization and providing direct service to others (Salamon et al., 2018) and TWO general types of military service in the US: active duty (full-time) and the Reserves/National Guard (part-time, but which the military can convert to full-time if needed).

ONE type of reaction to going on a Spring Break volunteer trip to help low-income orphans in another country, namely *personal transformation*, that led college students to stay involved with this cause (Cox & McAdams, 2012).

Possible Class Activities

1. Clary and colleagues (1998) developed a questionnaire to assess people's possible reasons for volunteering. This questionnaire is available online at: https://generosityresearch.nd.edu/assets/13636/clary_snyder_volunteer_function_inventory_scale.pdf. Your instructor may wish to have students complete the questionnaire on their own time and then discuss in class or have students fill it out during class time.

2. I have found that nothing captures the essence of military life like having a veteran in the classroom (which I am not) to share their experiences and answer questions. If the instructor or a student has served and is willing to share, that's

great. If not, the instructor may know people around campus who would be willing to come into class (in person or virtually) and speak.

3. The class can discuss the different theories of low youth political involvement (Table 11.1) and see which theory or theories students find most plausible.

Notes

1 In the US, for example, many states offer extensive opportunities for early voting and voting by mail. However, not all do. Further, due to an insufficient number of voting locations in some communities, waiting times can be quite long (Quealy & Parlapiano, 2021).

2 My parents, both of whom were born in the 1930s, are/were highly active in civic engagement. Both of them served for many years on committees to raise money for charitable and cultural organizations. My father (who lived to age 83) maintained his weekly card games until late in his life, and my mother (who is still alive) continues to volunteer.

3 US military service is typically classified as either active duty (full-time employment in the military) or National Guard and Reserves (part-time commitments that the military can convert to full-time combat deployments if additional troops are needed) (US Department of Veterans Affairs, 2015). As of 2020, the US military consisted of roughly 1.4 million active-duty personnel and 1 million (combined) Guard and Reserves (Statista, 2021c). The statistics reported in the text combine all these forms of service. Statista (2021b) reports that there were 600,000 US active-duty personnel age 25 and under in 2020 (with the minimum age being 18; 17 with parental permission). Based on the overall ratio of active-duty to Guard/Reserve personnel, we can assume there were roughly 450,000 Guard/Reserve personnel under 25, for 1,050,000 total military personnel under 25. The closest figure I could find for the relevant total (civilian and military) population was 30 million among 18–24-year-olds in 2020 (Annie E. Casey Foundation, 2021). Dividing the 1,050,000 by 30 million (again, a rough calculation) yields 3.5% of US 18–24/25-year-olds serving in the military in 2020.

4 Anderson (2015) discusses the emergence of protest and political organizing groups for high school students, typically those asking for a voice in school policies that affect them. Should these kinds of groups thrive, they will likely provide a training experience for future young-adult protesters.

5 US House, US Senate, and state elections for governor and legislatures occur in November of every even-numbered year. Presidential elections occur every four years. Years such as 2012, 2016, and 2020, with both presidential and lower-office elections, are known as presidential years. Those without presidential elections, such as 2010, 2014, and 2018 are known as midterm or off-year elections.

6 Wattenberg (2015) notes that some countries have compulsory voting laws. Even without requiring people to show up at the polls (which many people would consider excessive), there are countries that stand out for their high youth turnout. Wattenberg notes that "Italy, Austria, Sweden, Denmark, and the Netherlands have recently been successful in getting young people to vote in satisfactory numbers without compelling them to do so. Why these countries have not experienced the problem of low youth turnout is an interesting puzzle that I leave to others to investigate" (p. 101).

7 I thank Texas Tech communications faculty member Melissa Gotlieb who, through her guest lecture a few years ago in my Development in Young Adulthood class, drew my attention to the role of communications media in young adults' political involvement.

8 Jauregui (2012) interviewed Father Jonathan Morris, a Catholic priest in New York, who offered his view of what it means to doubt the existence of God. As Jauregui wrote, Morris "included himself and Mother Teresa among the ranks of people who have had doubt about their faith, recalling that the famous nun's diaries were 'full of spiritual conflict.' Morris also said that questioning one's faith could be a positive thing leading to a mature acceptance of their beliefs." Anyone remember the term from Chapter 4, "Identity," for continually re-examining your identity? It's exploration in depth.

12

Government Policies to Regulate and Assist Emerging Adults

Providing educational, economic, social, and health supports will help young adults assume adult roles, develop marketable skills, and adopt healthy lifelong habits that will benefit them, their children, and the nation. ... [Young adults] are too rarely treated as a distinct population in policy, program design, and research. Instead, they are often grouped with adolescents or, more often, with all adults.

— *National Research Council (2015, p. 1)*

In the US and other countries, the government and young adults interact in two ways: government regulation of the age at which people (or companies) can do things (e.g., get a driver's license, buy alcohol, vote in elections), and government programs aimed at helping young people make the transition to adulthood (e.g., financial assistance for independent housing). This brief chapter reviews these topics.

Age-Related Regulations

Eligibility ages for "adult" behaviors vary for different domains of life. In the US, one can obtain a driver's license at 16; vote, sign a contract, and serve in the military at 18; buy alcohol or tobacco products at 21 (the age for both previously was 18); and rent a car at age 25.[1] Many observers see little logic or consistency in these different age thresholds. Greenblatt (2010) observed the following:

> To many young people, rental-car restrictions [requiring one to be 25] are more than an annoyance. They're also a confusing contradiction, in terms of what society expects of them. After all, states trust people to drive at a much younger age … By the time adolescents become adults, they are accustomed to such inconsistent treatment. Practically from puberty, young people are bombarded with mixed signals about the scope of their rights and the depth of their responsibilities.

DOI: 10.4324/9781003156567-16

As a regulation for both businesses and young adults, the Credit CARD Act (Cothern, 2021) limited companies' ability to issue credit cards to individuals under 21 (see Chapter 7). For example, companies must consider applicants' independent ability to pay. This regulation appears to be linked directly to young adults' decision-making abilities.

Back in Chapter 5, we discussed how certain "finishing touches" on the development of a mature and efficient brain continue into people's twenties. Greenblatt (2010) takes up this issue, noting that whereas brain development research might suggest delaying the ages at which we allow people to drive or purchase alcohol or tobacco, "The conclusion that 25 might be the most scientifically defensible age for any of those things is simply a nonstarter politically." Instead, legal determinations of maturity are "rooted in a mix of culture, convenience and historical precedent."

As societal awareness of emerging adulthood – and brain development within this stage – grows, it is possible that public opinion toward changing some legal age thresholds may shift. After all, the argument for lowering the US voting age from 21 to 18 – because soldiers could be sent to risk their lives in the Vietnam War at 18 but did not have a say in the policy through voting until age 21 – carried the day in 1971. That year, ratification of the 26th Amendment to the US Constitution lowered the voting age to 18.

Government Policies/Programs to Ease the Transition to Adulthood

Among OECD countries (those with the most advanced economies; Kenton, 2020), there is great variation in the degree to which government assists young people in their transition to adulthood (Thévenon, 2015). Such assistance may cover areas such as housing, employment, tertiary (higher) education, and childrearing. To "examine how countries are helping young adults to enter into adult life, i.e. to live out of parental home, pursue their studies, enter the labour market and getting access to economic independence" (p. 6), Thévenon conducted elaborate statistical analyses to classify 36 OECD countries according to the extent of government (vs. private or family) assistance to young people (Table 12.1). Placement in the categories depicted in Table 12.1 is approximate, with some countries exhibiting properties of two categories. For example, the US, Australia, Portugal, and some eastern European countries, which were classified as having comparatively high but limited assistance, arguably could also have been classified as having lower government housing and education assistance.

As shown in Table 12.1, Nordic and Scandinavian countries (first column) tend to be the most generous in government spending on young adults, whereas southern Europe/Mediterranean countries (fourth column) are the least generous. Perhaps, at least in part, because of the lack of housing assistance from countries in the fourth column, grown children tend to live at home the longest (Thévenon, 2015). Nations in the second and third columns tend to rely more on private funding (e.g., corporate foundations) and families themselves to assist young adults. The following sections go into a little more depth on some examples of government programs.

TABLE 12.1 Classification of Countries According to Their Extent of Government Assistance to Help Young People Make the Transition to Adulthood

Considerable Public Spending and Awarding of Grants	Comparatively High Public and Private Assistance, but Somewhat Limited	Low Public Benefits, Instead Indirect Aid (Money to Families to Distribute among Themselves)	Lower Levels of Government Housing Benefits and Education Spending
Denmark	United States	Slovak Republic	Italy
Finland	Australia	Czech Republic	Spain
Iceland	United Kingdom	Estonia	Greece
France	Canada	Germany	
Netherlands	New Zealand	Ireland	
Sweden		Belgium	
		(and many others)	

Source: Based on Thévenon (2015, Figure 1).

Housing Assistance for Young Adults in Sweden

Sweden is one country known for providing government assistance to help lower-income young adults (18–28) obtain their own housing. According to a European Commission document (not dated),

> If you are between 18 and 28, you can get housing allowance for housing costs exceeding SEK [Swedish krona] 1,800 [approximately $200 US] and for a maximum surface area of 60 m² of dwelling space. The most you can receive is SEK 1,300 [$140 US]. You must live and be registered at the address where you are applying for the allowance. There are some exceptions to this requirement.
>
> If you live alone, you must earn less than SEK 86,720 [$9,500 US] in the year in which you apply for the allowance. If you are married or cohabiting, your combined income must be less than SEK 103,720 [$11,000 US]. Income may in this case be salary, but it also includes other remuneration such as scholarships and study grants.

Grown children in Sweden indeed leave their parents' home at a young age: "The most common age to leave home is between 18 and 19, compared to the [European Union] average of 26" (Savage, 2019). However, the trend does not stem only from government housing assistance in Sweden. Citing demographer Gunnar Andersson, Savage notes that

> Sweden's "culture of individualism" dates back centuries, with teenagers in rural communities typically leaving home to go and work on another farm. In more recent years the norm of young people living alone has, [Andersson] says, remained realistic thanks to Sweden's strong welfare state which, in theory, should enable them to have access to affordable housing, healthcare and education without relying on relatives or partners for help.

Health Insurance in the US

Health insurance in the US comes from government programs (e.g., Medicare for adults 65 years and older and Medicaid for low-income individuals of any age) and private for-profit and non-profit insurance companies. More Americans (47%) receive their health insurance through their employers, who contract with a private insurer, than in any other way (Hiltzik, 2016). Prior to the passage of the Affordable Care Act (ACA; also known as Obamacare) in 2010, "dependent children often 'aged out' of their parents' health plan at age 19, or 22 if they were full-time students" (Andrews, 2013). Among its many provisions, the ACA required insurance companies to allow grown children to remain on their parents' plans until age 26. Shortly after the ACA went into effect, 7.8 million young adults ages 19–25 who previously would have been on their own to find health insurance now had it through their parents (Andrews, 2013). And, because young adults are generally healthy and may not have perceived themselves to need health insurance, many of them may not even have sought out health insurance before the ACA. According to US Census Bureau (2018) data, the uninsured rate for 25-year-olds dropped from roughly 35% in 2010 to 26% in 2013 to 17% in 2015.

Aging Out of Foster Care in the US

According to a definition provided by the Texas Children's Commission (TCC, 2015),

> Foster care is … when the state takes custody of your child and places him in someone else's home. Foster parents … are approved by the state to care for children in their home. So, when your child can't live safely at home and there is no appropriate relative or family friend who is willing and able to care for your child, [Child Protective Services, CPS] will put your child in foster care. This means that some other adult will be taking care of your child for you.

As implied in this statement, foster-care placement occurs only after CPS has convinced a judge that the removal of a child from their parental home is necessary to preserve the child's safety or both parents have consented to the removal (TCC, 2015). The Texas chapter of Court Appointed Special Advocates (CASA, 2019) notes also that "Ultimately, the goal of foster care is to safely reunite a child with their family of origin, but sometimes that is not an option and the parents' rights are terminated." Following termination of parental rights, some children may be adopted, either by their foster parents or other parents (CASA, 2019).[2]

A 2007 *New York Times* article on foster care began on a poignant note:

> When current and former foster children formed a group to help youths who had turned 18 and were "aging out" of the system, one of the first things they did was hold a luggage drive … "We saw that a lot of the kids were taking their clothes out in garbage bags," said Chilton Brown, 23, a former foster child who spent ages 3 to 18 as a ward of the state, bouncing around 15 family homes or group residences.
>
> *(Eckholm, 2007)*

Being in that type of situation clearly makes those who age out of foster care a vulnerable population (Osgood et al., 2010).[3] Alluding to the family problems that led to children being put into the foster-care system in the first place, Osgood and colleagues (2010) noted that "After the difficulties that youth in foster care have faced earlier in life, their need for continuing assistance from adults is no doubt greater than that of most other youth" (p. 213).

Many states have since acted to make the transition out of foster care and into adulthood somewhat less difficult, offering transition programs (e.g., housing, counseling) and even extending the age to which these youths can remain in care. The *Times* article presented the following statistics on the 24,000 annual aged-out foster youth (as of 2007):

> Four in ten were high school graduates. The average youth had been unemployed half the time since leaving care; most jobs were in fast food, averaging just $600 per month. More than one in four males had spent time in jail.
>
> *(Eckholm, 2007)*

According to the US government's Office of Planning, Research, and Evaluation (OPRE, 2018),

> In 2008, the [federal] Fostering Connections to Success and Increasing Adoptions Act amended Title IV-E of the Social Security Act by giving states the option to extend the age of eligibility for federally funded foster care to 21. In doing so, the federal government provided states with a financial incentive to allow young people to remain in foster care until their 21st birthday.

To remain eligible for this federal funding, states were required to ensure that youth in the program remained active in education, job training, and/or employment (OPRE, 2018). At least one state, Washington, has created a system for aiding aged-out foster youth (up through age 23), which it calls the Independent Youth Housing Program (Washington State Department of Commerce, not dated). The program provides funding for rent, utilities, and other living expenses, with youth also required to participate in planning their futures (i.e., working with a case manager and on independent-living goals).

General Conclusions on Programs to Facilitate the Transition to Adulthood

The Child Trends organization (Hadley et al., 2010) published a list of programs that research has shown to work, not work, or show mixed results in aiding older youths' transition to adulthood. Effective programs include education and employment training for low-income youth; mentoring; case management; and childcare for those with children. As you may have noticed, most of the programs and laws reviewed above are *targeted*. In other words, they apply only to lower-income or vulnerable populations (e.g., foster youth). An exception among the discussed policies is the US law requiring insurance companies to continue covering grown children on their parents' health-insurance policies, which applies to all families with health insurance. Such programs are known as *universal*.[4] In an era in which federal government spending (and budget deficits) have increased tremendously to help the public cope with COVID-19 (in the US, at least), targeting programs to the neediest people (known as means-testing) may seem most logical. Zhou (2021), however, makes a case for universal programs, arguing that "Though they're usually framed as ways of curbing government spending, means-tested benefits are often more expensive to provide, on average, than universal benefits, simply because of the administrative support needed to vet and process applicants." Also, notes Zhou, targeted/means-tested benefits impose many burdens on potential recipients to document their income and other assets. Some means-tested programs are said to require the completion of a 17-page form or 90-minute interview, as well as showing as many as 10 documents about one's assets (Zhou, 2021). Because emerging adulthood is a relatively new stage of life (dating back to Arnett [2000]), it is likely that countries, states, and cities will continue having policy discussions on how much the healthy development of young adults should fall to the young adults themselves, their parents, companies, and governments.

Notes

1 One can readily find lists on the internet of legal rights, privileges, and responsibilities that take effect at different ages. Endlich Heffernan (2020) lists 50 things one can do in the US upon turning 18. The list contains many prerogatives that likely never would have occurred to most observers, such as "Use a meat/deli slicer at a grocery store job" and "Buy spraypaint." At 21, among other things, you can gamble in a casino, obtain a pilot's license, and become an Uber driver (Allen, 2020).

2 These summaries of foster care and adoption should not be taken as proper legal advice. Those interested in becoming foster or adoptive parents should meet with a qualified attorney. Also, the above descriptions apply only to the US state of Texas. Policies may be different in other states or in other countries.

3 Osgood and colleagues (2010) include foster youth along with youth involved with the mental health, juvenile justice, (adult) criminal justice, special education, and health care systems, and runaway/homeless youth, as what they consider seven vulnerable populations. They also note that "One commonality is that males, the poor, and youth of color are over-represented in every group" (p. 214). These vulnerable groups appear to marry at the same rate as the general population, but the vulnerable groups are more likely to have children young (Osgood et al., 2010). Full discussion of policies aimed at all of these groups is beyond the scope of this book. To summarize briefly, however, Osgood et al. identify four areas for policy improvement: program eligibility criteria that are unnecessarily stringent and thus do not cover youth who could benefit from the program, inadequate funding, lack of coordination between the aforementioned systems, and lack of training in developmental issues (i.e., regarding the youths' age-specific needs) among those who provide services and work with youth.

4 In fact, because families with health insurance presumably are more advantaged than are those without insurance, this provision might be said to "target" better-off people.

13

Conclusion

You are now almost finished with your journey of learning about the journeys through emerging adulthood. Please note that "journeys" is plural, as there are many ways to move toward and through emerging adulthood. Remember the so-called "spaghetti graph" (Figure 1.2 in Chapter 1) that illustrates how, in virtually every arena of life (residential, as was depicted in Figure 1.2 but also romantic relationships, financial matters, etc.), people progress in different speeds and with different arcs. By "arc," I refer to the shape of a person's trajectory graph. The shape might be a relatively straight upward line if people make steady progress year after year (e.g., regular pay raises and promotions in one's job). Or the shape might loop up and down like a roller-coaster if, for example, someone begins college, drops out after a year, enters a community college and receives a two-year degree, takes time off from school to save enough money to switch to a state university, and finally completes a bachelor's degree. During some parts of the transition to adulthood, some individuals may feel "lost" in life, as did the 24-year-old caller to a television program whose question prompted Oprah Winfrey's answer:

> the 20s are the time when you're finding out who you are. And so if you're ever going to be lost, 24 is the time to be seeking and finding yourself. So don't – this is what I say to people in their 20s, don't beat yourself up about it … you always feel like you're not doing enough, you're not getting ahead. You wish you were doing more, and why – why aren't things more settled? They're not supposed to be in your 20s.
>
> *(CNN, 2003)*

Additional evidence of people's different journeys through emerging adulthood comes in the form of Osgood and colleagues' (2005) groupings of young adults into fast starters (in marriage, work, family formation), educated singles, parents without careers, and so forth. Some young people have helicopter parents or homes to which the grown children boomerang. People also form their identities differently from each other (if they form one at all), some by taking a moratorium period to explore different options extensively (do I want to become a lawyer or a teacher

DOI: 10.4324/9781003156567-17

or a journalist?) and then selecting the one that seems best (identity achievement). Others adopt their career plans or belief systems from their parents or other significant people in their lives (foreclosure).

Having listed all the ways in which individual young adults may differ from each other in their life pathways, I should note that there are also social and environmental forces that make individuals act more similarly to each other. If you grow up in Arkansas or Oklahoma, for example, chances are good that you will marry at a younger age than if you grow up in New York or Massachusetts, based on these states' typical ages at first marriage (Cahn & Carbone, 2010). Different parts of the US have different religious, cultural, and political norms, which we cannot avoid entirely (if we even wanted to). The country in which one grows up also is associated with typical marriage ages (Chapters 1 and 8). We are each partly an independent actor and partly the product of our environment.

Societal changes – seemingly happening more quickly than ever (Friedman, 2016) – are also affecting emerging-adult development. As Cherlin (2009) noted in the quote to open Chapter 8, never have patterns of marital, relationship, and family life transformed so quickly and in so many ways as they have in the past 50 years! Extensive change has also hit many other domains such as education and work. During my twenties, which I spent in undergraduate college (1980–1984) and graduate school (1984–1989), there were no websites, online classes, Zoom meetings of coworkers, smartphones, or dating apps. Yes, we had supermarkets in my youth, but not with the numerous choices of food products available today (Iyengar et al., 2000). Choices are everywhere today, from satellite television systems with 500 channels to types of religious services tailored for every preference (from emerging churches to megachurches). It is almost certain that these new developments have changed how young people today learn, work, develop romantic relationships, shop, and worship. Whether these changes are for the better is a separate matter!

How we deal with institutions also may have a dramatic impact on young–adult development, opportunities, and success. Silva (2013) documents the many ways in which bureaucratic hassles that do not faze socially advantaged individuals and families (who are used to filling out forms and interacting with authorities) can sometimes be insurmountable for those from more modest economic backgrounds. For example, one young man interviewed by Silva was unable to submit a financial-aid application to attend community college because his mother, apparently concerned over privacy and security, would not share with him the family financial information the application required.[1] Another young man experienced a delay of several weeks in receiving his GI Bill check to pay for textbooks, putting him behind in his classes.

However, despite all the possible hurdles they can encounter and all the twists and turns their journeys can take, most young people fare reasonably well – if not thrive – as they become adults. University of Michigan researcher John Schulenberg and colleagues examined longitudinal data on nearly 3,000 young people who had been doing well as high school seniors. Schulenberg and colleagues looked at how, by the time participants were 26, they were doing in the eight domains of education, employment, financial independence, romance, leisure, health/lifestyle, citizenship, and religion. More specifically, the Michigan researchers used a set of criteria[2] to categorize each participant at 26 as either "thriving," "making it" (i.e., doing OK) or "floundering" in each domain (Institute for Social Research, 2002b; Schulenberg et al., 2004). (Some readers may recall from Chapter 2 that Furstenberg and Kmec [2000] used a similar approach in their Philadelphia study.) Averaging over the eight domains, 36.5% of Schulenberg and colleagues' participants were thriving by age 26 (thriving in specific domains ranging from 28% in employment and health/lifestyle to 51% in romance). A higher percentage (43.6%) were making it (from 29% in the financial domain to 58% in employment). Finally, 19.8 were floundering (from 14% in employment to 29% financially). Although most individuals do well during their transition to adulthood, about 20% have a harder time.

During an appearance on NBC's Today Show (2010), Jeff Arnett was asked how parents could distinguish when a grown child of theirs was simply going through the typical ups and downs of young adulthood from when there might be a serious problem. "You need to worry if there's not a plan," Arnett suggested.

> If your emerging adult is not headed in any direction at all. If they're trying something at least, even if it's something that fails and they have to try again, they're doing fine and it may take them most of their 20s to find what they really want to do. But, if they don't have a plan, they seem depressed and defeated, then it's time to worry.

To end on a positive note, thanks to more than 20 years of research by Arnett and many others, the field knows a lot more about emerging-adult development than it did prior to 2000. Armed with this information, professionals who counsel young adults are now examining the best ways to reach this population (NeMoyer et al., 2020). Setbacks during the transition to adulthood are not uncommon, but most people's life trajectories eventually do point in an upward direction.

Notes

1 This is not to say that members of minority groups do not have perfectly valid reasons for being skeptical of providing their financial information to institutions. One recent example, of course, was the subprime home-lending scandal, in which banks were much more likely to give high-interest loans to Black applicants than to White applicants, even when credit scores were equal between the two groups (Baptiste, 2014).

2 Brief examples of these criteria include the following (Schulenberg et al., 2004). For romantic relationships, the researchers defined thriving as being engaged or married with no divorces; making it as cohabiting, dating at least twice a month, or remarried after a divorce; and floundering as dating once a month or less frequently. For health/lifestyle, they defined thriving as no cigarette smoking, marijuana use, or any other illegal drug use, and no binge drinking; making it as engaging in limited substance use; and floundering as two or more of these forms of substance use at ages 18, 22, and 26; or three or more forms of substance use at 26.

References

Abt, T. (2019). *Bleeding out: The devastating consequences of urban violence - and a bold new plan for peace in the streets*. New York: Basic Books.

Adkins, D. E., Wang, V., & Elder, Jr., G. H. (2009). Structure and stress: Trajectories of depressive symptoms across adolescence and young adulthood. *Social Forces*, *88*, 31–60. doi:10.1353/sof.0.0238

Allen, A. (2020). 21 things you can do at 21. *Society 19*. Retrieved from https://www.society19.com/things-you-can-do-at-21/

Allen, D. N., & Becker, M. L. (2019). Clinical interviewing. In G. Goldstein, D. N. Allen, & J. DeLuca (Eds.), *Handbook of psychological assessment* (pp. 307–336). Elsevier Academic Press. doi:10.1016/B978-0-12-802203-0.00010-9

Alsop, R. (2008). *The trophy kids grow up: How the Millennial Generation is shaking up the workplace*. Jossey-Bass.

Altucher, K. A. & Williams, L. B. (2003). Family clocks: Timing parenthood. In P. Moen (Ed.), *It's about time: Couples and careers* (pp. 49–59). ILR Press.

Amato, P. R. (2011). Transitions and sequences: Early family formation among women in emerging adulthood. In F. D. Fincham & M. Cui (Eds.), *Romantic relationships in emerging adulthood* (pp. 27–43). Cambridge University Press.

American Association of Community Colleges (2021). *Fast facts 2021*. Retrieved from https://www.aacc.nche.edu/wp-content/uploads/2021/03/AACC_2021_FastFacts.pdf

American College Health Association. (2021). *National College Health Assessment*. Retrieved from https://www.acha.org/NCHA/About_ACHA_NCHA/Overview/NCHA/About/About_NCHA.aspx?hkey=75eaa64f-e82c-4cfd-a19c-4e3f9bf126ee

American College of Obstetricians and Gynecologists. (2021). *Having a baby after age 35: How aging affects fertility and pregnancy*. Retrieved from https://www.acog.org/womens-health/faqs/having-a-baby-after-age-35-how-aging-affects-fertility-and-pregnancy

American Psychiatric Association. (2013). *Diagnostic and statistical manual of mental disorders* (5th edition).

APA Style. (2019). *Racial and ethnic identity*. American Psychological Association. Retrieved from https://apastyle.apa.org/style-grammar-guidelines/bias-free-language/racial-ethnic-minorities

Ames, G. M., & Cunradi, C. (2004). Alcohol use and preventing alcohol-related problems among young adults in the military. *Alcohol Research and Health*, *28*, 252–257. Retrieved from https://pubs.niaaa.nih.gov/publications/arh284/252-257.pdf

Anderson, K. G. (2010). Life expectancy and the timing of life history events in developing countries. *Human Nature, 21*, 103–123. https://doi.org/10.1007/s12110-010-9087-z

Anderson, M. D. (2015, November 23). The other student activists: Throughout history, protests spearheaded by teens have helped facilitate change, too. *The Atlantic*. Retrieved from https://www.theatlantic.com/education/archive/2015/11/student-activism-history -injustice/417129/

Anderson, P. & Baumberg, B. (2006). *Alcohol in Europe: A public health perspective*. Institute of Alcohol Studies (UK). Retrieved from https://ec.europa.eu/health/archive/ph _determinants/life_style/alcohol/documents/alcohol_europe_en.pdf

Andrews, M. (2013, October 1). Young adult insurance quandary: Stay with parents, or go it alone? *NBC News*. Retrieved from https://www.nbcnews.com/healthmain/young-adult -insurance-quandary-stay-parents-or-go-it-alone-8c11300070

Ankrom, S. (2020). DSM-5 criteria for diagnosing panic disorder. *Verywell Mind*. Retrieved from https://www.verywellmind.com/diagnosing-panic-disorder-2583930

Annie E. Casey Foundation. (2021). Adult population by age group in the United States. *Kids Count Data Center*. Retrieved from https://datacenter.kidscount.org/data/tables/6538 -adult-population-by-age-group#detailed/1/any/false/574,1729,37,871,870,573,869,36 ,868,867/117,2801,2802,2803/13515,13516

Arias, E., Tejada-Vera, B., & Ahmad. F. (2021, February). Provisional life expectancy estimates for January through June, 2020. *Vital Statistics Rapid Release*; no 10. National Center for Health Statistics. https://doi.org/10.15620/cdc:100392

Arnett, J. J. (2000). Emerging adulthood: A theory of development from the late teens through the twenties. *American Psychologist, 55*, 469–480. doi:10.1037/0003-066X.55.5.469

Arnett, J. J. (2001). Conceptions of the transition to adulthood: Perspectives from adolescence through midlife. *Journal of Adult Development, 8*, 133–143. doi:10.1023/A:1026450103225

Arnett, J. J. (2004). *Emerging adulthood: The winding road from the late teens through the twenties*. Oxford University Press.

Arnett, J. J. (2007). Emerging adulthood, a 21st century theory: A rejoinder to Hendry and Kloep. *Child Development Perspectives, 1*, 80–82. doi:10.1111/j.1750-8606.2007.00018.x

Arnett, J. J. (2015a). *Emerging adulthood: The winding road from the late teens through the twenties* (2nd edition). Oxford University Press.

Arnett, J. J. (2015b, August 25). What really motivates workers in their 20s. *Harvard Business Review*. Retrieved from https://hbr.org/2015/08/what-really-motivates-workers-in-their-20s

Arnett, J. J. (2016). Does emerging adulthood theory apply across social classes? National data on a persistent question. *Emerging Adulthood, 4*, 227–235. doi:10.1177/2167696815613000

Arnett, J. J. (2018). *Adolescence and emerging adulthood: A cultural approach* (6th edition). Pearson.

Arnett, J. J., & Taber, S. (1994). Adolescence terminable and interminable: When does adolescence end? *Journal of Youth and Adolescence, 23*, 517–537. https://doi.org/10.1007/BF01537734

Arum, R., & Roksa, J. (2011). *Academically adrift: Limited learning on college campuses*. University of Chicago Press.

Bachman, J. G., Wadsworth, K. N., O'Malley, P. M., Schulenberg, J., & Johnston, L. D. (1997). Marriage, divorce, and parenthood during the transition to young adulthood: Impacts on drug use and abuse. In J. Schulenberg, J. L. Maggs, & K. Hurrelmann (Eds.), *Health risks and developmental transitions during adolescence* (pp. 246–279). Cambridge University Press.

Baptiste, N. (2014, October 13). Staggering loss of Black wealth due to subprime scandal continues unabated. *The American Prospect*. Retrieved from https://prospect.org/justice/ staggering-loss-black-wealth-due-subprime-scandal-continues-unabated/

Barlette, K. G. (2008, January 2). Marriage doesn't validate commitment. *Albany Times Union*. Retrieved from https://blog.timesunion.com/kristi/2008/01/02/marriage-doesnt -validate-commitment/

Barmak, S. (2010, September 3). Why 30 is the new 20. *Toronto Star*. Retrieved from https://www .thestar.com/news/insight/2010/09/03/why_30_is_the_new_20.html

Barnard College. (not dated). The LeClair Affair: The incident. *Barnard College Archives*. Retrieved from https://barnardarchives.omeka.net/exhibits/show/introduction/leclairaffair/page1

Barroso, A. & Minkin, R. (2020, June 24). Recent protest attendees are more racially and ethnically diverse, younger than Americans overall. *Pew Research Center*. Retrieved from https://www.pewresearch.org/fact-tank/2020/06/24/recent-protest-attendees-are-more-racially-and-ethnically-diverse-younger-than-americans-overall/

Batman, K. (2020, December 25). 'It's a brotherhood that's unbreakable and it's not going to change': Nonprofit organization creates a lifeline for veterans. KSN-TV, Wichita, Kansas. Retrieved from https://www.ksn.com/news/local/its-a-brotherhood-thats-unbreakable-and-its-not-going-to-change-nonprofit-organization-creates-a-lifeline-for-veterans/

Bauman, K. (2017, April). Mapping the transition to adulthood: A bird's-eye view of enrollment, employment, independence, and marriage. Presented at the annual meeting of the Population Association of America, Chicago. Retrieved from https://www.census.gov/content/dam/Census/library/working-papers/2017/demo/SEHSD-WP2017-20.pdf

Baumeister, R. F. (2000). Gender differences in erotic plasticity: The female sex drive as socially flexible and responsive. *Psychological Bulletin, 126*, 347–374. doi:10.1037/0033-2909.126.3.347

Baunach, D. M. (2012). Changing same-sex marriage attitudes in America from 1988 through 2010. *Public Opinion Quarterly, 76*, 364–378. doi:10.1093/poq/nfs022

BBC. (2018). Cameroon country profile. *BBC News*. Retrieved from https://www.bbc.com/news/world-africa-13146029

Beck, J. (2016, January 5). When are you really an adult? *The Atlantic*. Retrieved from https://www.theatlantic.com/health/archive/2016/01/when-are-you-really-an-adult/422487/

Benes, A., & Walker, M. (2021, June 28). PYDin3: Do you have a plan? Insights into emerging adulthood [podcast]. Nebraska Extension, University of Nebraska-Lincoln. Retrieved from https://www.buzzsprout.com/1723242/8777544-do-you-have-a-plan-insights-into-emerging-adulthood

Bennett, T. (2017, August 9). DSM-5 Major depressive disorder: Causes, symptoms, treatment. *Thriveworks*. Retrieved from https://thriveworks.com/blog/major-depressive-disorder/

Bennett, W. L., Wells, C., & Rank, A. (2009). Young citizens and civic learning: Two paradigms of citizenship in the digital age. *Citizenship Studies, 13*, 105–120. doi:10.1080/13621020902731116

Berkowitz, S. A, Gold, R., Domino, M. E., & Basu S. (2021) Health insurance coverage and self-employment. *Health Services Research, 56*, 247–255. doi:10.1111/1475-6773.13598

Bharadwaj, A., & Dvorkin, M. A. (2019, July 10). The rise of automation: How robots may impact the U.S. labor market. *Regional Economist*. St. Louis Federal Reserve Bank. Retrieved from https://www.stlouisfed.org/publications/regional-economist/second-quarter-2019/rise-automation-robots

Bieber, C. R. (2020). Dependents: Who you can claim on your taxes. *Credit Karma*. Retrieved from https://www.creditkarma.com/tax/i/who-you-can-claim-dependent

Bishop, B. (2009). *The big sort: Why the clustering of like-minded America is tearing us apart*. Mariner Books.

Blais, A. (2000). *To vote or not to vote? The merits and limits of rational choice theory*. University of Pittsburgh Press.

Blakemore, S.-J. (2018). *Inventing ourselves: The secret life of the teenage brain*. Public Affairs Books.

Bogle, K. A. (2008). *Hooking up: Sex, dating, and relationships on campus*. New York: NYU Press.

Bohanan, L. & Cohen, C. J. (2020, July 23). Millennials and Gen Z want affordable child care: Findings from Next100 and GenForward. *The Century Foundation*. Retrieved from https://thenext100.org/millennials-and-gen-z-want-affordable-child-care/

Bolzman, K. (2019). Before spending more on vocational training, Let's ensure it meets market needs. *Catalyst*. Retrieved from https://catalyst.independent.org/2019/05/20/before-spending-more-on-vocational-training-lets-ensure-it-meets-market-needs/

Bonnie, R. J., Stroud, C. & Breiner, H. (Eds.) (2014). Investing in the health and well-being of young adults. Committee on Improving the Health, Safety, and Well-Being of Young Adults; Board on Children, Youth, and Families; Institute of Medicine; National Research Council. Retrieved from https://www.issuelab.org/resources/21000/21000.pdf

Borden, N. M., Forseen, S. E., & Stefan, C. (2015). *Imaging anatomy of the human brain: A comprehensive atlas including adjacent structures.* DemosMEDICAL.

Bos, M. G. N., Wierenga, L. M., Blankenstein, N. E., Schreuders, E., Tamnes, C. K., & Crone, E. A. (2018). Longitudinal structural brain development and externalizing behavior in adolescence. *Journal of Child Psychology and Psychiatry, 59*, 1061–1072. doi:10.1111/jcpp.12972

Bound, J., & Turner, S. (2002). Going to war and going to college: Did World War II and the G.I. Bill increase educational attainment for returning veterans? *Journal of Labor Economics, 20*, 784–815.

Brière, F. N., Rohde, P., Seeley, J. R., Klein, D., & Lewinsohn, P. M. (2014). Comorbidity between major depression and alcohol use disorder from adolescence to adulthood. *Comprehensive Psychiatry, 55*, 526–533. doi:10.1016/j.comppsych.2013.10.007

Brown, S. L. (2005). How cohabitation is reshaping American families. *Contexts, 4*, 33–37.

Bruner, R. (2021, October 29). Young people are leaving their jobs in record numbers – and not going back. *TIME*. Retrieved from https://time.com/6111245/young-workers-quitting/

Buchholz, K. (2019). When people get married around the world. *Statista*. Retrieved from https://www.statista.com/chart/19119/global-marriage-ages/

Budiman, A. (2020, August 20). Key findings about U.S. immigrants. *Pew Research Center*. Retrieved from https://www.pewresearch.org/fact-tank/2020/08/20/key-findings-about-u-s-immigrants/

Cafasso, J. (2018, September 18). What is synaptic pruning? *Healthline*. Retrieved from https://www.healthline.com/health/synaptic-pruning

Cahn, N. & Carbone, J. (2010). *Red families v. blue families.* Oxford University Press.

Cakir, S. G. (2014). Ego identity status and psychological well-being among Turkish emerging adults. *Identity, 14*, 230–239. https://doi.org/10.1080/15283488.2014.921169

Calabrese, E. J. (2016). The emergence of the dose-response concept in biology and medicine. *International Journal of Molecular Sciences 17*, Article No. UNSP 2034.

Campbell, A. F. (2017, July 13). Rahm Emanuel's plan to push Chicago teens to go to college, explained. *Vox*. Retrieved from https://www.vox.com/policy-and-politics/2017/4/12/15245236/chicago-public-school-graduation-requirement-for-college

Cantwell, B. (2021, September 22). A partial reset. *Revue*. Retrieved from https://www.getrevue.co/profile/cant_b/issues/a-partial-reset-759784

Carbone, J., & Cahn, N. (2014). *Marriage markets: How inequality is remaking the American family.* Oxford University Press.

Casey, B., Jones, R. M., & Somerville, L. H. (2011). Braking and accelerating of the adolescent brain. *Journal of Research on Adolescence, 21*, 21–33. doi:10.1111/j.1532-7795.2010.00712.x

Casselman, B. (2015, May 5). Enough already about the job-hopping Millennials. *Five–Thirty-Eight*. Retrieved from https://fivethirtyeight.com/features/enough-already-about-the-job-hopping-millennials/

Catani, M., Dell'acqua, F., & Thiebaut De Schotten, M. (2013). A revised limbic system model for memory, emotion and behaviour. *Neuroscience and Biobehavioral Reviews, 37*, 1724–1737. https://doi.org/10.1016/j.neubiorev.2013.07.001

Center for Community-Engaged Learning. (2011). *Frequently asked questions about service-learning.* http://ccel-app.umn.edu/info/FAQ.html

Center for Engaged Learning. (not dated). *Service-learning.* Retrieved from https://www.centerforengagedlearning.org/resources/service-learning/

Center for Functional MRI. (not dated). *Structural MRI imaging.* Retrieved from http://fmri.ucsd.edu/Howto/3T/structure.html

Centers for Disease Control and Prevention. (2020a). *National Survey of Family Growth*. US Department of Health & Human Services. Retrieved from: https://www.cdc.gov/nchs/nsfg/index.htm

Centers for Disease Control and Prevention. (2020b). *Dietary guidelines for alcohol*. US Department of Health & Human Services. Retrieved from https://www.cdc.gov/alcohol/fact-sheets/moderate-drinking.htm

Centers for Disease Control and Prevention. (2021). *CDC Museum COVID-19 timeline*. US Department of Health & Human Services. Retrieved from https://www.cdc.gov/museum/timeline/covid19.html

Chaiyasong, S., Huckle, T., Mackintosh, A.-M., Meier, P., Parry, C. D. H., Callinan, S., et al. (2018). Drinking patterns vary by sex, age and country-level income: Cross-country analysis of the International Alcohol Control Study. *Drug and Alcohol Review, 37*(S2), S53–S62. doi:10.1111/dar.12820

Chalabi, M. (2014, October 9). Dear Mona, does living together before marriage increase the risk of divorce? *Five-Thirty-Eight*. Retrieved from https://fivethirtyeight.com/features/does-living-together-before-marriage-increase-the-risk-of-divorce/

Chan, M., Tsai, K. M., & Fuligni, A. J. (2015). Changes in religiosity across the transition to young adulthood. *Journal of Youth and Adolescence, 44*, 1555–1566. doi:10.1007/s10964-014-0157-0

Chao, G. T., & Gardner, P. D. (2007a). *What do young adults want?* Michigan State University Collegiate Employment Research Institute/MonsterTrak. Retrieved from https://ceri.msu.edu/_assets/pdfs/young-pro-pdfs/JobChar4-16.pdf

Chao, G. T., & Gardner, P. D. (2007b). *Today's young adults: Surfing for the right job*. Michigan State University Collegiate Employment Research Institute/MonsterTrak. Retrieved from https://ceri.msu.edu/_assets/pdfs/young-pro-pdfs/Young-Adults-Right-Job.pdf

Chapman, A. (2014). Single-parent families. In M. J. Coleman & L. H. Ganong (Eds.), *The social history of the American family: An encyclopedia* (pp. 1188–1193). Sage. doi:10.4135/9781452286143.n476

Chen, M. K., Chevalier, J. A., Rossi, P. E., & Oehlsen, E. (2019). The value of flexible work: Evidence from Uber drivers. *Journal of Political Economy, 127*, 2735–2794. doi:10.1086/702171

Cherlin, A. J. (2009). *The marriage-go-round: The state of marriage and the family in America today*. Knopf.

Chicago Public Schools. (2020). *Chicago Public Schools announces 97.5 percent of seniors submitted concrete post-secondary plan as part of Learn.Plan.Succeed*. Retrieved from https://www.cps.edu/press-releases/chicago-public-schools-announces-97.5-percent-of-seniors-submitted-concrete-post-secondary-plan-as-part-of-learn.plan.succeed/

Child & Family Research Partnership. (2018, June). *The evidence base: Predictors of father involvement*. University of Texas-Austin. Retrieved from http://childandfamilyresearch.utexas.edu/predictors-father-involvement

Clance, P. R., & Imes, S. A. (1978). The imposter phenomenon in high achieving women: Dynamics and therapeutic intervention. *Psychotherapy: Theory, Research & Practice, 15*, 241–247. doi:10.1037/h0086006

Clark, K. B., & Clark, M. P. (1947). Racial identification and preference in Negro children. In T. M. Newcomb & E. L. Hartley (Eds.), *Readings in social psychology* (pp. 169–178). Henry Holt and Company.

Clark University Poll. (2015). *About the Clark University Poll*. Retrieved from http://www2.clarku.edu/clark-poll-emerging-adults/

Clary, E. G., Snyder, M., Ridge, R. D., Copeland, J., Stukas, A. A., Haugen, J., & Miene, P. (1998). Understanding and assessing the motivations of volunteers: A functional approach. *Journal of Personality and Social Psychology, 74*, 1516–1530. doi:10.1037/0022-3514.74.6.1516

Claxton, S. E., & van Dulmen, M. H. M. (2013). Casual sexual relationships and experiences in emerging adulthood. *Emerging Adulthood, 1*, 138–150. doi:10.1177/2167696813487181

Cloudpay. (2019, April 18). *A guide to pay parity laws around the world*. Retrieved from https://www.cloudpay.com/resources/a-guide-to-pay-parity-laws-around-the-world

CNN. (2003, December 9). *Transcript of Oprah Winfrey appearance on Larry King Live*. Retrieved from https://transcripts.cnn.com/show/lkl/date/2003-12-09/segment/00

CNN.com (2010, May 14). *Study: White and black children biased toward lighter skin*. Retrieved from http://www.cnn.com/2010/US/05/13/doll.study/

Coaston, J. (2019, May 28). The intersectionality wars. *Vox*. Retrieved from https://www.vox.com/the-highlight/2019/5/20/18542843/intersectionality-conservatism-law-race-gender-discrimination

Coates, T.-N. (2009). *The beautiful struggle*. Penguin Random House.

Cohen, P. (2012, December 11). More women are doctors and lawyers than ever – but progress is stalling. *The Atlantic*. Retrieved from https://www.theatlantic.com/sexes/archive/2012/12/more-women-are-doctors-and-lawyers-than-ever-but-progress-is-stalling/266115/

Cohen, P., Kasen, S., Chen, H., Hartmark, C., & Gordon, K. (2003). Variations in patterns of developmental transitions in the emerging adulthood period. *Developmental Psychology, 39*, 657–669. doi:10.1037/0012-1649.39.4.657

College Confidential. (2018). *Elite colleges & universities with highest percentage of small classes (under 20 per class)*. Retrieved from https://talk.collegeconfidential.com/t/elite-colleges-universities-with-highest-percentage-of-small-classes-under-20-per-class/2023022

Conner, B. (2021, February 17). *History & hope: Former Woolworth busboy recounts memory of A&T Four sit-in at Greensboro restaurant*. WXII 12 TV, Winston-Salem, North Carolina. Retrieved from https://www.wxii12.com/article/greensboro-woolworth-bus-boy-aandt-four-sit-in-restaurant/35492920#

Cooper, D. T. & Klein, J. L. (2018). College students' online pornography use: Contrasting general and specific structural variables with social learning variables. *American Journal of Criminal Justice, 43*, 551–569. doi:10.1007/s12103-017-9424-4

Côté, J. E. (2006). Emerging adulthood as an institutionalized moratorium: Risks and benefits to identity formation. In J. J. Arnett & J. L. Tanner (Eds.), *Emerging adults in America: Coming of age in the 21st century* (pp. 85–116). American Psychological Association.

Côté, J. E. (2014). The dangerous myth of emerging adulthood: An evidence-based critique of a flawed developmental theory. *Applied Developmental Science, 18*, 177–188. doi:10.1080/10888691.2014.954451

Cothern, (2021). Credit CARD Act: Credit Card Accountability Responsibility and Disclosure Act of 2009. *Credit Karma*. Retrieved from https://www.creditkarma.com/credit-cards/i/card-act

Cottle, M. (2018, May 7). Planned parenthood was always meant to be controversial. *The Atlantic*. Retrieved from https://www.theatlantic.com/politics/archive/2018/05/cecile-richards-legacy/559781/

Court Appointed Special Advocates (Texas Chapter). (2019, December 16). *CASA deep dive: Adopting a child from foster care*. Retrieved from https://texascasa.org/2019/12/16/casa-deep-dive-adopting-a-child-from-foster-care/

Cox, K., & McAdams, D. P. (2012). The transforming self: Service narratives and identity change in emerging adulthood. *Journal of Adolescent Research, 27*, 18–43. doi:10.1177/0743558410384732

Cramer, K. J., & Bartels, L. M. (2020). *Conceptions of good citizenship in the class of 1965*. Center for the Study of Democratic Institutions, Vanderbilt University. Retrieved from https://www.vanderbilt.edu/csdi/includes/WP_2_2020_final.pdf

Crandall, C. S., Priesler, J. J., & Aussprung, J. (1992). Measuring life event stress in the lives of college students: The Undergraduate Stress Questionnaire (USQ). *Journal of Behavioral Medicine, 15*, 627–662. Research Gate doi:10.13140/RG.2.2.16623.38566

Crenshaw, K. (1989). Demarginalizing the intersection of race and sex: A black feminist critique of antidiscrimination doctrine, feminist theory and antiracist politics. *University of Chicago Legal Forum*, 139–167.

Crist, C. (2021, July 12). What you need to know about the delta variant. *WebMD*. Retrieved from https://www.webmd.com/lung/news/20210712/what-to-know-about-covid-delta-variant

Crocetti, E., Rubini, M., & Meeus, W. (2008). Capturing the dynamics of identity formation in various ethnic groups: Development and validation of a three-dimensional model. *Journal of Adolescence, 31*, 207–222. doi:10.1016/j.adolescence.2007.09.002

Crocetti, E., Tagliabue, S., Sugimura, K., Nelson, L. J., Takahashi, A., Niwa, T., Sugiura, Y., & Jinno., M. (2015). Perceptions of emerging adulthood: A study With Italian and Japanese university students and young workers. *Emerging Adulthood, 3*, 229–243. doi:10.1177/2167696815569848

Cui, M., Darling, C. A., Coccia, C., Fincham, F. D., & May, R. W. (2019). Indulgent parenting, helicopter parenting, and well-being of parents and emerging adults. *Journal of Child and Family Studies, 28*, 860–871. doi:10.1007/s10826-018-01314-3

Dafny, N. (2020). Overview of the nervous system. *Neuroscience Online*. Retrieved from https://nba.uth.tmc.edu/neuroscience/m/s2/chapter01.html

Dailey, R. M. (2020). *On-again, off-again relationships: Navigating (in)stability in romantic relationships.* Cambridge: Cambridge University Press.

Dailey, R. M., Pfiester, A., Jin, B., Beck, G., & Clark, G. (2009). On-again/off-again dating relationships: How are they different from other dating relationships? *Personal Relationships, 16*, 23–47. doi:10.1111/j.1475-6811.2009.01208.x

Dailey, R. M., Rossetto, K. R., Pfiester, R. A., & Surra, C. A. (2009). A qualitative analysis of on-again/off-again romantic relationships: "It's up, it's down, all around." *Journal of Social and Personal Relationships, 26*, 443–466. doi:10.1177/0265407509351035

Dalton, R. J. (2008). Citizenship norms and the expansion of political participation. *Political Studies, 56*, 76–98. https://doi.org/10.1111/j.1467-9248.2007.00718.x

Darlow, V., Norvilitis, J. M., & Schuetze, P. (2017). The relationship between helicopter parenting and adjustment to college. *Journal of Child and Family Studies, 26*, 2291–2298. doi:10.1007/s10826-017-0751-3

Deci, E. L., & Ryan, R. M. (1987). The support of autonomy and the control of behavior. *Journal of Personality and Social Psychology, 53*, 1024–1037. doi:10.1037/0022-3514.53.6.1024

DeLuca, S., Clampet-Lundquist, S., & Edin, K. (2016). *Coming of age in the other America.* Russell Sage Foundation.

Desjardins, R., & Warnke, A. J. (2012). Ageing and skills: A review and analysis of skill gain and skill loss over the lifespan and over time. OECD Working Paper No. 72. Retrieved from https://www.oecd.org/officialdocuments/publicdisplaydocumentpdf/?cote=EDU/WKP(2012)9&docLanguage=En

Diamond, L. M. (2003). Was it a phase? Young women's relinquishment of lesbian/bisexual identities over a 5-year period. *Journal of Personality and Social Psychology, 84*, 352–364. doi:10.1037/0022-3514.84.2.352

Diamond, L. M. (2008). *Sexual fluidity: Understanding women's love and desire.* Harvard University Press.

Dik, B. J., Eldridge, B. M., Steger, M. F., & Duffy, R. D. (2012). Development and validation of the Calling and Vocation Questionnaire (CVQ) and Brief Calling Scale (BCS). *Journal of Career Assessment, 20*, 242–263. doi:10.1177/1069072711434410

Dimock, M. (2019, January 17). Defining generations: Where Millennials end and Generation Z begins. *Pew Research Center*. Retrieved from https://www.pewresearch.org/fact-tank/2019/01/17/where-millennials-end-and-generation-z-begins/

DK. (2014, October 29). Why young people don't vote. *The Economist*. Retrieved from https://www.economist.com/the-economist-explains/2014/10/29/why-young-people-dont-vote

Duris, J. (2009). Erleben des erwachsenwerdens und bewertung von alltäglichen risikosituationen [Experiencing growing up and evaluating everyday risky situations]. Magistra [master's] thesis, University of Vienna.

Dutra-Thomé, L. (2013). Emerging adulthood in southern Brazilians from differing socioeconomic status: Social and subjective markers. Doctoral dissertation, Universidade Federal Do Rio Grande Do Sul. Retrieved from http://www.lume.ufrgs.br/bitstream/handle/10183/76534/000886149.pdf

Eckholm, E. (2007, January 27). Offering help for former foster care youths. *New York Times*. Retrieved from https://www.nytimes.com/2007/01/27/us/27foster.html

Edin, K., & Tach, L. (2011) Becoming a parent: Social contexts of fertility during young adulthood. In A. Booth, S. L. Brown, N. S. Landale, W. Manning, & S. M. McHale (Eds.), *Early adulthood in a family context* (pp. 185–207). Springer. doi:10.1007/978-1-4614-1436-0_12

Edwards-Levy, A. (2020, June 30). Most Americans favor mask requirements, poll finds. *Huffington Post*. Retrieved from https://www.huffpost.com/entry/mask-requirements-huffpost-yougov-poll_n_5efbb870c5b6ca9709163993

Elias, V., Fullerton, A. & Simpson, J. (2013). Long-term changes in attitudes toward premarital sex in the United States: Reexamining the role of cohort replacement. *Journal of Sex Research, 52,* 129–139. doi:10.1080/00224499.2013.798610

Endlich Heffernan, L. (2020, December 23). 50 things you can do when you turn 18 (who knew?). *Grown & Flown*. Retrieved from https://grownandflown.com/50-things-do-when-you-turn-18/

Epstein, D. (2019). *Range: Why generalists triumph in a specialized world*. Riverhead Books.

Erikson, E. (1968). *Identity: Youth and crisis*. Norton.

Eriksson, P. L., Wängqvist, M., Carlsson, J., & Frisén, A. (2020). Identity development in early adulthood. *Developmental Psychology, 56,* 1968–1983. doi:10.1037/dev0001093

European Community. (not dated). *Employment, social affairs & inclusion: Sweden - housing allowance.* Retrieved from https://ec.europa.eu/social/main.jsp?catId=1130&langId=en&intPageId=4807

European Monitoring Centre for Drugs and Drug Addiction. (2017). *European drug report 2017: Trends and developments*. Retrieved from https://www.emcdda.europa.eu/publications/edr/trends-developments/2017

Evans, T. (2015, July 14). This is what the first 36 hours of Marine boot camp is like. *Business Insider*. Retrieved from https://www.businessinsider.com/this-is-what-the-first-36-hours-of-marine-boot-camp-is-like-2015-7

Facio, A., Prestofelippo, M. E., & Sireix, M. C. (2017). Positive development in Latin American emerging adults. In L. M. Padilla-Walker & L. J. Nelson (Eds), *Flourishing in emerging adulthood: Positive development during the third decade of life* (pp. 449–461). Oxford University Press.

Facio, A., Resett, S., Micocci, F., & Mistrorigo, C. (2007). Emerging adulthood in Argentina: An age of diversity and possibilities. *Child Development Perspectives, 1,* 115–118. doi:10.1111/j.1750-8606.2007.00025.x

Fadjukoff, P., Pulkkinen, L., & Kokko, K. (2016). Identity formation in adulthood: A longitudinal study from age 27 to 50. *Identity, 16,* 8–23. doi:10.1080/15283488.2015.1121820

Federal Reserve Board (2016). Experiences and perspectives of young workers. Retrieved from https://www.federalreserve.gov/econresdata/2015-experiences-and-perspectives-of-young-workers-201612.pdf

Fernández Águeda, B. (2009, June). Urban planning in industrial cities: The reversibility of decay. Paper presented at City Futures Conference, Madrid, Spain. Retrieved from https://www.researchgate.net/publication/49911741_Urban_Planning_in_Industrial_Cities_the_Reversibility_of_Decay/figures?lo=1

Fieldstadt, E. (2018). November 26). America's biggest megachurches, ranked. *CBS News*. Retrieved from https://www.cbsnews.com/pictures/30-biggest-american-megachurches-ranked/9/

Fingerman, K. L., Cheng, Y. P., Wesselmann, E. D., Zarit, S., Furstenberg, F., & Birditt, K. S. (2012). Helicopter parents and landing pad kids: Intense parental support of grown children. *Journal of Marriage and Family, 74,* 880–896. doi:10.1111/j.1741-3737.2012.00987.x

Fingerman, K. L., Huo, M., & Birditt, K. S. (2020). A decade of research on intergenerational ties: Technological, economic, political, and demographic changes. *Journal of Marriage and Family, 82,* 383–403. doi:10.1111/jomf.12604

Fingerman, K. L., Huo, M., Kim, K., & Birditt, K. S. (2017). Coresident and noncoresident young adults' daily experiences with parents. *Emerging Adulthood, 5,* 337–350. doi:10.1177/2167696816676583

Fingerman, K. L., Miller, L. M., Birditt, K. S., & Zarit, S. (2009). Giving to the good and the needy: Parental support of grown children. *Journal of Marriage and Family, 71,* 1220–1233. doi:10.1111/j.1741-3737.2009.00665.x

Finkel, E. J., Eastwick, P. W., Karney, B. R., Reis, H. T., & Sprecher, S. (2012). Online dating: A critical analysis from the perspective of psychological science. *Psychological Science in the Public Interest, 13,* 3–66. https://doi.org/10.1177/1529100612436522

Fish, T. (2021, June 20). The 12 most educated countries in the world *Newsweek.* Retrieved from https://www.newsweek.com/most-educated-countries-world-1600620

Flanagan, C. (2014, March 15). The dark power of fraternities. *The Atlantic.* Retrieved from https://www.theatlantic.com/magazine/archive/2014/03/the-dark-power-of-fraternities /357580/

Fox, L. (2014, March 20). The science of cohabitation: A step toward marriage, not a rebellion. *The Atlantic.* https://www.theatlantic.com/health/archive/2014/03/the-science-of -cohabitation-a-step-toward-marriage-not-a-rebellion/284512/

Fresquez, B., & Rabinowitz, A. (2020, October 1). Prioritizing transfer for tomorrow's higher education landscape. *American Talent Initiative.* Retrieved from https://americantalenti nitiative.org/prioritizing-transfer-for-tomorrows-higher-education-landscape/

Frey, W. H. (2018, January 26). Old versus young: The cultural generation gap. *Trend Magazine/ Pew Charitable Trusts.* Retrieved from https://www.pewtrusts.org/en/trend/archive/winter -2018/old-versus-young-the-cultural-generation-gap

Friedan, B. (1963). *The feminine mystique.* Norton.

Friedman, T. (2016). *Thank you for being late: An optimist's guide to thriving in the age of accelerations.* Farrar, Straus, and Giroux.

Fry, R. (2017, January 18). U.S. still has a ways to go in meeting Obama's goal of producing more college grads. *Pew Research Center.* Retrieved from https://www.pewresearch.org/ fact-tank/2017/01/18/u-s-still-has-a-ways-to-go-in-meeting-obamas-goal-of-producing -more-college-grads/

Fry, R., Passel, J. S., & Cohn, D. (2020, September 4). A majority of young adults in the U.S. live with their parents for the first time since the Great Depression. *Pew Research Center.* Retrieved from https://www.pewresearch.org/fact-tank/2020/09/04/a-majority-of -young-adults-in-the-u-s-live-with-their-parents-for-the-first-time-since-the-great -depression/

Furman, W., & Hand, L. S. (2006). The slippery nature of romantic relationships: Issues in definition and differentiation. In A. Booth & A. C. Crouter (Eds.), *Romance and sex in adolescence and emerging adulthood: Risks and opportunities* (pp. 171–178). Lawrence Erlbaum.

Furstenberg, F. F., Jr., & Kmec, J. A. (2000, June). Racial differences in the transition to adulthood: A follow-up study of the Philadelphia Youth Study. Presentation at Harvard University Inequality Summer Institute. Retrieved from https://citeseerx.ist.psu.edu/viewdoc/ download?doi=10.1.1.568.9515&rep=rep1&type=pdf

Galanaki, E., & Leontopoulou, S. (2017). Criteria for the transition to adulthood: Developmental features of emerging adulthood, and views of the future among Greek studying youth. *Europe's Journal of Psychology, 13,* 417–440. https://doi.org/10.5964/ejop.v13i3.1327

Galarnyk, M. (2018). Explaining the 68-95-99.7 rule for a normal distribution. *Towards Data Science.* Retrieved from https://towardsdatascience.com/understanding-the-68-95-99-7 -rule-for-a-normal-distribution-b7b7cbf760c2

Gates, M. A., Holowka, D. W., Vasterling, J. J., Keane, T. M., Marx, B. P., & Rosen, R. C. (2012). Posttraumatic stress disorder in veterans and military personnel: Epidemiology, screening, and case recognition. *Psychological Services*, *9*, 361–82. doi:10.1037/a0027649

Gentry, B. (2018). *Why youth vote: Identity, inspirational leaders and independence.* Springer.

Glenn, N. D., Uecker, J., & Love, R. W. B. (2010). Later first marriage and marital success. *Social Science Research*, *39*, 787–800. doi:10.1016/j.ssresearch.2010.06.002

Go Overseas. (2013). *Why are gap years more common in Europe than the US?* Retrieved from https://www.gooverseas.com/blog/why-gap-years-more-common-in-europe-us

Goldberg, S. K., & Conron, K. J. (2018, July). *How many same-sex couples in the US are raising children?* Williams Institute, UCLA Law School. Retrieved from https://williamsinstitute.law.ucla.edu/publications/same-sex-parents-us/

Goldin, C., & Katz, L. F. (2002). The power of the pill: Oral contraceptives and women's career and marriage decisions. *Journal of Political Economy*, *110*, 730–770. doi:10.1086/340778

Gonzalez, E. (2016, May 13). Adrián González pushes for Spanish accents on MLB jerseys. *Los Angeles Times*. Retrieved from https://www.latimes.com/sports/sportsnow/la-sp-sn-adrian-gonzalez-pushing-spanish-accents-jerseys-20160513-snap-htmlstory.html

Gordon, K. (2012, June 17). Blessed after 40: For central Ohioans who become dads later in life, the first Father's Day is all the more special. *Columbus Dispatch*. Retrieved from https://web.archive.org/web/20120623030007/http:/www.dispatch.com/content/stories/local/2012/06/17/blessed-after-40.html

Gordon, L. (2020, June 16). Endangered: Large university lecture hall classes. *Ed Source*. Retrieved from https://edsource.org/2020/are-the-days-numbered-for-the-large-university-lecture-hall-class/633619

Green, K., & Kreamer, K. (2018). 3 reasons that career and technical education doesn't preclude college. *Hechinger Report*. Retrieved from https://hechingerreport.org/opinion-3-reasons-career-and-technical-education-doesnt-preclude-college/

Greenblatt, A. (2010, March 24). What is the age of responsibility? *Governing*. Retrieved from https://www.governing.com/archive/what-is-the-age.html

Greenwood, J., Guner, N., & Kopecky, K. (2019). The wife's protector: A quantitative theory linking contraceptive technology with the decline in marriage. University of Pennsylvania Population Center Working Paper (PSC/PARC), 2019–28. Retrieved from https://repository.upenn.edu/psc_publications/28

Griffin, R. M. (2021). How different antidepressants work. *WebMD*. Retrieved from https://www.webmd.com/depression/how-different-antidepressants-work

Grosemans, I., Hannes, K., Neyens, J., & Kyndt, E. (2020). Emerging adults embarking on their careers: Job and identity explorations in the transition to work. *Youth & Society*, *52*, 795–819. doi:10.1177/0044118X18772695

Gurrentz, B. (2018, November 15). Living with an unmarried partner now common for young adults. US Census Bureau. https://www.census.gov/library/stories/2018/11/cohabitation-is-up-marriage-is-down-for-young-adults.html

Gustavson, K., Knudsen, A. K., Nesvåg, R., Knudsen, G. P., Vollset, S. E., & Reichborn-Kjennerud, T. (2018). Prevalence and stability of mental disorders among young adults: Findings from a longitudinal study. *BMC Psychiatry 18*, Article No. 65. doi:10.1186/s12888-018-1647-5

Guttmacher Institute. (2019). *Unintended pregnancy in the United States.* Retrieved from https://www.guttmacher.org/fact-sheet/unintended-pregnancy-united-states

Guzzo, K. B., & Dorius, C. (2016). Challenges in measuring and studying multipartnered fertility in American survey data. *Population Research and Policy Review*, *35*, 553–579. doi:10.1007/s11113-016-9398-9

Haardörfer, R., Windle, M., Fairman, R. T., & Berg, C. J. (2021). Longitudinal changes in alcohol use and binge-drinking among young-adult college students: Analyses of predictors across system levels. *Addictive Behaviors*, *112*, 1–8. doi:10.1016/j.addbeh.2020.106619

Haber, S. N. (2011). Neuroanatomy of reward: A view from the ventral striatum. In J. A. Gottfried (Ed.), *Neurobiology of sensation and reward* (235–261). CRC Press/Taylor & Francis. doi:10.1201/b10776-15

Hadley, A. M., Mbwana, K., & Hair, E. C. (2010, March). What works for older youth during the transition to adulthood: Lessons from experimental evaluations of programs and interventions. *Child Trends*. Retrieved from http://www.childtrends.org/wp-content/uploads/2013/03/Child_Trends-2010_03_09_FS_WWOlderYouth.pdf

Hagerty, B. B. (2016). *Life reimagined: The science, art, and opportunity of midlife*. Riverhead Books.

Hahnenberg, E. P. (2020). The meaning of calling in a culture of choice. *Reflections*. Retrieved from https://reflections.yale.edu/article/seize-day-vocation-calling-work/meaning-calling-culture-choice

Han, F.-B., & Dong, J.-M. (2009). "Helicopter parents" in colleges of China. *College & University*, *84*, 75–78.

Harrington, B. C., Jimerson, M., Haxton, C., & Jimerson, D. C. (2015). Initial evaluation, diagnosis, and treatment of anorexia nervosa and bulimia nervosa. *American Family Physician, 91*, 46–52. Retrieved from https://www.aafp.org/afp/2015/0101/p46.html

Hart, R., & Lancaster, S. L. (2019). Identity fusion in U.S. military members. *Armed Forces & Society*, 45, 45–58. doi:10.1177/0095327X17737021

Hendry, L. B., & Kloep, M. (2007). Conceptualizing emerging adulthood: Inspecting the emperor's new clothes? *Child Development Perspectives*, 1, 74–79. doi:10.1111/j.1750-8606.2007.00017.x

Henig, R. M. (2010, August 18). What is it about 20-somethings? *New York Times Magazine*. Retrieved from https://www.nytimes.com/2010/08/22/magazine/22Adulthood-t.html

Henig, R. M. (2012). What's the 'best age' to have a baby? *Psychology Today*. Retrieved from https://www.psychologytoday.com/us/blog/cusp/201211/whats-the-best-age-have-baby

Henig, R. M., & Henig, S. (2012). *Twenty-something: Why do young adults seem stuck?* Plume.

Henrich, J., Heine, S. J., & Norenzayan, A. (2010). Beyond WEIRD: Towards a broad-based behavioral science. *Behavioral and Brain Sciences*, *33*, 111–135. doi:10.1017/S0140525X10000725

Hiekel, N. (2014). *The different meanings of cohabitation across Europe: How cohabiters view their unions and differ in their plans and behaviors*. Amsterdam University Press. Retrieved from https://www.researchgate.net/publication/313878453_The_different_meanings_of_cohabitation_across_Europe_How_cohabiters_view_their_unions_and_differ_in_their_plans_and_behaviors

Hiltzik, M. (2016, March 29). Where America gets its health coverage: Everything you wanted to know in one handy chart. *Los Angeles Times*. Retrieved from https://www.latimes.com/business/hiltzik/la-fi-hiltzik-gaba-20160329-snap-htmlstory.html

Hodgkinson, S. C., Colantuoni, E., Roberts, D., Berg-Cross, L., & Belcher, H. M. E. (2010). Depressive symptoms and birth outcomes among pregnant teenagers. *Journal of Pediatric & Adolescent Gynecology, 23*, 16–22. doi:10.1016/j.jpag.2009.04.006

Hofer, J., Kärtner, J., Chasiotis, A., Busch, H., & Kiessling, F. (2007). Socio-cultural aspects of identity formation: The relationship between commitment and well-being in student samples from Cameroon and Germany. *Identity*, 7, 265–288. doi:10.1080/15283480701600744

Hoff, K. A., Briley, D. A., Wee, C. J. M., & Rounds, J. (2018). Normative changes in interests from adolescence to adulthood: A meta-analysis of longitudinal studies. *Psychological Bulletin*, *144*, 426–451. doi:10.1037/bul0000140

Holland, J. L. (1959). A theory of vocational choice. *Journal of Counseling Psychology*, *6*, 35–45.

Hollén, L., Dörner, R., Griffiths, M. D., & Emond, A. (2020). Gambling in young adults aged 17–24 years: A population-based study. *Journal of Gambling Studies, 36*, 747–766. doi:10.1007/s10899-020-09948-z

Holzer, H. J., & Lerman, R. I. (2007). *America's forgotten middle-skill jobs*. Urban Institute. Retrieved from http://webarchive.urban.org/publications/411633.html

Honwana, A. (2013). *Lugard Lecture 2013: Youth, waithood, and protest movements in Africa*. 5th European Conference on African Studies. Retrieved from https://repositorio.iscte-iul.pt /bitstream/10071/7528/1/Halcinda_Honwana_ECAS_2013.pdf

Horwitz, A. V. (2021). *DSM: A history of psychiatry's bible*. Johns Hopkins University Press.

Human Rights Campaign. (not dated). *Marriage equality around the world*. Retrieved from https:// www.hrc.org/resources/marriage-equality-around-the-world

Huston, T. L., Coughlin, J. P., Houts, R. M., Smith, S. E., & George, L. J. (2001). The connubial crucible: Newlywed years as predictors of delight, distress, and divorce. *Journal of Personality and Social Psychology, 80*, 237–252. doi:10.1037//O022-3514.80.2.237

Ifedi, A. (2018, October 19). How Nigeria is changing what we've learned about improving education. *World Economic Forum*. Retrieved from https://www.weforum.org/agenda /2018/10/how-nigeria-is-changing-what-weve-learned-about-improving-education/

Institute for Social Research. (2002a). *Family values: Belief in marriage and family life remains strong. ISR Update, 2, 1*. Retrieved from https://web.archive.org/web/20070330023739/http:/ www.isr.umich.edu/home/news/update/2002-11.pdf

Institute for Social Research. (2002b). *From adolescence to adulthood: Many flourish, but a few flounder ISR Update, 2, 1*. Retrieved from https://web.archive.org/web/20070330023739/http:/ www.isr.umich.edu/home/news/update/2002-11.pdf

Institute of Education Sciences. (2021). *International Educational Attainment. Condition of Education*. U.S. Department of Education, National Center for Education Statistics. Washington, DC. Retrieved from https://nces.ed.gov/programs/coe/indicator/cac

International Labour Organization. (2020). *Global employment trends for youth 2020*. Retrieved from https://www.ilo.org/wcmsp5/groups/public/---dgreports/---dcomm/---publ/ documents/publication/wcms_737648.pdf

Irish News. (2017, June 5). *Why don't young people vote?* Retrieved from https://www.irishnews .com/magazine/daily/2017/06/05/news/why-don-t-young-people-vote--1045599/

Iyengar, S., & Lepper, M. R. (2000). When choice is demotivating: Can one desire too much of a good thing? *Journal of Personality and Social Psychology 79*, 995–1006.

Iyengar, S., Wells, R. E., & Schwartz, B. (2006). Doing better but feeling worse: Looking for the "best" job undermines satisfaction. *Psychological Science, 17*, 143–50.

Jamison, T. B., & Proulx, C. M. (2013). Stayovers in emerging adulthood: Who stays over and why? *Personal Relationships, 20*, 155–169. doi:10.1111/j.1475-6811.2012.01407.x

Jauregui, A. (2012, June 26). Young Americans losing faith? New poll shows 31 percent of adults under 30 doubt God exists. *Huffington Post*. Retrieved from https://www.huffpost.com/ entry/young-adults-losing-faith-americans-under-30-doubt-god-exists_n_1627333

Jekielek, S. & Brown, B. (2005). *The transition to adulthood: Characteristics of young adults ages 18 to 24 in America*. Annie E. Casey Foundation, Population Reference Bureau, and Child Trends. Retrieved from https://web.archive.org/web/20050629112457/https:/www.prb .org/pdf05/TransitionToAdulthood.pdf

Jennings-Edquist, G. (2020, October 22). 20s, 30s, 40s: Does the age you become a parent actually matter? *ABC Everyday*. Retrieved from https://www.abc.net.au/everyday/does-the-age -you-become-a-parent-actually-matter/12742736

Johnson, J. (2020a, May 22). Everything you need to know about the occipital lobe. *Medical News Today*. Retrieved from https://www.medicalnewstoday.com/articles/occipital-lobe

Johnson, J. (2020b, May 26). All about the parietal lobe. *Medical News Today*. Retrieved from https://www.medicalnewstoday.com/articles/parietal-lobe

Jung, E., Hwang, W., Kim, S., Sin, H., Zhao, Z., Zhang, Y., et al. (2020). Helicopter parenting, autonomy support, and student wellbeing in the United States and South Korea. *Journal of Child and Family Studies, 29*, 358–373. doi:10.1007/s10826-019-01601-7

Jung, W. H., Lee, S., Lerman, C., & Kable, J. W. (2018). Amygdala functional and structural connectivity predicts individual risk tolerance. *Neuron, 98*, 394–404. doi:10.1016/j. neuron.2018.03.019

Kahne, J., & Middaugh, E. (2012). Digital media shapes youth participation in politics. *Kappan Magazine* (Phi Delta Kappa). Retrieved from https://ypp.dmlcentral.net/sites/default/files/publications/Digital_Media_Shapes_Participation.pdf

Kelly, O. (2020). How clinical interviews help diagnose mental illness. *Verywell Mind*. Retrieved from https://www.verywellmind.com/structured-clinical-interview-2510532

Kelty, R., Kleykamp, M., & Segal, D. R. (2010). The military and the transition to adulthood. *The Future of Children, 20*, 181–207. Retrieved from https://futureofchildren.princeton.edu/sites/futureofchildren/files/media/transition_to_adulthood_20_01_fulljournal.pdf

Kennedy, S., & Ruggles, S. (2014). Breaking up is hard to count: The rise of divorce in the United States, 1980–2010. *Demography, 51*, 587–598. doi:10.1007/s13524-013-0270-9

Kentnor, H. (2015). Distance education and the evolution of online learning in the United States. *Curriculum and Teaching Dialogue, 17*, 21–34.

Kenton, W. (2020, November 22). Organisation for Economic Co-operation and Development (OECD). *Investopedia*. Retrieved from https://www.investopedia.com/terms/o/oecd.asp

Kimmel, M. (2008). *Guyland: The perilous world where boys become men / Understanding the critical years between 16 and 26*. Harper.

Kirkpatrick, T. (2019, September 12). Watch these Marine recruits take on the infamous 'Reaper.' *We Are the Mighty*. Retrieved from https://www.wearethemighty.com/military-life/marine-recruits-take-on-reaper/

Kirkpatrick Johnson, M., Crosnoe, R., & Elder, G. H. Jr. (2011). Insights on adolescence from a life course perspective. *Journal of Research on Adolescence, 21*, 273–280. doi:10.1111/j.1532-7795.2010.00728.x

Kolevska, A. (2017). *Dimensions of emerging adulthood and a sense of adulthood in Macedonian emerging adults*. Master's thesis, Ss. Cyril and Methodius University, Skopje.

Koolschijn, P. C. M. P., & Crone, E. A. (2013). Sex differences and structural brain maturation from childhood to early adulthood. *Developmental Cognitive Neuroscience, 5*, 106–118.

Kornrich, S., & Furstenberg, F. F. (2013). Investing in children: Changes in parental spending on children, 1972–2007. *Demography, 50*, 1–23. doi:10.1007/s13524-012-0146-4

Kouros, C. D., Pruitt, M. M., Ekas, N. V., Kiriaki, R., & Sunderland, M. (2017). Helicopter parenting, autonomy support, and college students' mental health and well-being: The moderating role of sex and ethnicity. *Journal of Child and Family Studies, 26*, 939–949. https://doi.org/10.1007/s10826-016-0614-3

Kragel, P. A., & LaBar, K. S. (2016). Decoding the nature of emotion in the brain. *Trends in Cognitive Sciences, 20*, 444–455. doi:10.1016/j.tics.2016.03.011

Kuh, G. D. (2003). What we're learning about student engagement from NSSE. *Change, 35*, 24–32.

Kuperberg, A. (2014a). Age at coresidence, premarital cohabitation, and marriage dissolution: 1985–2009. *Journal of Marriage and Family, 76*, 352–369. doi:10.1111/jomf.12092

Kuperberg, A. (2014b). Does premarital cohabitation raise your risk of divorce? *Council on Contemporary Families*. Retrieved from https://sites.utexas.edu/contemporaryfamilies/2014/03/10/cohabitation-divorce-brief-report/

Laboratory for the Study of Anxiety Disorder. (2021). *Generalized anxiety disorder*. University of Texas-Austin. Retrieved from https://labs.la.utexas.edu/telch/anxiety-and-its-disorders/generalized-anxiety-disorder/

Lachman, M. E. (2004). Development in midlife. *Annual Review of Psychology, 55*, 305–331. doi:10.1146/annurev.psych.55.090902.141521

Lee, J. S. & Waithaka, E. N. (2017). The intersections of marginalized social identities in the transition to adulthood: A demographic profile. *Emerging Adulthood, 5*, 151–163. doi:10.1177/2167696816659021

Lefkowitz, E. S., & Gillen, M. M. (2005). "Sex is just a normal part of life": Sexuality in emerging adulthood. In J. J. Arnett & J. L. Tanner (Eds.), *Emerging adults in America: Coming of age in the 21st century* (pp. 235–255). American Psychological Association.

LeMoyne, T., & Buchanan, T. (2011). Does "hovering" matter? Helicopter parenting and its effect on well-being. *Sociological Spectrum, 31*, 399–418. doi:10.1080/02732173.2011.574038

Lerma, G. (2011, August 26). Bid day brings joy to many Red Raiders. *Daily Toreador.* Retrieved from http://www.dailytoreador.com/news/article_b6e4a74c-cfa5-11e0-b719 -001a4bcf6878.html

Levinger, G., 1965. Marital cohesiveness and dissolution: An integrative review. *Journal of Marriage and the Family 27*, 19–28.

Levinson, D. J. (1978). *The seasons of a man's life.* Ballantine.

Lipka, M. (2014, November 13). 7 key takeaways about religion in Latin America. Pew Research Center. Retrieved from https://www.pewresearch.org/fact-tank/2014/11/13/7-key -takeaways-about-religion-in-latin-america/

Lippman, L. H., & McIntosh, H. (2010). The demographics of spirituality and religiosity among youth: International and U.S. patterns (Publication #2010-21). *Child Trends.*

Livingston, G. (2018, January 18). They're waiting longer, but U.S. women today more likely to have children than a decade ago. *Pew Research Center.* Retrieved from https://www .pewresearch.org/social-trends/2018/01/18/theyre-waiting-longer-but-u-s-women -today-more-likely-to-have-children-than-a-decade-ago/

Luempert, A. J. (2021). Latinx college students' transition to adulthood: The intersections of childhood economic pressure, biculturalism, and familism. Doctoral dissertation, Department of Human Development and Family Sciences, Texas Tech University.

Luker, K. (1984). *Abortion & the politics of motherhood.* University of California Press.

Lumina Foundation. (2021). *We're tracking America's progress toward the 60% attainment goal.* Retrieved from https://www.luminafoundation.org/stronger-nation/report/#/progress

Luyckx, K., Goossens, L., & Soenens, B. (2006). A developmental contextual perspective on identity construction in emerging adulthood: Change dynamics in commitment formation and commitment evaluation. *Developmental Psychology, 42*, 366–380. doi:10.1037/0012-1649.42.2.366

Luyckx, K., Klimstra, T. A., Duriez, B., Van Petegem, S., & Beyers, W. (2013). Personal identity processes from adolescence through the late 20s: Age trends, functionality, and depressive symptoms. *Social Development, 22*, 701–721.

Lyness, J. L., Lipetz, M. E., & Davis, K. E. (1972). Living together: An alternative to marriage. *Journal of Marriage and the Family, 34*, 305–311.

Macapagal, K., Greene, G. J., Rivera, Z., & Mustanski, B. (2015). "The best is always yet to come": Relationship stages and processes among young LGBT couples. *Journal of Family Psychology, 29*, 309–320. doi:10.1037/fam0000094

Macklin, E. D. (1972). Heterosexual cohabitation among unmarried college students. *The Family Coordinator, 21*, 463–472.

Maganga, T. (August 20, 2020). *Youth demonstrations and their impact on political change and development in Africa.* African Centre for the Constructive Resolution of Disputes (ACCORD). Retrieved from https://www.accord.org.za/conflict-trends/youth-demonstrations-and -their-impact-on-political-change-and-development-in-africa/

Mai, J. K., Majtanik, M., & Paxinos, G. (2016). *Atlas of the human brain* (4th edition). Academic Press.

Mak, K. K. L., Kleitman, S., & Abbott M. J. (2019). Impostor phenomenon measurement scales: A systematic review. *Frontiers in Psychology, 10*, Article No. 671. https://www.frontiersin .org/article/10.3389/fpsyg.2019.00671

Malamud, O. (2010), Breadth versus depth: The timing of specialization in higher education. *Labour, 24*, 359–390. doi:10.1111/j.1467-9914.2010.00489.x

Marcia, J. E. (1966). Development and validation of ego-identity status. *Journal of Personality and Social Psychology, 3*, 551–558. doi:10.1037/h0023281

Marcia, J. E. (1980). Identity in adolescence. In J. Adelson (Ed.), *Handbook of adolescent psychology* (pp. 159–187). Wiley.

Marte, J. (2015, May 9). Why parenting is even more daunting for millennials than it was for their parents – or their grandparents. *Washington Post*. Retrieved from https://www .washingtonpost.com/news/get-there/wp/2015/04/29/the-catch-22-many-millennial -parents-face/

Massachusetts Office of Problem Gambling Services (2021). *Identifying a gambling disorder.* Retrieved from https://www.mass.gov/info-details/identifying-a-gambling-disorder

Mathews, T. J., & Hamilton, B. E. (2002, December 11). Mean age of mother, 1970–2000. *National Vital Statistics Reports, 51* (Article 1). National Center for Health Statistics. Retrieved from https://www.cdc.gov/nchs/data/nvsr/nvsr51/nvsr51_01.pdf

Mathews, T. J., & Hamilton, B. E. (2016, January). Mean Age of Mothers is on the Rise: United States, 2000–2014. *National Center for Health Statistics*. Retrieved from https://www.cdc .gov/nchs/products/databriefs/db232.htm

Mayhew, M. J., Rockenbach, A. B., Bowman, N. A., Seifert, T. A., Wolniak, G. C., with Pascarella, E. T., & Terenzini, P. T. (2016). *How college affects students: 21st century evidence that higher education works.* Jossey-Bass.

McIlvain, G., Clements, R. G., Magoon, E. M., Spielberg, J. M., Telzer, E. H., & Johnson, C. L. (2020). Viscoelasticity of reward and control systems in adolescent risk taking. *NeuroImage 215*, 116850.

McNamara Barry, C., & Abo-Zena, M. M. (Eds.) (2014). *Emerging adults' religiousness and spirituality: Meaning-making in an age of transition.* Oxford University Press.

Medina, L. D., Sabo, S., & Vespa, J. (2020). Living longer: Historical and projected life expectancy in the United States, 1960 to 2060. Current Population Reports, P25-1145, U.S. Census Bureau. Retrieved from https://www.census.gov/content/dam/Census/library/ publications/2020/demo/p25-1145.pdf

Meeus, W. (2011). The study of adolescent identity formation 2000–2010: A review of longitudinal research. *Journal of Research on Adolescence, 21*, 75–94. doi:10.1111/j.1532-7795.2010.00716.x

Meeus, W., van de Schoot, R., Keijsers, L., Schwartz, S. J., & Branje, S. (2010). On the progression and stability of adolescent identity formation. A five-wave longitudinal study in early-to-middle and middle-to-late adolescence. *Child Development, 81*, 1565–1581.

Mehta, C. M., Arnett, J. J., Palmer, C. G., & Nelson, L. (2020). Established adulthood: A new conception of ages 30 to 45. *American Psychologist, 75*, 431–444. https://doi.org/10.1037 /amp0000600

Menand, L. (2014, July 14). How women got in on the Civil Rights Act. *The New Yorker*. Retrieved from https://www.newyorker.com/magazine/2014/07/21/sex-amendment

Michalski, D. S., & Fowler, G. (2016, January). *Doctoral degrees in psychology: How are they different, or not so different?* American Psychological Association, Psychology Student Network. Retrieved from https://www.apa.org/ed/precollege/psn/2016/01/doctoral-degrees

Mickelson, K. D., & Biehle, S. N. (2017). Gender and the transition to parenthood: Introduction to the special issue. *Sex Roles, 76*, 271–275. doi:10.1007/s11199-016-0724-9

Miller, A. (2015-present). *Vietnam-era antiwar protests - Timeline and maps 1963–1975.* Mapping American Social Movements Project, University of Washington. Retrieved from https:// depts.washington.edu/moves/antiwar_map_protests.shtml

Miller-Tutzauer, C., Leonard, K. E., & Windle, M. (1991). Marriage and alcohol use: A longitudinal study of "maturing out." *Journal of Studies on Alcohol, 52*, 434–440. doi:10.15288/jsa.1991.52.434

Mitra, D., & Arnett, J. J. (2021). Life choices of emerging adults in India. *Emerging Adulthood, 9*, 229–239. doi:10.1177/2167696819851891

Moen, P., & Sweet, S. (2002). Two careers, one employer: Couples working for the same corporation. *Journal of Vocational Behavior 61*, 466–483. doi:10.1006/jvbe.2002.1886

Montenegro, R. (2014, October 20). Why young people don't vote: Part apathy, part frustration, part ignorance. *Big Think*. Retrieved from https://bigthink.com/politics-current-affairs/ why-young-people-dont-vote-part-apathy-part-frustration/

Moody, J. (2020). How a gap year prepares students for college. *US News & World Report*. Retrieved from https://www.usnews.com/education/best-colleges/articles/2019-03-08 /what-a-gap-year-is-and-how-it-prepares-students-for-college

Moore, R., Ames, G., & Cunradi, C. (2007). Physical and social availability of alcohol for young enlisted naval personnel in and around home port. *Substance Abuse Treatment, Prevention, and Policy, 2,* Article No. 17. doi:10.1186/1747-597X-2-17

Morgan, E. M. (2012). Contemporary issues in sexual orientation and identity development in emerging adulthood. *Emerging Adulthood, 1,* 52–66. doi:10.1177/2167696812469187

Morris, M. (2017, June 8). Why don't young people vote? Because school teaches us nothing about politics. *The Guardian*. Retrieved from https://www.theguardian.com/commentisfree /2017/jun/08/young-people-vote-school-teach-politics-curriculum-election

Mosher, W. D. Jones, J., & Abma, J. C. (2012, July 24). Intended and unintended births in the United States: 1982–2010. *National Health Statistics Reports* (No. 55). Retrieved from https://www.cdc.gov/nchs/data/nhsr/nhsr055.pdf

Munno, D. W., & Syed, N. I. (2003). Synaptogenesis in the CNS: An odyssey from wiring together to firing together. *Journal of Physiology, 552.*1, 1–11. doi:10.1113/jphysiol.2003.045062

Murphy, R., & Hallahan, B. (2016). Differences between DSM-IV and DSM-5 as applied to general adult psychiatry. *Irish Journal of Psychological Medicine, 33,* 135–141. doi:10.1017/ ipm.2015.54

Nation Master. (2003–2021). *Military: Service age and obligation: Countries compared.* Retrieved from https://www.nationmaster.com/country-info/stats/Military/Service-age-and-obligation

National Center for Education Statistics. (2011). Number and percentage of 18- to 24-year-olds in the armed forces, by age group and sex: 2000 through 2008. Youth Indicators 2011. America's Youth: Transitions to Adulthood. Retrieved from https://nces.ed.gov/pubs2012 /2012026/tables/table_29.asp

National Center for Health Statistics. (2021). Births and natality. *Centers for Disease Control and Prevention (CDC).* Retrieved from https://www.cdc.gov/nchs/fastats/births.htm

National Congregations Study. (2019). *American congregations at the beginning of the 21st century.* Retrieved from https://sites.duke.edu/ncsweb/files/2019/03/NCSII_report_final.pdf

National Institute on Alcohol Abuse and Alcoholism. (2016). *Alcohol use disorder: A comparison between DSM–IV and DSM–5.* Retrieved from https://pubs.niaaa.nih.gov/publications/ dsmfactsheet/dsmfact.pdf

National Institute on Alcohol Abuse and Alcoholism. (not dated). *What is a standard drink?* Retrieved from https://www.niaaa.nih.gov/alcohols-effects-health/overview-alcohol -consumption/what-standard-drink

National Institute on Drug Abuse. (2018). Comorbidity: Substance use disorders and other mental illnesses. *DrugFacts.* Retrieved from https://www.drugabuse.gov/publications/ drugfacts/comorbidity-substance-use-disorders-other-mental-illnesses

National Institute of Mental Health. (2021). *Major depression.* Retrieved from https://www.nimh .nih.gov/health/statistics/major-depression

National Research Council. (2015). *Investing in the health and well-being of young adults.* National Academies Press. doi:10.17226/18869

National Survey of Student Engagement (2007). *Experiences that matter: Enhancing student learning and success annual report 2007.* Center for Postsecondary Research, School of Education, Indiana University Bloomington. Retrieved from https://nsse.indiana.edu/research/ annual-results/past-annual-results/nsse-annual-report-2007.html

National Women's History Alliance. (2021). *Timeline of legal history of women in the United States.* Retrieved from https://nationalwomenshistoryalliance.org/resources/womens-rights -movement/detailed-timeline/

Nauta, M. M. (2010). The development, evolution, and status of Holland's theory of vocational personalities: Reflections and future directions for counseling psychology. *Journal of Counseling Psychology, 57,* 11–22. doi:10.1037/a0018213

Nelson, L. (2015, February 4). The big problem Obama's free community college plan ignores. *Vox.* Retrieved from https://www.vox.com/2015/2/4/7977413/college-completion-free-tuition

Nelson, L. J., Badger, S., & Wu, B. (2004). The influence of culture in emerging adulthood: Perspectives of Chinese college students. *International Journal of Behavioral Development, 28,* 26–36. doi:10.1080/01650250344000244

NeMoyer, A., Cruz-Gonzalez, M., Alvarez, K., Kessler, R. C., Sampson, N. A., Green, J. G., & Alegría, M. (2020, online first). Reducing racial/ethnic disparities in mental health service use among emerging adults: Community-level supply factors. *Ethnicity & Health.* doi:10.1080/13557858.2020.1814999

Neubauer, B. E., Witkop, C. T., & Varpio, L. (2019). How phenomenology can help us learn from the experiences of others. *Perspectives on Medical Education, 8,* 90–97. doi:10.1007/s40037-019-0509-2

NeuroRelay . (2012, October 7). *Female brain versus male brain.* Retrieved from http://neurorelay.com/2012/10/07/female-brain-versus-male-brain/

Newman, K. (2012). *The accordion family: Boomerang kids, anxious parents, and the private toll of global competition.* Beacon Press.

Nguyen, A.-M. D., & Benet-Martínez, V. (2013). Biculturalism and adjustment: A meta-analysis. *Journal of Cross-Cultural Psychology, 44,* 122–159. doi:10.1177/0022022111435097

Niehuis, S., Lee, K.-H., & Oblad, T. (2013). Cohabitation before marriage. In R. E. Emery & G. J. Golson (Eds.), *Cultural sociology of divorce: An encyclopedia* (pp. 276–280). Sage Publications. doi:10.4135/9781452274447.n101

Niehuis, S., Reifman, A., Al-Khalil, K., Oldham, C. R., Fang, D., O'Boyle, M., & Davis, T. H. (2019). Functional magnetic resonance imaging activation in response to prompts of romantically disillusioning events. *Personal Relationships, 26,* 209–231. doi:10.1111/pere.12272

Niehuis, S., Reifman, A., Feng, D., & Huston, T. (2016). Courtship progression rate and declines in expressed affection early in marriage: A test of the disillusionment model. *Journal of Family Issues, 37,* 1074–1100. doi:10.1177/0192513X14540159

Niehuis, S., Reifman, A., Weiser, D., Punyanunt-Carter, N., Flora, J., Arias, V. S., & Oldham, C. R. (2020). Guilty pleasure? Communicating sexually explicit content on dating apps and disillusionment with app usage. *Human Communication Research, 46,* 55–85. https://doi.org/10.1093/hcr/hqz013

Núñez, J., & Flanagan, C. (2016). Political beliefs and civic engagement in emerging adulthood. In J. J. Arnett (Ed.), *The Oxford handbook of emerging adulthood* (pp. 481–496). Oxford University Press.

O'Boyle, M. W. (2008). Book review of Daniel Romer and Elaine F. Walker (Eds.). Adolescent psychopathology and the developing brain. *Journal of Youth and Adolescence, 37,* 481–483. doi:10.1007/s10964-007-9252-9

Obidoa, C. A., Dodor, B. A., Tackie-Ofosu, V., Obidoa, M. A., Kalisch, H. R., & Nelson, L. J. (2019). Perspectives on markers of adulthood among emerging adults in Ghana and Nigeria. *Emerging Adulthood, 7,* 270–278. doi:10.1177/2167696818778906

Oesterle, S., Hawkins, J. D., Hill, K. G., & Bailey, J. A. (2010). Men's and women's pathways to adulthood and their adolescent precursors. *Journal of Marriage and Family 72*(5), 1436–1453. doi:10.1111/j.1741-3737.2010.00775.x

Office of Planning, Research, and Evaluation. (2018). *Housing for young adults in extended federally funded foster care.* Administration for Children & Families, US Department of Health and Human Services. Retrieved from https://www.acf.hhs.gov/opre/report/housing-young-adults-extended-federally-funded-foster-care

Ogolsky, B. G., & Monk, J. K. (2019). Dating and couple formation. In B. H. Fiese, M. Celano, K. Deater-Deckard, E. N. Jouriles, & M. A. Whisman (Eds.), *APA handbook of contemporary family psychology: Vol. 1. Foundations, methods, and contemporary issues across the lifespan* (pp. 427–443). doi:10.1037/0000099-024

Olmstead, S. B., Roberson, P. N. E., Pasley, K., Fincham, F. D. (2015). Hooking up and risk behaviors among first semester college men: What is the role of pre-college experience? *Journal of Sex Research, 52*, 186–198. doi:10.1080/00224499.2013.843147

Olson, J. (2020, June 27). Four Minnesota bars linked to youth COVID-19 surge. *Star Tribune.* Retrieved from https://www.startribune.com/four-bars-linked-to-covid-19-surge-in -young-adults/571513112/

O'Neill, S. E., Parra, G. R., & Sher, K. J. (2001). Clinical relevance of heavy drinking during the college years: Cross-sectional and prospective perspectives. *Psychology of Addictive Behaviors, 15*, 350–359. doi:10.1037/0893-164X.15.4.350

Organization for Economic Cooperation and Development. (2021a). Gender wage gap. *OECD iLibrary.* Retrieved from https://www.oecd-ilibrary.org/employment/gender-wage-gap/ indicator/english_7cee77aa-en

Organization for Economic Cooperation and Development. (2021b). Young self-employed. *OECD iLibrary.* Retrieved from https://data.oecd.org/entrepreneur/young-self-employed .htm

Osborne, C., Michelsen, A., & Bobbitt, K. (2017, August). *Fatherhood EFFECT evaluation final report: A comprehensive plan for supporting Texas fathers and families.* Child & Family Research Partnership, University of Texas-Austin. Retrieved from https://childandfamilyresearch .utexas.edu/sites/default/files/CFRPReport_R0140817_FatherhoodEFFECT.pdf

Osgood, D. W., Foster, E. M. & Courtney, M. E. (2010). Vulnerable populations and the transition to adulthood. *Future of Children, 20*, 209–229. doi:10.1353/foc.0.0047

Osgood, D. W., Ruth, G., Eccles, J. S., Jacobs, J. E., & Barber, B. L. (2005). Six paths to adulthood. In R. A. Settersten Jr., F. F. Furstenberg, Jr., & R. G. Rumbaut (Eds.), *On the frontier of adulthood: Theory, research, and public policy* (pp. 320–355). University of Chicago Press.

Oswalt, S. B., Lederer, A. M., Chestnut-Steich, K., Day, C. Halbritter, A., & Ortiz, D. (2020). Trends in college students' mental health diagnoses and utilization of services, 2009–2015. *Journal of American College Health, 68*, 41–51. doi:10.1080/07448481.2018.1515748

Othering and Belonging Institute (2021). Maps of city segregation. University of California, Berkeley. Retrieved from https://belonging.berkeley.edu/

Padilla-Walker, L. M., & Nelson, L. J. (2012). Black hawk down? Establishing helicopter parenting as a distinct construct from other forms of parental control during emerging adulthood. *Journal of Adolescence, 35*, 1177–1190. doi:10.1016/j.adolescence.2012.03.007

Palkovitz, R., Copes, M. & Woolfolk, T. (2001). "It's like… you discover a sense of being": Involved fathering as an evoker of adult development. *Men and Masculinities, 4*, 49–69. doi:10.1177 /1097184X01004001003

Park, B.-y., Seo, J., Yi, J., & Park, H. (2015). Structural and functional brain connectivity of people with obesity and prediction of body mass index using connectivity. *PLoS ONE 10*(11): e0141376. doi:10.1371/journal.pone.0141376

Parker, P. D., Thoemmes, F., Duineveld, J. J., & Salmela-Aro, K. (2015). I wish I had (not) taken a gap-year? The psychological and attainment outcomes of different post-school pathways. *Developmental Psychology, 51*, 323–333. doi:10.1037/a0038667

Pedersen, E. R., Larimer, M. E., & Lee, C. M. (2010). When in Rome: Factors associated with changes in drinking behavior among American college students studying abroad. *Psychology of Addictive Behaviors, 24*, 535–540. doi:10.1037/a0019863

Petts, R. J. (2009). Trajectories of religious participation from adolescence to young adulthood. *Journal for the Scientific Study of Religion, 48*, 552–571. doi:10.1111/j.1468-5906.2009.01465.x

Pew Research Center (2011, October 5). A profile of the modern military. In *War and sacrifice in the post-9/11 era.* Retrieved from https://www.pewresearch.org/social-trends/2011/10 /05/chapter-6-a-profile-of-the-modern-military/

Pew Research Center (2012, March 15). The boomerang generation: Who are the boomerang kids? *Pew Research Center.* Retrieved from https://www.pewresearch.org/social-trends /2012/03/15/who-are-the-boomerang-kids/

Pharo, H., Sim, C,. Graham, M., Gross, J., & Hayne, H. (2011). Risky business: Executive function, personality, and reckless behavior during adolescence and emerging adulthood. *Behavioral Neuroscience, 125*, 970–978.

Pitzer, L., Fingerman, K. L., & Lefkowitz, E. S. (2011). Development of the Parent Adult Relationship Questionnaire (PARQ). *International Journal of Aging & Human Development, 72*, 111–135. doi:10.2190/AG.72.2.b

Pleck, E. H. (2012). *Not just roommates: Cohabitation after the sexual revolution*. University of Chicago Press.

Polling Report. (2021). *Polling Report compilation of surveys on LGBT issues*. Retrieved from https://pollingreport.com/lgbt.htm

Powell, D., Freedman, G., Jensen, K., & Preston, V. (2021). "Talking" as a romantic interaction: Is there consensus? *Journal of Couple & Relationship Therapy, 20*, 1–21. doi:10.1080/153326 91.2020.1867684

Preetz, R., Filser, A., Brömmelhaus, A., Baalmann, T., & Feldhaus, M. (in press). Longitudinal changes in life satisfaction and mental health in emerging adulthood during the COVID-19 pandemic: Risk and protective factors. *Emerging Adulthood*. doi:10.1177/21676968211042109

Prikhidko, A., & Swank, J. M. (2018). Motherhood experiences and expectations: A qualitative exploration of mothers of toddlers. *The Family Journal, 26*, 278–284. doi:10.1177/1066480718795116

PsyToolKit . (2021). *Stroop task*. Retrieved from https://www.psytoolkit.org/experiment-library /stroop.html

Public Religion Research Institute. (2021, July 8). *The American religious landscape in 2020*. https://www.prri.org/research/2020-census-of-american-religion/

Putnam, R. D. (2000). *Bowling alone: The collapse and revival of American community*. Touchstone Books/Simon & Schuster. doi:10.1145/358916.361990

Quealy, K., & Parlapiano, A. (2021, January 4). Election day voting in 2020 took longer in America's poorest neighborhoods. *New York Times*. Retrieved from https://www.nytimes .com/interactive/2021/01/04/upshot/voting-wait-times.html

Queensland Brain Institute (2019). *The limbic system*. Retrieved from https://qbi.uq.edu.au/brain /brain-anatomy/limbic-system

Radloff, L. S. (1977). The CES-D scale: A self-report depression scale for research in the general population. *Applied Psychological Measurement, 1*, 385–401. https://doi.org/10.1177 /014662167700100306

Räikkönen, E., Kokko, K., Chen, M., Pulkkinen, L. (2012). Patterns of adult roles, their antecedents and psychosocial wellbeing correlates among Finns born in 1959. *Longitudinal and Life Course Studies, 3*, 211–227. doi:10.14301/llcs.v3i2.180

Rankin, S., Garvey, J. C., & Duran, A. (2019). A retrospective of LGBT issues on U.S. college campuses: 1990–2020. *International Sociology, 34*, 435–454. doi:10.1177/0268580919851429

Ravert, R. D. (2009). "You're only young once": Things college students report doing now before it is too late. *Journal of Adolescent Research, 24*, 376–396. doi:10.1177/0743558409334254

Reczek, C. (2020). Sexual- and gender-minority families: A 2010 to 2020 decade in review. *Journal of Marriage and Family, 82*, 300–325. doi:10.1111/jomf.12607

Regnerus, M., & Uecker, J. (2011). *Premarital sex in America: How young Americans meet, mate, and think about marrying*. Oxford University Press.

Reid, J. (2012). *Let the people in: The life and times of Ann Richards*. University of Texas Press.

Reifman, A. (2011a, September 1). How fraternities and sororities impact students (or do they?). *Psychology Today Blog*. Retrieved from https://www.psychologytoday.com/us/blog/the -campus/201109/how-fraternities-and-sororities-impact-students-or-do-they

Reifman, A. (2011b, October 1). Stress in college students. *Psychology Today Blog*. Retrieved from https://www.psychologytoday.com/us/blog/the-campus/201110/stress-in-college-students

Reifman, A. (2017). Fraternities. In K. L. Nadal (Ed.), *The Sage encyclopedia of psychology and gender* (pp. 584 585). Sage.

Reifman, A. (2020, December). Marital paradigms: A teaching activity to help understand marriage-age trends. *Relationship Research News, 19* (4). Accessible at: https://iarr.org/relationshipresearchnews.html

Reifman, A., Arnett, J. J., & Colwell, M. J. (2007a, Summer). Emerging adulthood: Theory, assessment, and application. *Journal of Youth Development, 2(1, electronic journal)*. Available at: https://jyd.pitt.edu/ojs/jyd/article/view/359/345

Reifman, A., Arnett, J. J., & Colwell, M. J. (2007b). The IDEA: Inventory of the dimensions of emerging adulthood (extended analyses to accompany Reifman, Arnett, & Colwell, 2007, journal of youth development). *Research Gate.* https://doi.org/10.13140/RG.2.1.3547.6886

Reifman, A., & Oblad, T. (2012, Fall). College students' and parents' communication and views of proper assistance with school-related matters. *AHEPPP Journal* [Association of Higher Education Parent/Family Program Professionals], *3*(2), 2–19. Available at: http://www.aheppp.org.

Reifman, A., Ro, H.-S., Barnes, G., & Feng, D. (2010). Drinking in youth ages 13–21 attending and not attending college. *Journal of the First-Year Experience and Students in Transition, 22,* 67–86.

Rhoades, G. K., Stanley, S. M., & Markman, H. J. (2012). The impact of the transition to cohabitation on relationship functioning: Cross-sectional and longitudinal findings. *Journal of Family Psychology, 26,* 348–358. doi:10.1037/a0028316

Robbins, A. (2004). *Pledged: The secret life of sororities.* Hyperion.

Robbins, A. (2019). *Fraternity: An inside look at a year of college boys becoming men.* Penguin Random House.

Robbins, A., & Wilner, A. (2001). *Quarterlife crisis: The unique challenges of life in your twenties.* Penguin Random House.

Rogers, B. P., Morgan, V. L., Newton, A. T., Gore, J. C. (2007). Assessing functional connectivity in the human brain by fMRI. *Magnetic Resonance Imaging, 25,* 1347–1357. doi:10.1016/j.mri.2007.03.007

Ross, M., Moore, K. A., Murphy, K., Bateman, N., DeMand, A., & Sacks, V. (2018). *Pathways to high-quality jobs for young adults.* Brookings Institution. Retrieved from https://www.brookings.edu/research/pathways-to-high-quality-jobs-for-young-adults/

Rostker, B. D. (2006). *The evolution of the all-volunteer force.* RAND Corporation. Retrieved from https://www.rand.org/pubs/research_briefs/RB9195.html

Rowe, A. (2018, June 25). *The parity paradox: Will more women in law school mean more women in the law? Best Lawyers "Women in the Law" 2018.* Retrieved from https://www.bestlawyers.com/article/women-now-outnumber-men-in-law-school/2029

Rumbaut, R. G., & Komaie, G. (2010). Immigration and adult transitions. *The Future of Children, 20,* 43–66. https://doi.org/10.1353/foc.0.0046

Rutter, L. A., & Brown, T. A. (2015). Reliability and validity of the dimensional features of generalized anxiety disorder. *Journal of Anxiety Disorders, 29,* 1–6. doi:10.1016/j.janxdis.2014.10.003

Salamon, L. M., Sokolowski, S. W., & Haddock, M. A. (2018). *The scope and scale of global volunteering: Current estimates and next steps. A background paper for the 2018 State of the World's Volunteerism report.* Retrieved from https://www.researchgate.net/publication/330543604_The_Scope_and_Scale_of_Global_Volunteering_Current_Estimates_and_Next_Steps_A_Background_Paper_for_the_2018_State_of_the_World%27s_Volunteerism_Report

Salmela-Aro, K., Taanila, A., Ek, E., & Chen, M. (2012). Role configurations in young adulthood, antecedents, and later wellbeing among Finns born in 1966. *Longitudinal and Life Course Studies, 3,* 228–242. doi:10.14301/llcs.v3i2.184

Sandberg-Thoma, S. E., Snyder, A. R., & Jang, B. J. (2015) Exiting and returning to the parental home for boomerang kids. *Journal of Marriage and Family, 77,* 806–818. doi:10.1111/jomf.12183

Sandefur, G. D., Eggerling-Boeck, J., & Park, H. (2005). Off to a good start? Postsecondary education and early adult life. In R. A. Settersten, Jr., F. F. Furstenberg, Jr., R. G. Rumbaut (Eds.), *On the frontier of adulthood: Theory, research, and public policy* (pp. 292–319). University of Chicago Press.

Sasse, B. (2017). *The vanishing American adult.* St. Martin's.

Sassler, S., Ciambrone, D. & Benway, G. (2008). Are they really mama's boys/daddy's girls? The negotiation of adulthood upon returning to the parental home. *Sociological Forum, 23,* 670–698. doi:10.1111/j.1573-7861.2008.00090.x

Savage, M. (2019, August 21). *Why so many young Swedes live alone.* British Broadcasting Corporation. Retrieved from https://www.bbc.com/worklife/article/20190821-why-so-many-young-swedes-live-alone

Schiffrin, H. H., Liss, M., Miles-McLean, H., Geary, K. A., Erchull, M. J., & Tashner, T. (2014). Helping or hovering? The effects of helicopter parenting on college students' well-being. *Journal of Child and Family Studies, 23,* 548–557. doi:10.1007/s10826-013-9716-3

Schnyders, C. M., & Lane, J. A. (2018). Gender, parent and peer relationships, and identification with emerging adulthood among college students. *Journal of College Counseling, 21,* 239–251. https://doi.org/10.1002/jocc.12106

Schoon, I., Chen, M., Kneale, D., & Jager, J. (2012). Becoming adults in Britain: Lifestyles and wellbeing in times of social change. *Longitudinal and Life Course Studies, 3,* 173–189. doi:10.14301/llcs.v3i2.181

Schulenberg, J., Bryant, A., & O'Malley, P. (2004). Taking hold of some kind of life: How developmental tasks relate to trajectories of well-being during the transition to adulthood. *Development and Psychopathology, 16,* 1119–1140. doi:10.1017/S0954579404040167

Schulenberg, J., Maggs, J. L., Long, S. W., Sher, K. J., Gotham, H. J., Baer, J. S., Kivlahan, D. R., Marlatt, G. A., & Zucker, R. A. (2001). The problem of college drinking: Insights from a developmental perspective. *Alcoholism: Clinical and Experimental Research, 25,* 473–477.

Schulenberg, J. E., Patrick, M. E., Johnston, L. D., O'Malley, P. M., Bachman, J. G., & Miech, R. A. (2021). *Monitoring the Future national survey results on drug use, 1975–2020: Volume II, College students and adults ages 19–60.* Institute for Social Research, The University of Michigan. Retrieved from http://monitoringthefuture.org/pubs/monographs/mtf-vol2_2020.pdf

Schwartz, S. J., Beyers, W., Luyckx, K., Soenens, B., Zamboanga, B. L., Forthun, L. F., Hardy, S. A., Vazsonyi, A. T., Ham, L. S., Kim, S. Y., Whitbourne, S. K., & Waterman, A. S. (2011). Examining the light and dark sides of emerging adults' identity: A study of identity status differences in positive and negative psychosocial functioning. *Journal of Youth and Adolescence, 40,* 839–859.

Schwartz, S. J., Luyckx, K., & Crocetti, E. (2014). What have we learned since Schwartz (2001)? A reappraisal of the field of identity development. In K. McLean & M. Syed (Eds.), *Oxford handbook of identity development* (pp. 539–561). Oxford University Press.

Schwartz, S. J., Montgomery, M. J., & Briones, E. (2006). The role of identity in acculturation among immigrant people: Theoretical propositions, empirical questions, and applied recommendations. *Human Development, 49,* 1–30. doi:10.1159/000090300

Scott, D. (2020, July 6). Covid-19 cases are rising, but deaths are falling. What's going on? Vox. Retrieved from https://www.vox.com/2020/7/6/21314472/covid-19-coronavirus-us-cases-deaths-trends-wtf

Scott, M. E., Schelar, E, Manlove, J., & Cui, C. (2009, July). Young adult attitudes about relationships and marriage: Times may have changed, but expectations remain high. *Child Trends® Research Brief.* Retrieved from https://www.childtrends.org/wp-content/uploads/2009/07/Child_Trends-2009_07_08_RB_YoungAdultAttitudes.pdf

Searing, L. (2019, December 23). The big number: Women now outnumber men in medical schools. *Washington Post.* Retrieved from https://www.washingtonpost.com/health/the-big-number-women-now-outnumber-men-in-medical-schools/2019/12/20/8b9eddea-2277-11ea-bed5-880264cc91a9_story.html

Segran, E. (2020). *The rocket years: How your twenties launch the rest of your life*. Harper.

Seiffge-Krenke, I. (2016). Leaving home: Antecedents, consequences, and cultural patterns. In J. J. Arnett (Ed.), *The Oxford handbook of emerging adulthood* (pp. 177–189). Oxford University Press.

Serafini, T. E. & Adams, G. R. (2002). Functions of identity: Scale construction and validation. *Identity, 2*, 361–389.

Serafini, T. E., Maitland, S. B, & Adams, G. R. (2006, March). *The Functions of Identity Scale: Revisions, validation and model testing*. Poster presented at the Biennial Meeting of the Society for Research on Adolescence, San Francisco, California.

Serido, J., & Shim, S. (2017). *APLUS Project website*. Retrieved from https://www.aplushappiness .org/

Settersten, Jr, R. A., & Ray, B. (2010). What's going on with young people today? The long and twisting path to adulthood. *The Future of Children 20*,19–41.

Seymour, T. (2017, June 24). What does the corpus callosum do? *Medical News Today*. Retrieved from https://www.medicalnewstoday.com/articles/318065

Shaw, V. (2015, February 10). Research highlights plight of 'Clipped-Wing' Generation. *Huffington Post*. Retrieved from https://www.huffingtonpost.co.uk/2015/10/01/research-highlights -plight-of-clipped-wing-generation_n_8230232.html

Sick, N. Vilter, C., & Spaulding, S. (2019, October). Young parents making their way: Combining education and work while parenting. *Urban Institute*. Retrieved from https://www.urban .org/research/publication/young-parents-making-their-way-combining-education-and -work-while-parenting

Siegel, D. (2021). *Dr. Dan Siegel's hand model of the brain*. Retrieved from https://drdansiegel.com /hand-model-of-the-brain/

Silva, J. M. (2013). *Coming up short: Working-class adulthood in an age of uncertainty*. Oxford University Press.

Sironi, M., & Furstenberg, F. F. (2012. Trends in the economic independence of young adults in the United States: 1973–2007. *Population Development and Review, 38*, 609–630. doi:10.1111/j.1728-4457.2012.00529.x

Sirsch, U., Dreher, E., Mayr, E., & Willinger, U. (2009). What does it take to be an adult in Austria? Views of adulthood in Austrian adolescents, emerging adults, and adults. *Journal of Adolescent Research, 24*, 275–292. https://doi.org/10.1177/0743558408331184

Smith, C., with Christofferson, K., Davidson, H., & Herzog, P. S. (2011). *Lost in transition: The dark side of emerging adulthood*. Oxford University Press.

Snyder, T. D. (1993). Education characteristics of the population. In T. D. Snyder (Ed.), *120 years of American education: A statistical portrait* (pp. 5–24). National Center for Education Statistics. Retrieved from https://web.archive.org/web/20050325202017/https://nces.ed.gov/ pubs93/93442.pdf

Sofola, B. (2019, August 4). Adult Kids: Parents should sympathise with children still living at home! *Vanguard*. Retrieved from https://www.vanguardngr.com/2019/08/adult-kids -parents-should-sympathise-with-children-still-living-at-home/

South Carolina Department of Health and Environmental Control. (2020, June 19). *DHEC warns of increased cases of COVID-19 in youth and young adults, latest COVID-19 update*. Retrieved from https://scdhec.gov/news-releases/dhec-warns-increased-cases-covid-19 -youth-young-adults-latest-covid-19-update-june-19

Southey, R. (1837) *Goldilocks and the three bears*. Longman, Rees, Orme, Green, and Longman.

Sperber, M. (2000). *Beer and circus: How big-time college sports is crippling undergraduate education*. Henry Holt and Company.

Spiegel, A. (2006, April 25). The mechanics of choice: More isn't always better [Radio story and transcript]. *National Public Radio*. Retrieved from https://www.npr.org/templates/story/ story.php?storyId=5361844

Srivastava, S., & Rani, K. S. (2014). *Textbook of human development: A lifespan developmental approach*. S. Chand & Co.

St-Esprit, M. (2019, March 6). The stigma of choosing trade school over college. *The Atlantic.* Retrieved from https://www.theatlantic.com/education/archive/2019/03/choosing -trade-school-over-college/584275/

Stanley, S. M., & Markman, H. J. (1992). Assessing commitment in personal relationships. *Journal of Marriage and Family, 54,* 595–608. doi:10.2307/353245

Stanley, S. M., Rhoades, G. K., & Fincham, F. D. (2011). Understanding romantic relationships among emerging adults: The significant roles of cohabitation and ambiguity. In F. D. Fincham & M. Cui (Eds.), *Romantic relationships in emerging adulthood* (pp. 234–251). Cambridge University Press.

Stanley, S. M., Rhoades, G. K., & Markman, H. J. (2006). Sliding vs. deciding: Inertia and the premarital cohabitation effect. *Family Relations, 55,* 499–509. doi:10.1111/j.1741-3729.2006.00418.x

Statista. (2019). *Percentage of educational attainment in the United States in 2018, by ethnicity.* Retrieved from https://www.statista.com/statistics/184264/educational-attainment-by -enthnicity/

Statista. (2021a). *Spain: Youth unemployment rate from 1999 to 2019.* Retrieved from https://www .statista.com/statistics/813014/youth-unemployment-rate-in-spain/

Statista. (2021b). *Number of active duty United States Armed Forces personnel in 2020, by age group.* Retrieved from https://www.statista.com/statistics/232711/number-of-active-duty-us -defense-force-personnel-by-age/

Statista. (2021c). *Active and reserve U.S. military force personnel numbers in 2020, by service branch and reserve component.* Retrieved from https://www.statista.com/statistics/232330/us-military -force-numbers-by-service-branch-and-reserve-component/

Steinberg, L. (2010). A dual systems model of adolescent risk-taking. *Developmental Psychobiology, 52,* 216–224.

Steinberg, L. (2014). *Age of opportunity: Lessons from the new science of adolescence.* Houghton Mifflin Harcourt, Boston.

Steinberg, L., & Morris, A. S. (2001). Adolescent development. *Annual Review of Psychology, 52,* 83–110. doi:10.1146/annurev.psych.52.1.83

Stephens, R. (2017). Mind the gap: The state of skills in the U.S. *Third Way.* Retrieved from https://www.thirdway.org/report/mind-the-gap-the-state-of-skills-in-the-u-s

Stingley, P. (2015, September 9). KU offering more classes with fewer students, but big lectures still part of the system. *The University Daily Kansan.* Retrieved from https://www.kansan .com/news/ku-offering-more-classes-with-fewer-students-but-big-lectures-still-part-of -the-system/article_fa827808-570a-11e5-9be0-4736a9beed15.html

Stroop, J. R. (1935). Studies of interference in serial verbal reactions. *Journal of Experimental Psychology, 18,* 643–662. doi:10.1037/h0054651

Student Conservation Association. (not dated). *Gap years: What does the research say?* Retrieved from https://www.thesca.org/connect/blog/gap-years-whats-does-research-say

Su, R., Tay, L., & Diener, E. (2014). The development and validation of Comprehensive Inventory of Thriving (CIT) and Brief Inventory of Thriving (BIT). *Applied Psychology: Health and Well-Being, 6,* 251–279. doi:10.1111/aphw.12027

Substance Abuse and Mental Health Services Administration. (2021). *Key substance use and mental health indicators in the United States: Results from the 2020 National Survey on Drug Use and Health* (HHS Publication No. PEP21-07-01-003, NSDUH Series H-56). Center for Behavioral Health Statistics and Quality. Retrieved from https://www.samhsa.gov/data/

Sumrak, T. (2017). *How do student loans affect your credit score?* LendingTree. Retrieved from https://www.lendingtree.com/student/do-student-loans-affect-your-credit-score/

Suri, M. (2020, November 18). India's attitude to arranged marriage is changing. But some say not fast enough. *CNN.com.* https://www.cnn.com/2020/11/18/asia/indian-arranged -marriage-dst-intl-hnk/index.html

Syed, M., & Mitchell, L. L. (2016). How race and ethnicity shape emerging adulthood. In J. J. Arnett (Ed.), *The Oxford handbook of emerging adulthood* (pp. 87–101). Oxford University Press.

Taber-Thomas, B., & Pérez-Edgar, K. (2015). Emerging adulthood brain development. In J. J. Arnett (Ed.), *The Oxford handbook of emerging adulthood* (pp. 126–141). Oxford University Press.

Tanielian, T., & Jaycox, L. H. (Eds.). (2008). *Invisible wounds of war: Psychological and cognitive injuries, their consequences, and services to assist recovery.* RAND Corporation.

Tanner, J. L., Reinherz, H. Z., Beardslee, W. R., Fitzmaurice, G. M., Leis, J. A., & Berger, S. R. (2007). Change in 12-month and lifetime prevalence of psychiatric disorders from ages 21, 26, to 30 in a community sample. *Journal of Nervous and Mental Disease, 195*, 298–306. doi:10.1097/01.nmd.0000261952.13887.6e

Tarnoff, C. (2016). The Peace Corps: Current issues. *Congressional Research Service.* Retrieved from https://ecommons.cornell.edu/bitstream/handle/1813/78321/CRS_Peace_Corp _Current_Issues.pdf?sequence=1

Texas Children's Commission. (2015). *Removal.* Retrieved from http://parentresourceguide.tex aschildrenscommission.gov/library_item/gov.texaschildrenscommission.parent_resource _guide/10

The Local. (2016). 80% of Spaniards under thirty still live at home with parents. *The Local Europe (Spain edition).* Retrieved from https://www.thelocal.es/20160301/80-of-spanish-young -adults-live-at-home-with-parents/

The Week. (2015). *The demographics of Occupy Wall Street: By the numbers.* Retrieved from https:// theweek.com/articles/480857/demographics-occupy-wall-street-by-numbers

Thévenon, O. (2015). *Aid policies for young people in Europe and the OECD countries.* Families and Societies Working Paper Series. Retrieved from http://www.familiesandsocieties.eu/wp -content/uploads/2015/04/WP34Thevenon2015-pp.1-53.pdf

Tobenkin, D. (2019, May 1). *Africa's education evolution: Nigeria, the awakening giant.* NAFSA (National Association for Foreign Student Affairs). Retrieved from https://www.nafsa.org /ie-magazine/2019/5/1/africas-education-evolution-nigeria-awakening-giant

Tobin, J. (2010). *JFK at the Union: The unknown story of the Peace Corps speech.* University of Michigan. Retrieved from https://peacecorps.umich.edu/Tobin.html

Today Show. (2010, August 24). Transcript of interview featuring Jeffrey Arnett. *NBC News.* Retrieved from https://archive.org/details/WBAL_20100824_110000_Today/start/6300 /end/6360

Topolewska-Siedzik, E., & Cieciuch, J. (2019). Modes of personal identity formation: A preliminary picture from the lifespan perspective. *Personality and Individual Differences, 138*, 237–242. doi:10.1016/j.paid.2018.09.041

Tosi, M. (2020) Boomerang kids and parents' well-being: Adaptation, stressors, and social norms. *European Sociological Review.* 36(3), 460–473. doi:10.1093/esr/jcz068

Tosi M. & Grundy E. (2018) Returns home by children and changes in parents' well-being in Europe. *Social Science & Medicine, 200*, 99–106. Open Access: doi:10.1016/j. socscimed.2018.01.016

Trafton, A. (2015, November 18). Neuroscientists reveal how the brain can enhance connections. *MIT News.* Retrieved from https://news.mit.edu/2015/brain-strengthen-connections -between-neurons-1118

Tunç, B., & Gülsoy, M. (2010). *Removal of brain tissue by Tm-fiber laser.* Presentation at the 15th National Biomedical Engineering Meeting (pp. 1–4). http://doi.org/10.1109/BIYOMUT .2010.5479794

Tutelian, L. (2008, August 21). Following the kids to college. *New York Times.* Retrieved from https://www.nytimes.com/2008/08/22/greathomesanddestinations/22college.html

UNESCO. (not dated). *Member states list.* Retrieved from https://en.unesco.org/countries

University Health Service. (2021). *The pill.* University of Michigan. Retrieved from https://uhs .umich.edu/contraception-pill

US Bureau of Labor Statistics. (2014, March 26). *America's young adults at 27: Labor market activity, education, and household composition: Results from a longitudinal survey.* https://www.bls.gov/ news.release/archives/nlsyth_03262014.pdf

US Bureau of Labor Statistics. (2017, May 22). *The Economics Daily: 69.7 percent of 2016 high school graduates enrolled in college in October 2016*. Retrieved from https://www.bls.gov/opub/ted/2017/69-point-7-percent-of-2016-high-school-graduates-enrolled-in-college-in-october-2016.htm

US Bureau of Labor Statistics. (2020, May 5). *Labor market activity, education, and partner status among Americans at age 33: Results from a longitudinal survey*. Retrieved from https://www.bls.gov/news.release/pdf/nlsyth.pdf

US Bureau of Labor Statistics. (2021, December 1). *NLSY97 data overview*. Retrieved from https://www.bls.gov/nls/nlsy97.htm

US Census Bureau. (2018, September 6). *Another look at health insurance coverage rates for young adults*. Retrieved from https://www.census.gov/newsroom/blogs/random-samplings/2018/09/another_look_at_heal.html

US Census Bureau. (2020, December). *Historical marital status tables (Figure MS-2)*. Retrieved from https://www.census.gov/data/tables/time-series/demo/families/marital.html

US Census Bureau. (2021, October 19). *CPS historical time series visualizations on school enrollment*. Retrieved from https://www.census.gov/library/visualizations/time-series/demo/school-enrollment-cps-historical-time-series.html

US Department of Health and Human Services. (2021, February 1). Annual update of the HHS poverty guidelines. *Federal Register*. Retrieved from https://www.federalregister.gov/documents/2021/02/01/2021-01969/annual-update-of-the-hhs-poverty-guidelines

US Department of Veterans Affairs (2015). *Veterans employment toolkit*. Retrieved from https://www.va.gov/vetsinworkplace/docs/em_activeReserve.asp

US Elections Project (not dated). *Voter turnout demographics [1984–2020]*. Retrieved from http://www.electproject.org/home/voter-turnout/demographics

Upwork. (not dated). *Freelancers Union and Upwork release new study revealing insights into the almost 54 million people freelancing in America*. Retrieved from https://www.upwork.com/press/releases/freelancers-union-and-upwork-release-new-study-revealing-insights-into-the-almost-54-million-people-freelancing-in-america

Van Epp, M. C., Futris, T. G., Van Epp, J. C., & Campbell, K. (2008). The impact of the PICK a Partner relationship education program on single army soldiers. *Family and Consumer Sciences Research Journal, 36*, 328–349. doi:10.1177/1077727X08316347

Vanhalst, J., Klimstra, T.A., Luyckx, K., Scholte, R. H. J., Engels, R. C. M. E., & Goossens, L. (2012). The interplay of loneliness and depressive symptoms across adolescence: Exploring the role of personality traits. *Journal of Youth and Adolescence, 41*, 776–787. doi:10.1007/s10964-011-9726-7

Vennum, A., Lindstrom, R., Monk, K., & Adams, R. (2014). "It's complicated": The continuity and correlates of cycling in cohabiting and marital relationships. *Journal of Social and Personal Relationships, 31*, 410–430. doi:10.1177/0265407513501987

Villines, Z. (2020, February 10). What is the best age to have a baby? *Medical News Today*. Retrieved from https://www.medicalnewstoday.com/articles/best-age-to-have-a-baby#psychology

Vosylis, R. & Klimstra, T. (in press). How does financial life shape emerging adulthood? Short-term longitudinal associations between perceived features of emerging adulthood, financial behaviors, and financial well-being. *Emerging Adulthood*. doi:10.1177/2167696820908970

Wallis, J. (2004). How much does a free T-shirt really cost? *Living a Better Life®*. Retrieved from http://www.betterbudgeting.org/2015/06/how-much-does-free-t-shirt-really-cost.html

Walsh, J. D. (2020, May 11). The coming disruption: Scott Galloway predicts a handful of elite cyborg universities will soon monopolize higher education. *New York Magazine*. Retrieved from https://nymag.com/intelligencer/2020/05/scott-galloway-future-of-college.html

Wang, H., Kim, K., Burr, J. A., Birditt, K. S., & Fingerman, K. L. (in press). Adult children's daily experiences with parental advice: The importance of life problems and relationship quality. *Journals of Gerontology, Series B: Psychological Sciences*. doi:10.1093/geronb/gbaa169

Wang, W. (2020). *The U.S. divorce rate has hit a 50-year low*. Institute for Family Studies. Retrieved from https://ifstudies.org/blog/the-us-divorce-rate-has-hit-a-50-year-low

Ward, R. A., & Spitze, G. D. (2007). Nestleaving and coresidence by young adult children: The role of family relations. *Research on Aging, 29*, 257–277. doi:10.1177/0164027506298225

Washington State Department of Commerce. (not dated). *Independent Youth Housing Program*. Retrieved from http://independence.wa.gov/programs/independent-youth-housing -program/

Watanabe, T. (2020, July 16). For the first time, Latinos are the largest group of Californians admitted to UC. *Los Angeles Times*. Retrieved from https://www.latimes.com/california/ story/2020-07-16/latinos-uc-berkeley-diverse-class-history

Waters, M. C., Carr, P. J., & Kefalas, M. J. (2011). Introduction. In M. C. Waters, P. J. Carr, M. J. Kefalas, & J. A. Holdaway (Eds.), *Coming of age in America: The transition to adulthood in the twenty-first century* (pp. 1–27). University of California Press.

Watson, S. (2020). Cisgender. *WebMD*. Retrieved from https://www.webmd.com/a-to-z-guides /cisgender-overview

Wattenberg, M. P. (2015). *Is voting for young people?* (4th edition). Routledge.

Watters, E. (2004). *Urban tribes: Are friends the new family?* Bloomsbury.

Wechsler, H., Lee, J. E., Hall, J., Wagenaar, A. C., & Lee, H. (2002). Secondhand effects of student alcohol use reported by neighbors of colleges: The role of alcohol outlets. *Social Science & Medicine, 55*, 425–435.

Wechsler, H., Lee, J. E., Kuo, M., Seibring, M., Nelson, T. F., & Lee, H. (2002). Trends in college binge drinking during a period of increased prevention efforts: Findings from 4 Harvard School of Public Health College Alcohol Study surveys: 1993–2001. *Journal of American College Health, 50*, 203–217. doi:10.1080/07448480209595713

Weinstein, A. M. (2017). An update overview on brain imaging studies of internet gaming disorder. *Frontiers in Psychiatry, 8*, Article 185. doi:10.3389/fpsyt.2017.00185

Weiss, R. E. (2021, June 14). Dealing with pregnancy in your twenties. *Verywell Family*. Retrieved from https://www.verywellfamily.com/pregnancy-in-your-twenties-4137939

Welte, J. W., Barnes, G. M., Tidwell, M.-C. O., Hoffman, J. H., & Wieczorek, W. F. (2015). Gambling and problem gambling in the United States: Changes between 1999 and 2013. *Journal of Gambling Studies, 31*, 695–715. doi:10.1007/s10899-014-9471-4

West-Bey, N., & Mendoza, M. (2019). *Behind the asterisk: Perspectives on young adult mental health from "small and hard-to-reach" communities*. Center for Law and Social Policy. Retrieved from https://www.clasp.org/sites/default/files/publications/2019/04/2019_behindtheasterisk.pdf

Whitford, E. (2021, November 9). A new push to create a 3-year degree option. *Inside Higher Ed*. Retrieved from https://www.insidehighered.com/news/2021/11/09/colleges-explore -new-three-year-bachelor%E2%80%99s-degree-program

Wider, W., Suki, N. M., Lott, M. L., Nelson, L. J., Low, S. K., & Cosmas, G. (in press). Examining criteria for adulthood among young people in sabah (East Malaysia). *Journal of Adult Development*. doi:10.1007/s10804-020-09367-9

Wilhelm, D., & Esdar, W. (2014). Helicopter parenting: Prävalenz sowie Einfluss von Bildungshintergrund und sozio-ökonomischem status [Prevalence and influence of educational background and socioeconomic status]. *Die Hochschule*: Journal für Wissenschaft und Bildung [The University: Journal for Science and Education], *23*, 66–76. Retrieved from https://www.pedocs.de/volltexte/2019/16244/pdf/t2242.pdf

Wilhelm, D., Esdar, W. & Wild, E. (2014). Helicopter parents – Begriffsbestimmung, entwicklung und validierung eines fragebogens [Definition, development and validation of a questionnaire]. *Zeitschrift für Hochschulentwicklung* [Journal for University Development], *9*, 70–83.

Williams, A. (2013, January 13). The end of courtship? *New York Times*. https://www.nytimes.com/2013/01/13/fashion/the-end-of-courtship.html

Willkomm, A. C. (2020). *Job vs. career: What's the difference?* Drexel University, Goodwin College of Professional Studies. Retrieved from https://drexel.edu/goodwin/professional-studies-blog/overview/2020/July/What-is-the-difference-between-a-job-and-a-career/

Willoughby, B. J., & Hall, S. S. (2015). Enthusiasts, delayers, and the ambiguous middle: Marital paradigms among emerging adults. *Emerging Adulthood*, *3*, 123–135. https://journals.sagepub.com/doi/abs/10.1177/2167696814548478

Wilson, B. (2008, May 8). For prospective moms, biology and culture clash. *National Public Radio*. Retrieved from https://www.npr.org/templates/story/story.php?storyId=90227229

Wilson, C. (2020, January 31). The moment when four students sat down to take a stand. *Smithsonian Magazine*. Retrieved from https://www.smithsonianmag.com/smithsonian-institution/lessons-worth-learning-moment-greensboro-four-sat-down-lunch-counter-180974087/

Wilson, C. A. (2018). *Living to work: The effects of occupational calling on mental health at work.* Master's thesis, Clemson University. Retrieved from https://tigerprints.clemson.edu/cgi/viewcontent.cgi?article=3898&context=all_theses

Wilson, V. (2020, September 16). Racial disparities in income and poverty remain largely unchanged amid strong income growth in 2019. *Economic Policy Institute*. Retrieved from https://www.epi.org/blog/racial-disparities-in-income-and-poverty-remain-largely-unchanged-amid-strong-income-growth-in-2019/

Wizarding World (2021). *How much magic can children do before they go to school?* Retrieved from https://www.wizardingworld.com/features/how-much-magic-can-you-do-before-hogwarts

Woolsey, T. A., Hanaway, J., & Gado, M. H. (2017). *The brain atlas: A visual guide to the human central nervous system.* Wiley-Blackwell.

World Health Organization. (2001). *The second decade: Improving adolescent health and development.* Retrieved from https://apps.who.int/iris/bitstream/handle/10665/64320/WHO_FRH_ADH_98.18_Rev.1.pdf

World Health Organization. (2021, November 28). *Update on omicron.* Retrieved from https://www.who.int/news/item/28-11-2021-update-on-omicron

World Health Organization. (2022). *Constitution.* Retrieved from https://www.who.int/about/governance/constitution

World Population Review. (2021). *Immigration by country 2021.* Retrieved from https://worldpopulationreview.com/country-rankings/immigration-by-country

Worldometer. (2021). *African countries by population.* Retrieved from https://www.worldometers.info/population/countries-in-africa-by-population/

Worldometer. (2020). *Main cities by population in India.* Retrieved from https://www.worldometers.info/world-population/india-population/

Wray-Lake, L., Arruda, E. H., & Schulenberg, J. E. (2020). Civic development across the transition to adulthood in a national U.S. sample: Variations by race/ethnicity, parent education, and gender. *Developmental Psychology*, *56*, 1948–1967. doi:10.1037/dev0001101

Wu, L. L., Martin, S. P., & England, P. (2017). The decoupling of sex and marriage: Cohort trends in who did and did not delay sex until marriage for U.S. women born 1938–1985. *Sociological Science*, *4*, 151–175. doi:10.15195/v4.a7

Wuthnow, R. (2007). *After the Baby Boomers: How twenty- and thirty-somethings are shaping the future of American religion.* Princeton University Press.

Yau, N. (2007–2021). Marital status by age. *Flowing Data*. Retrieved from https://flowingdata.com/2016/12/08/marital-status-by-age/

Yılmaz, H. (2020). Türkiyede helikopter ebeveynlik eğilimi ve helikopter ebeveynlerin demografik özellikleri [Helicopter parenting tendencies in Turkey and demographic characteristics of helicopter parents]. *Sosyal Politika Çalışmaları Dergisi [Journal of Social Policy Studies]*, *20*, 133–160. doi:10.21560/spcd.v20i54504.540233

Zapp, (2019). *2019 Money matters on campus*. Lumina Foundation. Retrieved from https://www.luminafoundation.org/resource/2019-money-matters-on-campus/

Zelizer, J. E. (2015). *The fierce urgency of now: Lyndon Johnson, Congress, and the battle for the Great Society*. Penguin.

Zhou, L. (2021, October 15). The case against means testing. *Vox*. Retrieved from https://www.vox.com/2021/10/15/22722418/means-testing-social-spending-reconciliation-bill

Index

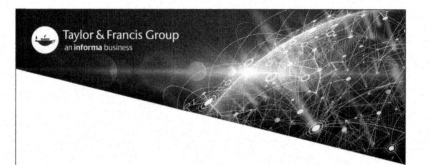